THE *Rules* WE BREAK

KATELYN TAYLOR

Playlist

Trevor's Playlist

Someone You Loved by Lewis Capaldi

You Proof by Morgan Wallen

The Hills by The Weeknd

Can't Hold Us by Macklemore, Ryan Lewis

Slayer by Bryce Savage

All I Do Is Win by DJ Khaled

All The Way Up by Fat Joe, Remy Ma, French Montana

Sweater Weather by The Neighbourhood

Take Me To Church by Hozier

Falling Like The Stars by James Arthur

Sage's Playlist

Nowhere To Go by Bad Omens

Sex With Me by Rhianna

Master Of Puppets by Metallica

Paint The Town Red by Doja Cat

Bad Blood by Taylor Swift

Greedy by Tate McRae

Riptide by Beartooth

Centuries by Fall Out Boy

Issues by Julia Michaels

Mine by Sleep Token

Say You Won't Let Go by James Arthur

Published by Katelyn Taylor

Cover art by Sammi Bee Designs

Edited by My Brother's Editor

Formatted by Katelyn Taylor

The Rules We Break is a work of fiction. Names, characters, incidents, and places are used fictitiously. Any resemblance to real people or events is coincidental.

The Rules We Break Copyright © 2024 by Katelyn Taylor

Dedication

To anyone who has ever loved and lost and you're not sure if you'll ever love again. I hope you find someone as sexy as Sage that can fuck like Trevor.

Trigger Warning

Your mental health is always first priority. Before continuing please make sure you review the potential triggers.

This book contains:

Domestic Violence/ Physical Abuse

Violence

Death of a parent

Explicit sexual scenes

Explicit language

Kidnapping

Prologue
TREVOR

Nineteen Years Ago

It's move-in day for our new neighbors.

I don't know much about them. I heard my parents talking about how they were lawyers or something. I guess Mom already went over there and invited them to dinner. She's always like that, getting to know all of the neighbors first, and letting the rest of the neighborhood know everything she learns. I've tried to tell her it's not cool to do that, but what parent listens to their twelve-year-old son when it comes to stuff like that?

Let's be real, though. What parents listen to their twelve-year-old son, period?

My dad owns a lot of buildings and houses, and despite him telling me a million times what he does with them, I never take too much time to listen. My mom is a full-time wife. At least that's what she says her job title is. One time I tried to tell her that I wasn't sure that was a real job, and she cried for a week, so I quickly learned to never talk about it again.

Don't get me wrong, my parents are great. They don't punish me, they give me anything and everything I want, and for the most part, they leave me alone. Sometimes too much. Rich kid problems, right?

Dad is already talking about me joining him at his company when I graduate college; meanwhile I'm more interested in football season coming up. I hope one day he will see that life isn't supposed to always be about just work and money. There is more to it, right? I hope there is, at least.

Grabbing a bottle of water from the fridge, I chug the majority of it before tossing it back in. Scooping up the football I brought inside, I head out to play some touch in the cul-de-sac with some of the neighbor guys. Some of them are on the team at school and aren't too bad. None of them besides me can even come close to throwing a spiral, though.

When I step outside, I walk down our winding driveway before I see the guys standing around a girl who looks to be at least a few years younger than us, despite how tall she seems. Her hair is long, curly, and a fire-engine red color. I've never seen someone with such red hair, not in person at least. Most redheads that I've met are more like an orange color. Not her, though.

She's pretty. Really pretty from what I can tell. I'm not sure I've seen a girl as pretty as her.

I watch as she talks, too far away to quite hear what she's saying, but I watch the way her aqua blue eyes widen slightly, almost making it hard to breathe for a second. What the heck? I pat my chest trying to clear whatever is stuck inside, but it won't budge.

I continue walking toward them, curious what this little redheaded girl wants when I hear a smooth voice.

"I'm going to play," she states so confidently, so truly, that it comes out as a fact instead of a question.

All of the guys laugh at her and it has me clenching my fist. I don't like that. Emmett Carson is laughing so hard he looks as if he can't breathe. Johnny laughs the loudest, pushing his black hair out of his face as he smiles in a mean way at her.

"No," he says. "Why don't you go play with your Barbies, little girl?"

I watch as her cheeks turn red, and she tucks a piece of her fiery locks behind her ear before glancing down at her shoes. I watch as the fight in her seems to escape like a deflating balloon. She's second guessing why she came over here in the first place, and all she wanted to do was play football with us.

"Shut it," I snap as I finally make it to the road, pushing through the still laughing guys until I'm in the middle of all of them.

I'm the captain of the football team, even as a sixth grader. Coach says I have good leadership skills, and people listen when I talk, so I use that power now. All of the guys have stopped laughing, all staring at me like they are waiting to hear me talk. Good.

Wow. She's even prettier up close than she was from my driveway. I take another step closer to her, a sweet smell suddenly filling my nose. It's like a fruit. Apples? Oranges?

Peaches.

She smells good. Really good. I take another step toward her, looking her over from head to toe before I turn my head to the side slightly.

"Have you played before?"

She pauses on my question for a second before she nods her head, rolling back her shoulders to stand taller as she does. I narrow my eyes at her like I'm weighing my options even though I already know I'm going to let the redheaded beauty play. I glance at Johnny who wordlessly tosses me the football before I turn back to her, holding it out for her to take.

"Let's see what you got," I say.

The girl takes the ball from my hand before she takes a step back. Part of me wants to tell her she needs to fix her footing. Coach has that permanently stuck in my head at this point, but it's not like she's even been quarterback before, so how would she know? She has a look of determination on her face, like it's all come down to this. She doesn't know that no matter how bad she is, she's still playing with us.

She pulls her arm back and throws it. It's not perfect, her technique could use some work, but I can help her with that. The fiery determination this girl has is more than enough to work with and just like that, the weird heavy feeling in my chest is back. Her aqua eyes come over to me, all the guys stunned in silence while I'm smiling like a fool because dang, I really like this girl.

I reach out for her, hooking my pinky with hers before dragging her over to be closer to me. Partly so we can play, and the other part because I already miss the smell of her. I breathe quietly so she can't hear me smelling her. Never thought I liked peaches so much.

"I'm Trevor," I say as I smile down at her. "And you are most definitely on my team, Little Red."

The nickname rolls off my tongue by accident. But it's perfect for her, and I instantly love it.

Little Red.

My Little Red.

Chapter 1
Trevor

Erica Pembrooke has been the love of my life since I was twelve years old. It was instant for me. We were inseparable for what seemed like forever at the time. She was two years younger than me, though, and when you're young, that tiny age difference can feel massive. So I waited until the time was right to make her mine.

When I was a sophomore in high school and Erica was in eighth grade, she got stood up for a dance. I was coming back from football practice, trying to catch a glimpse of her in the dress I helped her pick out before she left when I saw her on the front porch of the house. My heart sank instantly when I saw the tears on her face as I slammed the door of my Mustang and rushed over to her.

She told me about how the guy never showed up, and she was too embarrassed to go inside. I was so fucking pissed. I was ready to hunt down this Jimmy Kowlitz and beat his ass for making my girl shed a single tear. Instead, I grabbed her hand, walked her over to my car, opening the door before letting her get inside. I took us to Moe's, the best little burger shop Grovebury had to offer, and we ate on the hood of my car out front.

I knew this was my chance, finally. I knew she was ready, or maybe I was sick of waiting for her. Either way, I grabbed her hand, pulling her to my chest before locking our pinkies together. It was our thing and just the touch of her silky skin against mine and the overwhelming scent of peaches had my heart jackhammering inside my chest. My eyes locked onto hers, those sparkling aqua blues, as I leaned in and stole Erica's first kiss. I wanted to be her last kiss, too, and everything in between.

We were happy for years, so fucking happy. But when it was time for me to go to college hours away, I got self-doubt. The guys on the football team had me convinced that I shouldn't go to college with a girlfriend. They said college girls were different, the parties were different, and Brighton University practically worshipped their football team. They told me if I didn't break up with Erica, we'd end up breaking up anyway.

At first I told them to fuck off, but I'm ashamed to admit fear crept in. I was worried about the distance, and if I'm honest, I was worried I'd do something I'd regret and hurt Erica. So, I ended things. Biggest fucking mistake of my life. Somehow the angel of a woman managed to stay my best friend, and when it was her turn to come to Brighton, I knew I was about to get my girl back, for good this time.

Plans don't always work out the way they do in your head, though. I always thought that when I saw Erica Pembrooke in a wedding dress, I'd be at the other end of the aisle, waiting for my bride. Instead, I was in the front pew, not even in the wedding party as I watched her marry my best friend, or I guess, former best friend. It hurt like hell, and I left shortly after the ceremony where I got trashed and woke up in bed with a few girls the next morning. It didn't matter, though. None of them were her.

It's been nearly ten years since I blew it with Erica, again. Sebastian stole her out from under me, and even though what he did was shitty, what I did after was worse. I'm thankful every day that Erica forgave me. Seb, not as much, but that's fine. All I need is Erica.

I take a sip of my bourbon, staring out the window at the cloud-covered sky. Man, they really do not exaggerate when they say Seattle is gray. I've been in the NFL for eight years, all of those were spent playing for the San Antonio Cobras. They were good to me, and I enjoyed Texas, but I knew it was time to come back to my roots. Be closer to my friends.

And her.

Don't worry if you hate me for being in love with a married woman, then rest assured I hate myself more. I know she's happily married, and I wish that I could say Sebastian Caldwell doesn't deserve her, but...he does. He treats her like she's a queen, a goddess, and that's the way it should be because she is.

I asked for the trade at the end of last season, and even though the majority of that reason was my redheaded best friend, it felt right. Our other friends and teammates from college all play for the Seattle Crusaders. Declan even came out of retirement to play one more season where we are all together. Slater is our running back, Declan our defensive end, Sebastian our tight end, and I'm the Crusaders' new quarterback.

From the outside, you'd think I had it all. I own multiple properties, have more money than I know what to do with, and I'm on the fast track to go down in the hall of fame. As far as companionship goes, my bed never goes cold. Women hear that I'm a professional football player, and their panties practically disintegrate right then and there. It was fun for a while, drowning my pain and heartache in booze and faceless nameless women. But it's grown a little boring. At the end of the day, I'll never have a real connection with any of them because it's against the rules. I'm safer that way.

I came up with the rules shortly after Erica and Sebastian had their twin girls, Daphne and Rosalie. Daphne looks like a spitting image of Sebastian, but Rosie...god. Some days when I stare at her for too long, she looks exactly like Erica, and it breaks my fucking heart. So, after that day, I came up with a list of rules, and they've proved to keep my heart locked down and my feelings unscathed since.

    1. No kissing on the mouth

    2. No sleepovers

    3. No women at my place

    4. No repeats

    5. No falling in love

Some have said my rules are too much, douchey even. But I never even touch a woman without laying out the ground rules. I'm out to have a good time, find a little peace where I can, and go home. I'm not trying to break anyone's heart. I wouldn't wish that feeling on my worst enemy.

When the plane lands, it doesn't take long before the stewardess I just fucked in the bathroom tells me it's safe to de-plane now, not so subtly slipping me her number. I give her a smile but toss her number in the trash on my way down the stairs. Sorry, babe. Rule number four.

Flying private definitely has its perks, and it gives me the chance to keep a low profile. That's the part you don't think about too much. When you're young and just getting into the game, you're almost desperate for someone to recognize you off the field, give you that validation that you're someone important. Now, I can't even go to the gym or grab a coffee without being swarmed. It's fucking exhausting.

I slide into the waiting town car as the flight crew loads my bags into the trunk. I already bought a condo up here while I was still in Texas, and I had all of my things shipped. It's all waiting for me, which is a nice relief. I pull out my phone, turning off Airplane Mode before shooting out a text.

Me: Just landed. I can't wait to see you.

Her reply comes instantly.

Erica: Yay! Me too.

I can't help but smile at that as I type out my next response.

Me: Dinner tonight?

The hope blooming in my chest at the idea of seeing Erica tonight shrivels up and dies when she texts me back.

Erica: Sorry. Seb and I have date night tonight. Rain check?

Blowing out a breath, I shake my head as I type out my response.

Me: Sure, no problem. Have fun.

Is this what living in Seattle is going to be like? I thought it would feel good being closer to Erica and the girls. But am I just going to get a front-row seat of how perfect Erica and Seb's life is? About how glaringly obvious it is that I don't belong in any of their lives?

Shaking my head, I decide to push away the self-deprecating shit and send another text. I need to get laid, and I know just the guy to be my wingman for the night.

Chapter 2
Trevor

"Dude, will you get off your fucking phone?" I shout over the thumping base of the club.

Slater continues tapping away on his phone as he rolls his eyes at me.

"Fuck you. Scar is just checking in."

I lift my drink to my lips, taking a sip before I speak.

"How is Freckles doing?"

Slater shoots me a look of irritation as he pockets his phone.

"She's fine. She says hi."

I smirk. "Well, if tonight doesn't go as planned, I could always come back to your place. I would make an exception to my no-repeat rule for her."

His fist slams into my arm, and I can't help but laugh.

"Shut your fucking mouth about my wife, Michaels."

Shaking my head at him with a chuckle, I look out from the VIP section to the club floor. It's pretty packed tonight, and everyone seems to be having a good time. The fact that I'm on my third drink tonight tells me I should be having a good time too. For some reason that's not the case, though. Maybe it's because of my lame wingman.

"I brought you because I thought you'd be fun. You're being a buzz kill."

Slater takes a sip of his seltzer water as he shrugs.

"I miss my girl, bro. She has a doctor's appointment tomorrow. I'm not looking to get trashed."

My brows furrow at that. "She good?"

Slater nods softly. "Just some scans. Routine."

"Good." I nod.

Scar just finished her chemo at the beginning of the year. Last I spoke to her, she was feeling good, getting back into things. It was scary there for a while. I didn't know if she was gonna make it, and if she didn't make it, there was no way Slater would have.

They are like Erica and me. They met as kids, became best friends, loved each other forever, but where I took my shot with Erica, Slater never did. He even went off and married someone else, all while leaving Scar on the sidelines. Eventually he pulled his head out of his ass. All it took was some well-timed jealousy, orchestrated by yours truly. One of my best friends finally got the girl, and I got a nice blow job out of it.

Win, win.

A couple blondes catch my eye across the room. As if they can feel my eyes on them, they both eagerly turn to face me, giving me a good view as they grind against each other, their dresses riding up with each move. I watch in interest as I lift my glass for another sip. I guess I could go for a couple girls tonight, especially when they are all too excited to touch each other.

I'm an asshole, I know, but it's not like any other red-blooded man wouldn't do the same thing if he was in my shoes.

Setting my drink down, I clap Slater on his back before moving across the VIP section, making my way down the stairs by the bar toward my latest interest for the night when a noise captures my attention.

"Just stop being a dick, and get me a drink, bar boy," a smooth voice snarks to my left.

A chuckle rumbles through me as I look to see a woman giving the bartender a hard time. That quick glance has me actually stopping in my tracks. Fucking hell. She's hot.

Long, sleek, black hair nearly hits her hips, her slim body covered by a tight black leather   dress that is one bounce away from her ass and tits falling out simultaneously. I also notice that both of her arms are covered in black tattoos. Normally, I'm not into women with tattoos, but on her, they look fucking good. She looks like that young, once wholesome, girl going through her rebellious stage. I've always loved a good rebel.

I change directions, abandoning the grinding blondes as I make my way next to her, listening in on the rest of the conversation.

"Listen, you little bitch. This shit is as fake as your tits. Now get the fuck out of here before I have you thrown out," the bartender says as he flicks her ID at her.

"Actually, my tits are all natural. I know it's hard to tell since you've only seen them on the porn you watch while you beat off in your mom's basement," she snarks back.

I do my best to smother my laugh. Who the hell is this spitfire?

"Fuck you! You stupid—"

"Alright," I cut in. "I think that's enough. What's going on?"

The bartender cuts an irritated look to me before he does a double take.

"Mr. Michaels, can I get you something?"

"She's with me." I nod at her.

His eyebrows raise in surprise. "W-well, I'm sorry, sir. She can't be in here. She has a fake ID. I'm not trying to lose my license or get this place shut down."

I nod, fishing into my pocket before pulling out a couple of hundreds. I throw them on the bar top at him as I speak.

"Another round of Pappy Van Winkle for me, and...what about you, Raven?"

The stunner screws her face up at me in disgust.

"That's not my name."

"Didn't ask for your name. Just asked for your drink."

She narrows her eyes slightly but obviously weighs her options before she turns to the bartender and smiles with a grin so sweet it could give you type 2 diabetes.

"Jameson on the rocks."

The bartender clenches his jaw at her but quickly scoops up the money I tossed at him before getting to work on our drinks. He's handing them to us in no time, moving to the other side of the bar to take care of the other thirsty clubbers. I raise my glass to hers before taking a sip. She watches me suspiciously before taking a drink of hers.

"So, what? You the owner or something? That how you got that prick to back down?"

I give her a disbelieving snort as I furrow my eyebrows.

"You don't know who I am?"

She looks around like I must be kidding before she laughs, tossing her head back and letting out a velvet-wrapped laugh that makes my dick twitch. Her slim throat exposed as she shakes her head and looks back at me.

"No but based on that answer, sounds like I don't want to," she goes to move past me when I catch the crook of her elbow.

"Are you always this snarky?"

"I don't know," she says. "Are you always this arrogant?"

I can't help but smirk as I crowd her, leaning my face down until I'm inches from hers.

"Always."

To my surprise, a smile spreads across her face, causing her eyes to practically sparkle in the strobe-light lit room. It takes several seconds for me to fully see her eye color. I thought my mind was playing tricks on me for a moment there, but her eyes are purple. Actually purple, like a soft violet. I've never seen anything like them in my life.

I don't realize that I'm still staring at them until she snaps her fingers in my face. I shake my head as I stand up to my full height, looking down at her petite frame. She can't be taller than   five-five, and since I'm standing around 6'1, I practically dwarf her. You wouldn't know it with the way she carries herself, her shoulders are thrown back, head held high. I'll bet that attitude intimidates weaker men every day of the week.

"How old are you?" I ask.

"What?"

"Your age, Raven. The bartender said you were underage."

"What's it to you?" she says with a lift of her chin.

"I need to know if you're jailbait or not."

She scoffs, rolling her eyes, but she doesn't pull out of my grasp which is a good sign.

"I'm twenty, k? No one has ever even questioned me until that douche."

"Not in an outfit like that, they wouldn't," I agree as I let my gaze roam over her once more, lingering on the curve of her ass wrapped in that leather dress before the milky flesh of her thigh is revealed.

"My eyes are up here, asshat," she snaps.

"And your ass is down here," I say matter-of-factly, bringing my eyes back up to her with a smirk.

She scoffs, pulling out of my grasp to walk away. I don't want her to walk away, though. Maybe it's because she's the first girl in here tonight who hasn't fallen all over herself to gain my attention. Or maybe it's the fiery attitude that has me simultaneously needing to slide between her legs while also needing to lift up that dress and spank her ass raw.

"Dance with me," I say as I fall into step with her.

She side-eyes me, looking me over for a moment before she shrugs and starts making her way to the dance floor. I have a feeling that is as close to a yes as I'll ever get from a woman like her, so I follow.

When we get to the middle of the room, she turns, raising her hands up as she moves to the music. I don't hesitate, wrapping my arm around her waist, plastering her body against mine. Her eyes flutter open at that, a sultry look worthy of a siren transforming her eyes into something hypnotic.

We move together flawlessly, each second her body coming closer and closer to me until there isn't an inch separating us anywhere. Those purple gems flick up to me before glancing down at my lips. I can't help but smirk, ready to make my move, when she grabs the front of my shirt and pulls me down to her, attempting to crush her lips to my own before I dodge her at the last moment. I feel her warm lips against my neck as I chuckle into her ear.

"Sorry, Raven. I don't do kisses."

I feel her huff against my skin, and I expect her to push me away, I don't expect her to latch on, her silky tongue running against my neck as she nips, kisses, and sucks against me. A groan rumbles through my chest as my cock hardens to a steel pipe.

My hands are everywhere, desperate to touch every inch of this raven-haired stunner in front of me. Her soft curves are perfect, giving me just enough to grab onto as I drag her against me harder this time. A sweet moan falls from her lips that has my cock twitching. Fuck. I want to hear that again.

I drag her against me again, this time grinding against her as I do, which causes her to let out an even louder moan than before. I slip my hand into the back of her hair, wrapping it around my fist before pulling gently so I can look into her eyes. Her jet-black hair is like silk in my hands as I keep my hold on her firm. She almost arches into it, like she's enjoying the slight pain I know my grip must be giving her.

Fuck. This girl is so goddamn hot.

I close the distance between us as I begin trailing a path over her cheek and down her neck, nipping at the sensitive flesh behind her ear that has her grip on my shirt tightening.

Pulling my head back to look at her, I watch as her eyes flutter open, need drenching the soft purple hues, her lips pink and swollen. A sense of pride runs through me that I did that. That I turned this spitfire into a needy little mess.

Slipping my hand underneath the tight fabric of her dress, I glide my fingertips up her silky smooth inner thigh before gripping her lace panties. Tugging them to the side, I run a finger through her slick pussy.

So fucking wet.

I drag my finger through her like we have all the time in the world before pausing on her clit. She lets out a shuddering breath before I begin rubbing slow circles that have her gyrating her hips in rhythm. I can't help but smirk at the neediness splashed across her face.

Without saying a word, I pull my hand out from under her dress, grab her hand, and begin tugging her through the heavily crowded dance floor. To my surprise, she follows me without a snarky word or jab. Is that all it took to shut her up?

When we make it through the crowds, I head for the employee-only hallway, ducking into a VIP room of sorts. It's usually a place for the performers to hang out before they go on. This definitely isn't my first time in Seattle, and the owner told both Slater and me when we got here that we are welcome to use it if we need a little space.

There is a long black couch in front of us, a marble coffee table in front of it, and a big screen TV to pretty much finish the room. It isn't the most luxurious room, but it'll do. The raven-haired girl stands in front of the arm of the couch, looking around the room before her eyes come up to me expectantly.

I close the distance between us, lifting up her dress before spinning her around, pushing her lower back to bend her over the arm of the couch. She obeys beautifully, like putty in my hands, as her ass arches into the air, causing her black lace-covered pussy to pop out. I hook my fingers around the scrap of fabric before dragging it down her legs and tossing it to the side.

Dropping to my knees, I brace my hands on the sides of her thighs, pulling her open for me before hovering just over her.

"You sure about this? I'm giving you an out if you want it."

Her head whips back to me, her eyes filled with outrage.

"When your mouth is an inch from my pussy? I think I'll pass. Now eat my cunt before I find someone else who will."

My fingers pinch the inside of her thigh in punishment before I bury my face in her, her taste spreading across my tongue as I devour her. She's so fucking sweet. I've fucked a lot of women, tasted all of their pussies, and this woman has got to have the best tasting cunt I've ever had. Maybe apart from one.

"Hell yes," she moans as her back arches against me even more, practically grinding herself against my face.

I give her what she wants, flicking my tongue against her clit before I slip a finger inside. Her tight pussy practically clenches around my finger before her hips begin slowly thrusting. I pull away from her as I speak against her inner thigh.

"You like riding my hand, baby? Like my mouth on your sweet little cunt?"

"Shut up and fuck me," she practically snarls before it gives way to a moan when I rub against her G-spot.

"Come on my tongue first," I say as I go back to work.

I flick my tongue against her, focusing on her clit as I continue finger fucking her. I feel Raven's legs begin to quake and her pussy contract around me before she loses it. Her screams are so loud, I wouldn't be surprised if security thought someone was being murdered back here. Her cum practically leaks down my finger, and I make sure not to waste a fucking drop as I lick and suck her clean.

When her orgasm has eased, I slowly stand, ready to line myself up to her when she surprises me, standing up and spinning around. I open my mouth to find out what the hell she's doing when she grabs a fist full of my shirt, dragging me in front of the couch before pushing me down. I mean, she probably thinks she's pushing me around. I outweigh the girl by well over eighty pounds and a handful of inches, but based on the look in her eye, I'm more than happy to do whatever she wants.

She comes to straddle me, reaching for my belt before quickly undoing my pants. I feel her silky smooth hand slip inside my pants, gripping my rock-hard cock before pulling it out. She runs her hand up and down a few times before she raises up on her knees.

"Condom," she demands.

I pat around in my pockets before I reach for my wallet, grabbing out the foil packet before tossing it at her.

"Put it on me," I say as I settle back into the couch.

Surprisingly, she obliges and rolls the latex over me in seconds.

"Are you gonna ride my cock, baby?" I ask with a smirk as my hands come to rest on her hips.

She lifts an unamused eyebrow at me.

"What does it look like?" she scoffs.

"Fuck. Are you always such a ball buster? That kind of attitude is gonna turn a lot of guys off."

She lowers herself down, sinking onto me until we are flush before she gives her hips a little wiggle.

"Not you, apparently," she says with a smart-ass smirk.

I try to roll my eyes in irritation, but when she lifts up and comes down on me again, they roll all the way back in pleasure instead. She begins riding me, bouncing up and down as she grinds herself against me. I have one hand on her hip and the other cupping her full ass. Shit. This girl fucks like a goddamn porn star. I'm used to being the dominant one, the one calling all the shots and doing eighty percent of the work. Right now all I can focus on is not coming too quickly because her pussy has got to be the tightest thing I've ever felt.

Her small hands come to rest on my shoulders as she throws her head back in pleasure.

"Fuck. You're huge," she gasps as she comes down on me again.

"Feel good? You like taking what you want?"

Her eyes come down to mine, the look in them bringing my impending orgasm closer to the surface.

"Always."

My hand massages her ass cheek before I clap down over it, causing the sound to ring out through the room as her back bows, her chest brushing against me. I release her hip as I use my hold on her ass to help her movements before my other hand comes up to cup her tits. They are practically falling out of this dress, and it doesn't take much effort to free one. I drag her against me, taking her nipple into my mouth as I do. My tongue swirls against her, teeth nipping against the sensitive skin in a way that has her shuttering and shaking.

"Fuck. That's a good tongue," she mutters as one of her hands goes behind my head, pushing me against her chest.

I pull my hand back before slapping the bare skin of her ass, causing her pussy to clench in response.

"Oh god!" she yelps.

I do it again and again, craving her pleasure even more than I crave my own. The fact that her pleasure seems to teeter the line of pain only elicits a deep desire in me to see how far I can push her. How far I can go before this tiny little raven shatters apart in my arms.

At least for tonight, it doesn't seem to be too much because one more spank, and she's falling over the edge, gasping and grinding against me as she rides out her orgasm. I feel my balls draw up before she reaches behind herself, cupping them before massaging them in a way that has my own orgasm slamming into me harder than a three-hundred-pound linebacker. She continues massaging me, practically forcing the cum out of me, before I collapse against the back of the couch.

I blink hard several times, my vision slightly blurred before I shake my head. Shit. I haven't fucked like that in a while.

It takes me a moment to realize that she isn't on my lap anymore. Instead, she's standing, slipping her panties back on before pulling down her dress. I sit up a little bit and get ready to give her the let-down talk, but before I can, she flattens out her hair and looks down at me.

"Thanks," she says before stepping toward the door and slipping out.

Several seconds go by, where I'm frozen in place. Wait, what? Thanks? She just rode my cock like it was her favorite thing in the world, came all over me, and then left with a thanks? No asking for my number, or even for another round? No trying to come back to my place?

Who the fuck *is* that chick?

Shaking my head, I stand, taking care of the condom before redoing my belt. When I step out of the room, I glance down the empty hallway before slowly making my way back out to the club floor. Everyone is partying, dancing, doing shots just like they were when we slipped away.

I make my way back to the VIP area where I see Slater is talking to a few of our teammates who must have shown up. I do my best not to keep my eyes out for that long black hair that feels like silk in my hands, but I don't do a good job. Who the fuck just bails like that? I mean, I guess she really doesn't know who I am. I'm the one that has to dip out, not the other way around.

I should probably be thankful. I think that was the easiest no-feelings-at-tached hookup I've ever had in my life. Instead, I'm a little fucking irritated.

Chapter 3
Sage

I woke up the next morning a little hungover and a lot tired. It wasn't just the two Jamesons I had last night before the douche bartender caught on to my fake. It wasn't even the one I had after that despite him catching on to me. It probably had something to do with the mid-grade tequila shots I did before even going out as a pregame. Tequila and I have always had a love-hate relationship. I love it, but it hates me.

I mean, upside if I puke, I can skip my hot yoga class for this week I guess.

Slowly, I push my covers to the side, peeling myself out of bed before making my way over to the bathroom. I feel a slight ache between my thighs, and flashes of last night come to the forefront of my mind. God. That was fun.

He thought I didn't know who he was, which is fine. I wasn't really interested in getting to know Trevor Michaels or anything. I grew up hearing my dad ramble on about him ever since he played for Brighton University. Last night I was really only interested in what he could do for me, though. Which turned out to be a free drink and a couple of orgasms, so I'd say he was an hour or so well spent.

I think he expected me to stick around, turn into a stage-five clinger or something, but that's not me. I'm not naïve enough to think men want anything more from me than enough time to get it up and get off. The few that do want more, I end up having to let them down. I'm not built like that, I don't do feelings and relationships and all of that stuff. Not anymore.

It's kinda weird to be back in Seattle. I was born and raised here, and though I was only gone for a little over two years, it feels like a lifetime ago. My dad was happy to help me get settled back in Seattle, after he gave me a three-hour lecture about how he was right and I was wrong, which was just a ball of fun. But after I endured that painful dinner, I left with an apartment leased in my name, a good-paying job, and a second chance. One I don't plan on wasting.

I begin washing away the smeared makeup from last night when my phone buzzes with an incoming FaceTime. I glance at who is calling before I answer as I continue washing my face.

"Bitch, did you forget to take off your makeup again last night?" Calista cackles through the phone.

I shoot her an irritated look before I roll my eyes. "Fuck off. I didn't get back until late."

"Ooo," she says with a waggle of her eyebrows. "Did you finally break that dry spell of yours and get some dick?"

I raise an unimpressed eyebrow at her as I begin moisturizing.

"I wouldn't necessarily call a week a dry spell, Cal," I snark.

"I would. That's a fucking lifetime." She laughs as a family sitting behind her looks at her in disdain.

"Will you quit talking about dick in a coffee shop? You're traumatizing children," I laugh.

She shrugs, seemingly unbothered as she adjusts her leather cut. Well, technically it's her man's, but still.

"So, how are you?" she asks, her voice lowering and tone softening.

I start to give her a bright smile before it slowly fades. I'm an excellent liar, a great bullshitter. Not with Calista, though. We practically lived together for two years. She knows everything about me. The good and the really bad.

"I'm better. Just a little—"

"On edge?" she questions.

I roll my lips together and nod. I watch as her eyes dart around the coffee shop before she leans closer to the phone, dropping her voice to a full-on whisper.

"He hasn't talked about you in a few weeks. Hammer said he's been strangely calm about the whole thing. He's even had Britt practically glued to his cock."

I swallow roughly at that as I nod. Hammer is Calista's husband and probably one of the only good ones. He's always treated me like a sister, always tried to help when he was allowed to, but unfortunately, he couldn't always protect me. Britt is one of the club girls who would constantly hang around, always hoping to be more than just a way to kill time for the guys. I never cared for her but to hear that she's been linked up with him actually makes me feel sympathy for her.

"I like the black," Calista says, very horribly transitioning topics.

I run my hand through the box-dyed hair and nod. "It's definitely better than the blue."

Calista wrinkles her nose up at the reminder. When I dyed my hair robin egg blue, it was cute for all of two days. Then it faded into this gross blueish green and practically fried my hair. I had to stop dying it for months just to get some length back. I've always changed the color of my hair, practically to any color of the rainbow, usually just depending on my mood. Before I left, though, I knew it was time for a change—a less recognizable one, just in case.

"I'll call you soon, okay?" Calista says.

I nod. "Make sure you delete our call history, just to be sure."

"Always," she sighs. "I miss you."

My heart pangs at her words. Calista is almost twelve years older than me, but it never felt like that. She wasn't just a best friend. She was like a sister. It almost killed me to leave her behind, knowing that I may never see her in person again. I knew I didn't have a choice, though.

"Miss you too. Talk soon," I say, emotion clogging my throat as I speak.

She gives me a sad smile and blows a kiss before the call ends. Blowing out a tired breath, I glance up to look in the mirror, my hands white knuckling the porcelain sink as I stare at myself.

Twenty years old, and I swear to God I've already lived enough life to be in my early forties at least. With that depressing thought in mind, I go about my morning routine before heading to the store to load up on supplies for the week. I won't have time soon since I'm starting work on Monday. Not sure what to expect from the job in all honesty. It's a great opportunity, but it isn't exactly my passion. I think Dad just gave me the job because he saw the others hiring in that position and thought he'd jump on the trend. Whatever, I'll ride it out while I can, save as much as I can and then get on my feet and the hell out of Seattle.

Chapter 4
Trevor

I try to ignore the heavy tension in the air as I take a bite of my chicken. The table is near silent, just sounds of clanking silverware and the occasional protest from one of the twins about eating their food.

"Baby girl," Sebastian says patiently to Rosalie who is currently crossing her arms, refusing to take a bite of her broccoli. "If you don't eat your broccoli, you won't grow up to be big and strong."

"I don't want to grow," she grumbles while Daphne happily munches away on her broccoli, avoiding her mashed potatoes like the plague.

Sebastian lets out an exasperated sigh, and I jump in before I can think better of it.

"Rosie, if you eat all of your broccoli, I'll take you out for ice cream soon."

She perks up at that, her bright red curls tumbling around her face as she turns to me.

"Really? You promise, Uncle Trev?"

I smile at her, her bright green eyes wide with hope.

"Of course, but you have to eat it all with no more fuss, okay?"

She nods excitedly and starts plowing through the green vegetable. A soft warm feeling takes up residence in my chest. That is until my eyes collide with Sebastian's. They are filled with anger and irritation as I watch him clench his fist on top of the table before gritting his teeth together.

"You can't just take my daughter out to ice cream for eating her vegetables, Trevor. She needs to eat them without incentive."

"I was just trying to hel—"

"Well, don't," he snaps in a tone that has that warm feeling shriveling up instantly, a pang of annoyance filling me instead. I nod as I look down at my plate, tightening my own jaw so I don't do something stupid like call him out for being a fucking prick in front of the girls. I hear Erica's soft, defeated sigh, and it hurts to know I'm the cause for her frustration. At least partially.

I glance at her out of the corner of my eye. Just enough so that I can see her but not enough that anyone would notice. I've practically perfected the move at this point. Ten years of watching my old best friend marry the love of my life, watching them have babies and build a life together. It wasn't like I could stare at her the way I used to.

At least, I try not to.

I've contemplated cutting Erica out of my life more times than I'd care to admit. The pain is too much to deal with some days. I question if her friendship is worth it. The constant ache in my chest when I'm around her is disrupting, frustrating, and agonizing because I know that if it was ever meant to go away, it would have by now. Erica Pembrooke is my great love, my soul mate, and she's married to someone else. As fate would have it, Erica is the love of my life, but I'm not hers, and that's been a real fucking hard pill to swallow.

So instead of being her husband, I'm her best friend. Instead of being the father of her children, I'm their "uncle." In all the times I've imagined cutting ties with Erica, I've come to my senses almost instantly. Having Erica in any capacity of my life is worth everything, so no matter how uncomfortable things are between me and Sebastian, no matter how hard it is to push down my feelings, I do it, happily, for her.

We finish up dinner and like the great team they are, they divide and conquer. Sebastian takes on getting the girls' teeth brushed and putting them to bed while Erica cleans up from dinner. I volunteer to help her and soon we are rinsing dishes and loading them into the dishwasher. We are silent for a little while before she speaks.

"I've missed you, Trev. It's good to have you here in town." She smiles softly as she hands me a dish.

I smile back at her, those bright green eyes practically staring into my soul as I do.

"I've missed you. So fucking much, Little Red."

"Ugh," she groans on a laugh. "Not the nickname. When are you gonna let that drop?" she says as her hand comes up to push against my chest.

I catch it before she can pull away, smiling at her as I bring our faces close to one another.

"Never."

Her smile slowly drops, her eyes flicking back and forth between my eyes and my lips. The look alone has my heart jack hammering in my chest, my stomach flipping as I slowly reach for the cup in her other hand, setting it down on the counter before resting my hand on the soft curve of her hip, her hand still captive in my grasp against my chest.

"Trevor," she whispers hoarsely.

I almost don't respond, letting the soft lilt of her voice saying my name wash over me. Maybe if I don't respond, she'll say it again. The look of fear, curiosity, and something that resembles want in her eyes has me answering, though.

"Yeah, Little Red?"

"Y-you should probably let me go," she says softly, her own words sounding so unsure.

She's right, I should. I know I should. But I can't help but lean into this reaction Erica is having to me. One I haven't seen in years. One I've been desperate for, longer than I could tell you.

"Should I?" I ask quietly, tightening my grip on both her hand and waist as if that will somehow keep her tethered to me. That it will somehow preserve this magic bubble we've found ourselves in.

Her breath hitches as I pull her toward me, just an inch or two. Enough for her chest to brush against mine, her head tilting up slightly to maintain eye contact with me. The hem of her T-shirt rises up just slightly, exposing a sliver of her creamy skin. My thumb rubs against the exposed skin before I can help myself, relishing the smooth feel of *her*.

I expect her to push me away, maybe even slap me and kick me out. I'm crossing lines here. I know it, I can feel it. But I've spent too goddamn long dreaming of this, practically desperate for just a moment, just one single moment, where she doesn't push me away after hugging me. Where she doesn't break eye contact because she feels Sebastian's eyes on us. So, as much of a piece of shit as it makes me, I hold her that much closer, hoping to soak in this moment just a little longer.

"Yes?" she breathes, the word sounding like a confused question rather than a statement.

Leaning forward, I bend down slightly until my mouth is only a few inches from her.

"Do you want me to let you go, Little Red?" I ask, purposefully letting my breath brush against her full red lips.

I hear her breath hitch once more, her chest now heaving as it rises and falls against mine. She closes her eyes as she speaks.

"We can't," she sighs sorrowfully, like the words pain her to say as much as they pain me to hear.

This is where a good man would pull away, let the married woman go, and berate himself later for being so slimy. When it comes to Erica, though, I just don't have that kind of self-control. Not when she feels it too.

"I love you," I say in a whisper as I bring my mouth closer to hers.

Her eyes are still closed as I wrap my arm around her lower back, pulling her until she's flush against me. She whimpers at the move, her hips involuntarily grinding against me for a moment as she does.

"Trev."

"I love you," I say again, determined not to let this moment slip between my fingertips, only an inch separating our lips now.

"I can't," she practically begs, like she doesn't have the will to stop this. Like she needs me to do it for her.

I pull her in a little more, my hand resting just above her perfect ass, keeping her flush against me as my lips barely touch hers while I speak.

"I. Love. You."

As if the wall she'd been building to hide her feelings for me has come crashing down in one move, she closes the remaining distance between us. Her lips are on mine, tongue stroking against me as she jumps into my arms. I catch her easily, encouraging her to wrap her legs around me as I hold her so tight, I fear I'll break her.

I can't believe it. I'm kissing Erica again after all this time. She tastes so goddamn sweet. Like she always did. Maybe better. I'm practically ravenous, desperate to take everything and anything she offers me right now. I feel her body wiggle against me, giving us that friction we both crave, silently begging me for what we both need.

I swipe the kitchen island clean before laying her down, her red hair fanning out around her like the halo of an angel. My angel. My Little Red.

"Trevor. I need—"

"I know what you need, baby. I need it too," I say, emotion tightening my throat as I quickly pull down her yoga pants and panties, exposing her beautifully bare pussy to me. Goddamn, I never thought I'd see this sight again.

I undo my pants pulling my cock out to see I'm already leaking pre-cum. Fuck, I've never needed anyone more than I need her right now. She looks at me with heavy-lidded eyes, need stricken across her face as she spreads her thighs open for me, gifting me the sight of her. My mouth salivates in remembrance of her taste, her smell. I want it all. But right now, I need to be inside her. I need to be close to her, to feel her.

Lining the head of my cock up with her entrance, I don't hesitate for a moment, pushing inside her with one long thrust. Her back bows as a sweet moan falls from her lips. I wrap my hands around her waist as I bring her closer to me, burying myself deeper inside her. I feel her pussy clench around me, like welcoming me home. Fuck. I've missed this. Missed her. This feels like so much more than fucking. It feels like the start of something, of what was always meant to be.

"Trevor," she gasps.

"Yes, Little Red?" I ask as I continue fucking her against the shiny quartz countertop.

"I love you so much. I've never stopped. I couldn't," she says as tears begin gathering in her eyes, sliding down her face.

I reach up to catch them, fucking her deeper as I get closer to her.

"No tears, baby. Anything but the tears," I practically beg.

"What do we do? I can't live without you. I need you," she says as she raises her hips and lets out a soft moan.

"I know, baby. I know. I'm not letting you go for anything. You hear me? I'll fight for you. Fight for us. I'll never let you go again."

"Don't Trev, ever. Please, please, please," she begs as I lower my hand to her clit, rubbing it in tight circles that have her body shuddering.

"You're so beautiful. So perfect. Come for me, Little Red. Give me what we both need. I need to know this is just about you and me. That you want me, that you need me like I need you."

Her eyes come to mine as I increase my speed, her mouth opening into a perfect O shape as she screams her release.

"Trevor! Trevor! Trevor!"

I fuck her through it, feeling her cunt grip me so tight, it practically sends me over the edge.

Trevor. Trevor.

"Trevor, hello? Anyone home?" Erica asks.

I blink hard before looking down at the dirty plate in my hand. I shake my head, glancing up to see a fully clothed yet worried-looking Erica.

"You okay? You spaced out for a while."

Jesus Christ.

Disappointment and a newfound pain I didn't know existed takes over me as I close my eyes and let out a heavy breath. I take a minute to do my best to separate reality from what was clearly an overly detailed delusion. *Way overly detailed.*

I muster up the best smile I can, but even I can feel how tight and fake it is. Erica's brows furrow with concern as I nod.

"I'm good."

Chapter 5
Trevor

I left before Seb was even done tucking the girls in. Usually, I'd try to stick around and at least attempt to say goodbye. Not yesterday, though. Not when I thought what I did, what I daydreamed I did. And the fact that disappointment weighed out remorse for it…well, I'm starting to think maybe coming to Seattle wasn't the best idea. That is if I don't want to implode Erica's life, my life, and everyone around us.

Gripping the steering wheel a little tighter, I pull into a parking spot at the stadium before turning off the engine of my Audi R8. I'm getting used to this thing, not quite sure I love it yet. My car collection is being shipped up here from Texas, and so I needed to get something for now. It's nice, don't get me wrong. But when I have classics like a 1969 Barracuda or a 1962 Ferrari 250 GTO, the thing kinda pales in comparison for me.

Flashes of yesterday's fantasy pass through my head, despite how much I try to push it to the side. It didn't even happen. It was a daydream. Obviously, I have one fucking hell of an imagination.

Shaking my head, I blow out a deep breath before hitting the side of my fist on the steering wheel. I throw open my door and get out, standing a little taller as I grab my bag and throw it over my shoulder while I make my way to the front of the building.

The thing is, even if I was willing to risk everything and shoot another shot with Erica, it would be a shot wasted. She loves Sebastian in a way that she never quite loved me. They balance each other. Even if it hurts to admit, they're good together. He makes her happy in a way I wish I could. Like I said, Erica is the love of my life, but I'm not hers. And if you love something, set it free, right?

Well, I've been out here for ten fucking years *trying*.

I push through the front doors, striding down the long entrance hallway and heading for the locker room. I've been to the practice field a few times. Before we started negotiations, Coach Aberton flew me out here to check out the facilities and meet some of the guys, even though I already know most of them.

Today is our first day of practice, and a sense of peace comes over me. My personal life may be a dumpster fire when you take into account the fact that I'm in love with a married woman, my best friends are wary of me, and my parents think I'm wasting my time playing a sport instead of taking my seat at the family business. When I'm on that field, though, all of it fades away, at least for a little while.

There was a time when a career in the NFL was a very unreal fantasy. My junior year of college, I got into a car accident. A bad one. I ended up breaking my throwing arm as well as destroying my life at the time with what came after. I didn't really have anyone for a while there, even Erica was distant, for obvious reasons, and so all I had to focus on was getting better. I worked with a private team of physical therapists, doctors, and trainers. The works. And somehow, amazingly, I was able to get drafted my senior year.

I know some of the guys are talking about retirement. Declan already did retire, technically. He's just back for the season. Erica told me Seb's contract is up after this season, and he's talking about just taking time to focus on them and the kids.

The only ones who are fully in it right now are Slater and me though obviously if Scarlett gets sick again, I know he will be out of here so fast, fines be damned. Me though, I'm happy to play until my fucking arm falls off. I don't have anyone sitting at home waiting for me. No one to talk about where I see my life going or how my day was. I can't lie that sometimes I crave a connection like I see all my friends have with their spouses. But then all it takes is one look at Erica, one so close but so far away glance, and the ache in my chest reminds me why I don't want to go looking for that. Because love is a fickle bitch, and you're never guaranteed a happily ever after. I just need to focus on my rules, on this season, and take everything else with a grain of salt.

"Ohhhh shittttt," Slater hoots when I round the corner and step into the locker room.

I can't help but smirk at his antics. Slater and I are probably the closest these days, mainly because his wife is also one of my closest friends.

"QB 1 is officially in the house. C'mon, rooks, make some noise!" Slater shouts at the rookies in the corner while he beats on the metal lockers like a pair of drums.

They all do as he says, quick to fit in with the team. It's not like college where we treat the lower classmen like shit or anything. Everyone has earned that jersey, and for that, they deserve respect. But some of these kids have been watching guys like Slater, Seb, Declan, and me for years. So typically there is a little bit of a shine to it for them.

"Hey, man. How ya doing?" Declan asks, coming around the corner to bump fists with me, his accent thicker than normal.

"Shit, Mikey. Knoxville made your accent real thick," Slater says, imitating Declan's accent terribly.

He rolls his eyes and punches Slater in the arm but doesn't respond because that's just Slater. Seb walks over to us in the next moment, fist bumping all the guys before he turns to face me. He doesn't offer more than a head dip, his eyes cold and hard on me before he turns to face our friends. I try not to let it bother me. I'm sure I'll be getting a lot of those looks this season. As long as it doesn't come onto the field, though, what can I do?

"Uh, Mr. Michaels?" a guy who has the face of a twenty-year-old kid but the body of a truck says.

"What's up?" I say with a head nod.

"I'm Brandon. Brandon Shuer. Fuck, this is embarrassing, but my mom wanted me to get your autograph if it's cool."

I can't help but grin at that. I've bagged a cougar or two in my day, and though I prefer my women to be around my age, if not a little younger, there is always an exception.

"For sure," I say as I take the pen and paper that I now see him holding at his side. I start signing it as I speak.

"So, is your mom hot? Should I jot down my number too?"

The kid grimaces, and Slater laughs while Declan tries to hold in his laugh as he shakes his head.

"C'mon, Trev. That's the man's mama."

I roll my eyes at our southern mama's boy before I hand the paper back to the kid.

"What's your position, Brenden?"

"It's Brandon," he corrects.

I just stare at him flatly to which he clams up for a moment before answering. "Left tackle."

"Aw, so you're gonna protect us?" Slater says with a bat of his eyes.

I can't help but scoff at my idiot friend.

"He's your running back. I'm quarterback. So—"

"I know," he cuts in quickly with a serious nod. "I got you guys."

Smirking, I nod as I clap his shoulder.

"Like the attitude. Don't be nervous, just play your game. Oh, and probably don't ask for any more signatures, especially not on day one of practice. Comes across a little..."

"Pathetic," Damion, one of our wide receivers, calls out.

Not the word I would have used, but it gets the point across. The kid screws up his face like he realizes what a rook he made himself look like before I slap him on the back.

"Hey, no sweat, man. Gotta do what you gotta do for your mom."

"Yeah," Slater says. "Sounds like Trev would be willing to help you do a lot of things for your mom."

The whole locker room erupts into laughter, even Brandon as he goes back over to his buddies. I get changed quickly and soon we are all making our way onto the field. Oh yeah. This is my therapy. My peace.

Once all the guys are warmed up and waiting on the turf, the coaches come in, Aberton standing front and center with his Crusaders polo, hat and black pants on. He looks every bit the NFL coach that he could, even has the premature graying at his temples to prove it.

"Alright, new season, new faces. Hopefully, you all stroked each other off in the locker room because we don't have time for that shit here. I'm Coach Aberton. This is your coaching staff," he says, not bothering to try to introduce the near dozen people standing behind him. "Hope you boys are ready to go all the way this year. I expect perfection out of each and every one of you."

"Before we get started I want to introduce someone—this is Sage. She is going to be the team's social media girl. She will be around a lot, filming you guys, doing interview questions. Participate," he nearly threatens as a small girl comes from the back of the group, standing next to Aberton and giving everyone a tight yet polite smile.

Wolf whistles instantly sound out just from the look of her. I mean, she's wearing a Crusaders T-shirt that couldn't be tighter on her tits, accompanied by some black yoga pants that look as if they were made as a second skin just for her. Not to mention the bombshell sleek black hair she has accented by those fucking purple eyes.

What. The. Fuck.

I thought she didn't know who I was? Was that bullshit? Had to have been. Not to sound cocky, but someone definitely couldn't be working for the Crusaders and not know who I am. What a little bit—

"My daughter," Aberton snaps, sending a venomous look to the guys who sounded off.

A hush falls over the room, and Aberton nods at that.

"Damn straight," he says before continuing on with his orientation spiel.

"Fuck. Who'd have thought Aberton could make a smoke show like that," I hear Damion whisper behind me, and I have to agree. Coach is not a good-looking guy by traditional standards, and Sage, well she looks even better in the daylight than she did in the dimly lit club.

I'm staring at her, unrelenting, practically daring her to look my way because once she does, she will know how royally she fucked up messing with me. I don't fuck around at work. There has to be a separation, and I have a strict no-repeats policy. Rule number four.

So, if she thinks this is going to turn into a thing, she will be sorely mistaken. The fact that she's Coach's daughter changes some things. I'll have to put her down a little easier than normal. Hopefully she doesn't run crying to daddy over it. It's not like Aberton will bench me, though. Even if I did eat his little girl's pussy before letting her ride my lap. Fuck. Kinda wish I did make exceptions to my rules. Girl fucked like a porn star.

She already tried to break rule number two, at the club, so she's definitely trouble. I'll just have to set her straight to make sure not a single rule is in danger of being broken because of Sage *Aberton*.

Chapter 6
Sage

Standing in front of the entire Crusaders team feels a lot like being a dangling ribeye in front of a starving pride of lions. Though, let's be honest, none of these men are starved for anything, least of all women, and most of them more accurately resemble pussies than lions. Okay, that was harsh. To be fair, I don't know any of them personally. Well, I guess that's not true. I sort of know one.

I feel him glaring daggers at me like if he continues, he can actually strike me down. Looks like someone had their Cheerios pissed in this morning. My dad dismisses me with a wave which I can't help but roll my eyes at. He's the arrogant type, all about what you can do for him and not as much about what he can do for you. There is a reason our relationship has been strained ever since Mom died. He threw himself into work and forgot that she didn't just leave him behind. She left me too. But that's a trauma dump for another day.

He talks for what feels like forever before he finally has the guys break up into offense, defense, and special teams. I pull out the brand new video camera Dad gave me this morning, compliments of the Seattle Crusaders, and begin recording. My dad also gave me the Crusaders T-shirt and yoga pants when I showed up in a black leather jacket and black jeans. Unfortunately for him, I don't think he was expecting the full-sleeve tattoos that now don my arms because he practically snarled at them before storming off to his coaches meeting.

Whatever.

I know most of the guys and their positions, at least the returning vets. The rooks will take a little to get the hang of, but Dad said he wants me to come up with unique content, so I'll probably be getting to know all of the guys in one way or another. I angle the camera down at the feet of the offensive players as they do the agility ladder that is laid out across the ground.

Slater Santos gives me the peace sign before sticking out his tongue when he gets to the end, and I can't help but laugh. Alright, good to know. Santos will be my golden boy for content. One by one, the guys take suit after Slater and throw up some type of gesture or smile until the last offensive player comes through. Trevor Michaels.

When he gets to the end, though, he looks down at me. Like literally, down at me, as if I were scum beneath his shoes. Like I was a bug begging to be squashed. The look instantly pisses me off and has me ready to chuck this crazy expensive camera at his stupid pretty boy face. Before I let my mouth run away from me on day one of this job, he's stepping to the side, sending me a withering glance that makes me feel two inches tall.

Fuck. Him.

I take back every decent thought I had about Trevor. He wasn't even that good anyway. His cock barely did the job. I had to climb on top of him and take control because he wouldn't know what to do with that thing if it stood up on its own and did the macarena. If he thinks I'll ever sleep with him again, he's got another thing coming. I don't double dip, and I most definitely do not fuck with pretty boy assholes. Saturday was a lapse of judgment, one that I will never be making again.

Once practice is over, all the guys head to the locker rooms while I pack up my things. Thankfully, I'm only required to come to two practices a week and obviously all games. Everything else I can do from the comfort of my apartment, which was the huge selling point for me.

I feel two heavy presences lurking over me, causing goosebumps to erupt on the back of my neck as I quickly whip my head up. It takes a moment for my heart to calm down as it bangs against my chest like a drum while I look at the two football players staring down at me. I stand to face them as best as I can, though they both still have almost a foot on me.

"Sorry, sweetheart. We didn't mean to scare you." Damion Andrews smiles in a way that makes my skin crawl.

I give him a tight smile, doing my best to remain pleasant since I'll be working with all of these guys for a minimum of five months or so. Maybe longer.

"No worries. What's up?"

"We just wanted to introduce ourselves. I'm Damion," he says, letting his words hang in the air for a few moments before I realize that's all he has to say. Or maybe he's waiting for starry-eyed recognition to flitter into my eyes.

Sorry bud, I know who you are, and if I'm honest. I'd have never picked him for my team.

My eyes swing over to his counterpart, dark hair, dark eyes, a few tattoos peeking out from the collar of his jersey, and the slight indentation that indicates he has a lip ring when he isn't on the field. He gives me a charming, albeit practiced, smile, but for some reason, I'm kind of digging on it. Dad gave me an entire speech about staying away from his players, that they don't need distractions, and he'll fire me if he finds out I've fucked any of them, blah, blah, blah. My dad should know me well enough though to know that when he tells me not to do something, it only makes me want to do it that much more.

I give him my most seductive smile as I take half a step toward him.

"Name?" I question, and this time I'm not playing dumb like I did with Trevor.

"Jackson Donatello," he says with a mischievous look in his eye.

"Sage."

"I know," he says in a way that tells me he's already cataloged everything about me, even if it's a part of his act to make a girl feel special.

"Donatello! Andrews! Hit the showers," my dad's voice booms through the room.

I don't suppress my eye roll. Fucking buzz kill. Andrews turns and jogs off first, clearly accepting the fact that I'm not even remotely interested. Donatello, on the other hand, bends down and grabs my bag, slinging it over his shoulder before gesturing for me to go first. I catch a glimpse of my dad's irritated face and can't help but smile.

"You're asking for trouble there, boy," I tease.

He glances over his shoulder at Dad before looking back at me.

"Maybe, but you look like the kind of trouble I'd like to get into," he says smoothly as we make it into the hallway.

"Oh, trust me. You'd never want to leave," I say, allowing a husky tone to wrap around my words.

I can practically see him salivating, and I know that I could drag him into a supply closet and fuck his brains out right here and now. But then I'd have to fend him off for the rest of the season. Best to hold out on him for a while, make the build up a good one, before I move on.

"See you around," I say as I take my bag from his shoulder, allowing my fingers to trail over him as I do.

He bites on the edge of his lip where I'm assuming his lip ring usually rests as he nods.

"Looking forward to it."

I give him a soft wink before turning on my heel and heading down the hallway. As soon as I push the doors to the parking lot open, a voice calls out.

"Hey!"

I slightly jump at the surprise before turning to see Trevor Michaels pushing off the wall and walking toward me.

"Were you waiting for me?" I ask with furrowed brows.

"Yeah, we gotta talk. I—"

"Listen, Saturday was fun and all, but you're definitely not the kind of fuck I'm willing to lose my job over, and I don't go back for seconds. Sorry to interrupt whatever lame pick up lines you practiced in the mirror while you quaffed your hair, but I'm not interested."

He stands there frozen for several seconds, like my words are taking a while to catch up to his underdeveloped brain before he squints and shakes his head.

"Wait. What?"

"What? Did the Wizard of Oz forget to give you a brain? That pretty boy package just a ruse so people don't catch on that the lights are on but nobody's home?" I question.

Trevor narrows his eyes at me.

"Are you calling me stupid?"

"Insinuating, actually. To which you proved my point. I gotta go. I—"

"Hold up, hold up. Let me get this straight. You knew who I was Saturday, obviously—"

"Obviously," I mimic with an eye roll, causing a fire to spark in his eyes.

Normally I'm not so childish or sassy. But he's so easy to rile up, it's kinda fun.

"So you lied."

I shrug.

"So you could sleep with me," he continues.

I let out a humorless laugh as I toss my head back before facing him again.

"Deflate that ego a bit, old man. You're the one who chased after me, the one who dragged me down a hallway and bent me over a couch. Not the other way around."

"You're the one who climbed on my dick like a cat in heat," he throws out, crossing his arms over his chest like he's got the upper hand.

"Had to," I shrug. "You weren't doing it right."

Irritation passes over his face, causing his jaw to clench so tight, you'd think it would break. He looks as if he's about ready to tear into me before he looks down at the ground and shakes his head.

"Whatever. Just wanted to make it clear there is no way in hell I'm going to fuck you again. So if you think just because you work for the team that I'm going to—"

"Grandpa, the fact that you think I've been sitting here pining over you for days is adorable, but completely off base. You aren't even my last hookup, dude."

Okay, that's a lie, but this guy seriously needs to be taken down a peg or ten. His ego is out of control.

He tilts his head to the side as he squints at me again. What, does he need glasses or some shit?

"Did you just call me grandpa?"

"Yeah."

"Why?"

I laugh. "Dude, you're old as fuck. What are you, thirty-nine, forty?" I say, throwing out ridiculous numbers that has smoke practically billowing out of his ears.

"I'm thirty-one, you fucking brat."

"Yikes," I say with a grimace. "It's called moisturizer. Might want to try it, Leatherface."

With that, I turn on my heel and start walking toward my car. I hear him cussing me out, but I'm kinda bored now, so I think I'll just go home and binge *That 70's Show* and order a pizza. Yeah, that sounds nice.

Chapter 7
Sage

The next day I spend nearly all day on my laptop. I compile the footage I got into a couple of cool videos that I'll be sending over to the marketing team for approval. I also scroll endlessly, taking note of trending content other teams are coming out with and how we can make ours a little different. I don't realize how buried I am in it all until my stomach lets out an almost feral growl. I glance down at the time in the lower right-hand corner to see it's already almost five in the afternoon, and all I've had is some leftover cold pizza and a protein shake.

Pushing my laptop to the side, I reach for my phone and look up some restaurants near me. Everything has changed in the last two years. I hardly recognize any of the places anymore. Looks like there is a place not far from my apartment called Blackwoods. It's like a bar/restaurant, I guess. It's on the outskirts of the city, but that means they probably aren't too busy tonight. Maybe I can just grab an order to go or something.

It doesn't take me long to scroll through their menu before I decide on the black and blue bacon burger. I order a side salad as well as the fries, telling myself that if I eat the salad, I won't be as hungry for the fries, even if I know that's a bald-faced lie. Leaving a single potato behind is not an option, but ordering the salad lets me pretend that I feel good about my choices, so it works.

The drive is quick, and when I get there, the sleek unsuspecting black brick building is actually a lot more packed than I would have expected. As I make my way through the doors, I see Milly J, a Seattle-native singer/songwriter, sitting in a corner booth with a few friends. To my other side, I see several guys that I recognize who play for the Mariners. My eyes begin cataloging my surroundings recognizing almost every person at least vaguely. What is this? A watering hole for the rich and influential? Makes a little more sense why my burger, fries, and salad is costing me over thirty bucks, I guess.

I see the hostess stand tucked away to the side and make my way over to it when I hear my name.

"Sage!"

I turn to see Erica sliding out of a booth and making her way over to me. We met when I started doing hot yoga a few weeks ago and hit it off. Mainly because we both seriously question why we even torture ourselves by spending our free time in the literal pits of hell. Her fire-engine red hair is piled on top of her head as she holds her arms out, grabbing me in for a hug.

I hug her back, though I'm definitely the first to let go. It's not that I don't like affection, I just didn't grow up in a touchy-feely home. It's just not me. I'll hug you if I like you, but it's for like .5 seconds, and then you need to let me go. Erica is a hugger, though. The kind that will hold you for several seconds longer than a typical hug would last, causing you to stand there awkwardly until they finally release you. If she wasn't so sweet, I'd probably be annoyed, but she kind of reminds me of Calista in the soft mothering way she seems to have about her, minus the infinite tattoos and tobacco addiction, so I tolerate it.

"Hey, what are you doing here?" I ask.

"Just grabbing some food with some friends. Come here. I want to introduce you to Seb."

She practically pulls my arm out of its socket as she drags me over to her table where I see six other people sitting. They aren't just six people, though. They are Crusader players.

"Seb, this is my friend I was telling you about, Sage." Erica smiles as she sits down at the edge of the booth next to who I now know as her husband.

He slings an arm around her as he nods politely at me.

"Small world."

"Yeah, no shit. I didn't know you were married to Caldwell," I say before nodding and smiling at Santos, Daniels, and the two brunette women next to them who I'm assuming are their wives.

My eyes come to the other side of the booth, landing on probably one of the only Crusader players I would prefer not to run into. Apparently the feeling is mutual because he is practically shooting daggers at me from the inside of the booth.

"How do you know her?" Trevor asks, his question clearly directed at Erica, but his eyes remain on me.

I raise an unimpressed eyebrow at him as I match his stare. Does he think he's intimidating? Like he can make me quiver in my boots? I want to laugh in his GQ-model-worthy face, but instead, I keep a blank mask on, determined to win this little stare off.

I'm competitive like that.

"We do hot yoga together," Erica says sweetly. "Oh my god. I'm such an idiot. I forgot you told me you were doing social media for a sports team. You didn't tell me it was the Crusaders!"

"Yeah, her dad is the coach. Nepotism at its finest," Trevor sneers.

"Trevor!" Erica admonishes, causing him to break my stare, his eyes coming to hers like a rubber band snapping into place.

"Kidding," he says, though it's more like the grumble of a child who's been scolded.

Instead of his shitty glare coming back to me like I expect, his eyes stay on Erica as she redirects the conversation, introducing me to Scarlett, Slater's wife, and Vi, Declan's wife.

Scarlett asks me how the job is going so far, and I answer her with a smile, though I can't help but steal a curious glance out of the corner of my eye. Trevor is still watching Erica, a distant look on his face like he's in another place entirely. No one seems to notice, more interested in Scarlett's and my conversation, except for Sebastian. He isn't looking at Trevor, but I watch as his grip on Erica tightens, scooting away from Trevor just the smallest amount and taking Erica with him. Letting it be known that he is a barrier between them, and it's going to stay that way.

Interesting. Does Trevor have a thing for his teammate's wife? That's some next level shady shit right there. I knew he was a self-absorbed douche, but I didn't peg him to be like that. Shows what I know, I guess.

"Why are you still standing? Sit!" Erica says, pulling my side gaze away from Trevor as I look at her bright smile.

I contemplate it for a moment. I like Erica, and Scarlett and Vi seem nice too. From what I've seen, Sebastian, Slater, and Declan are good guys off the field as well as on, but when my eyes drop to the last member of the group, my interest dissipates.

"I'm gonna pass," I say, my eyes staying on Trevor, making the reason for my refusal extremely clear, and I couldn't give a fuck. I give Erica a shrug before saying my goodbyes.

I'm able to get my food almost instantly, and with one more wave to the back booth, I'm out the door and heading home. The entire walk to my car, though, I feel eyes on me, hot like lasers digging into my back. God, have I said that Trevor Michaels is a total prick yet? Because he's the prickiest.

"So, what was with the other day?" Erica asks breathlessly, sweat running down her forehead as the music thumps.

As much as I hate how miserable hot yoga can be, at least it's not totally silent like the traditional kind. I just don't think I could get behind that.

"What do you mean?" I ask, genuinely seeming confused even if I'm full of shit.

Erica must be able to tell too because she just lifts a brow as we move into another position. I shake my head, looking toward the wall as I speak.

"Michaels just isn't my cup of tea, that's all."

She is quiet for a few moments, so I'm assuming she's going to drop it when her voice comes out, a little softer than before.

"Go easy on him. I know how he comes across, but that's not the real Trevor. He's having a hard time adjusting up here. He doesn't really have anyone—"

"But you?" I guess gently.

Her eyes come to mine, a tint of sadness in them as she shrugs softly and nods.

"Am I missing something between you two?"

Erica bites her lip as the instructor moves positions yet again.

"We dated forever ago. For a while. He was that first love, you know?"

"Really? How did Seb feel about that when he found out?" I ask.

She winces slightly. "Well, he knew. Seb and Trevor were roommates in college while I was still in high school. They were best friends actually, practically inseparable."

"Oh no," I laugh. "Did you Yoko them?"

A teasing smile plays at my face, but when I look over at Erica, she isn't smiling. A complicated look crosses her face, one of guilt, shame, and hurt that has my smile dropping.

"Sorry," I mutter, feeling like an asshat for poking fun.

Erica swallows roughly, shaking her head before she speaks softly.

"It was hard for those first couple of years. I think things are getting better, but then again, sometimes I think this is the best they will ever get."

The nosey part of me wants to continue to pry, but the sensible part of me can tell that Erica is on the verge of tears, and so, I let it go. Once class is over, we are gathering up our things before walking out to the parking lot.

"So, we're having this get together at the house this weekend. You should come. You can finally meet the girls. Scarlett, Slater, Declan, and Vi will all be there," she smiles.

I want to ask if Trevor prickface Michaels will be there, but I go with my best judgment and keep my mouth shut. I'm ready to turn her down when she cuts in.

"Please, I know that you don't like to talk about your personal life much, but I know that you're alone way too much. I feel protective of you, like you're my baby sister, and I'm an only child so let me have this," she says with a laugh that has me giving her half a smile.

"Fine, but there better be alcohol."

Erica laughs. "See? Just like a big sister to sneak her underage sister booze."

I shake my head and laugh as I push some fallen hair out of my face.

"So, I'll see you there? Saturday? I'll text you the address."

I nod, causing Erica to let out a little yelp of excitement before she wraps me up in a hug. I hug her back for a second longer than normal, which is progress for me, but she still continues to hold on for several more seconds before she lets go and waves goodbye.

I'd never admit it out loud, but when Erica said that I was alone too much, it struck a nerve. I'm an only child too. I didn't have siblings to grow up with, and then when my mom died and my dad buried himself in work, I really was alone almost all of the time. He was home for dinner and gone before I left for school the next day. I practically raised myself, and until I met Calista, I didn't really know what it meant to have a true friend. And now that I'm gone, I'm back to having no one. So I'll go to the party thing, I guess. Even if I know Trevor fucking Michaels will no doubt be there.

Chapter 8
Trevor

I take a sip of my bourbon, before looking around the backyard. Besides the wives, I'm the only one drinking. The coaching staff doesn't approve of drinking during the season, even if it's only practice right now. They can kiss my ass, though. I'd quit football before I give up my bourbon.

Okay, maybe that's an exaggeration, but I do like it. It brings on a calming numbness that sweeps over my body entirely, allowing me to finally relax when I do indulge.

I watch as the kids run around the backyard, playing some game Erica set up for them while a handful of the Crusader players and their wives mingle. Sebastian is barbecuing as Erica and Scarlett are prepping food. Vi is sitting in the lounger next to me, looking pretty fucking pregnant while Declan plays with their two boys, Tucker and Rodney.

"You okay, Trev?" Vi's soft voice asks.

I turn to face her, giving her a smooth wink as I take another drink.

"I'm doing just fine, baby doll. How are you doing? Don't you know it's unfair to mankind for a woman to be nearly eight months pregnant and still look as sexy as you do?"

Vi blushes but rolls her eyes as Declan comes over, smacking me on the back of the head as he does.

"Stop fucking flirting with my wife, asshole," he grumbles as he lifts Vi to stand before taking her place and pulling her down to sit on his lap.

Slater and Scar come out with Erica and Sebastian closely following them as they set up the table to my left with all of the food.

"Aw come on, Daniels. Sharing is caring. Just ask Slater. I'm an excellent sharer," I say with a wink in Scarlett and Slater's direction.

To my surprise, Scarlett is the one who laughs while Slater is the one who sends me a death glare. Maybe it's the fact that this is my fourth drink of the day, or I just don't give a fuck anymore, but my mouth keeps running.

"I mean, it's only fair, right. I've fucked Seb's wife. I've messed around with Slater's. Vi is the only one left out," I tease with a waggle of my eyebrows that has concern knitting Vi's brows while what looks like thunder passes across Declan's face. He practically gnashes his teeth at me as he speaks.

"Show some fucking respect, or I'll teach ya some," he says, his southern drawl coming out thicker than normal.

"I mean no disrespect," I say with my hands thrown up. "I'm just saying, I'm here if you ever need a little spice in your life. I'm not doing anything else, obviously," I snort in a self-deprecating way that has everyone around us staring at me uncomfortably.

I glance around not sure why no one is laughing. I'm fucking hilarious. I'm just joking, obviously. Declan could snap me in two if he wanted, and I'm pretty sure if I fucked Vi, I'd send her into early term labor, so pass. Still, everyone is just staring at me, varying looks of irritation and disappointment.

Whatever.

Forcing myself out of the chair, I stumble only for a step or two before I make my way inside to the bar, draining the last bit of bourbon as I walk inside. I grab the bottle, filling my glass almost all the way to the top when I turn, slamming into someone almost instantly. My bourbon sloshes over the side, soaking the person in front of me and draining the glass.

"Damn it," I grumble. "This shit is expensive."

"Yeah? What about my fucking jacket," a smooth voice says filled with irritation.

I look up from my glass to see a tiny yet mighty Sage looking pretty pissed off as she tries to rub the bourbon off her leather jacket. She's wearing a plain white T-shirt that has got a little on it as well—just a few drops making the material almost see through, but not quite enough. Shame. I think the only redeemable thing about the woman at this point is her body. It's certainly not her fucking mouth.

She paired the outfit with a pair of skintight black jeans and some Doc Martens that make her look every bit the edgy chick I know she is.

"Your scene kid clothes? What I did is an improvement—anything is, really," I laugh as I lift the nearly empty glass, determined to get at least a few drops out of it.

She shoots me a dangerous look as she peels her jacket off and takes it over to the kitchen island, grabbing some paper towels before dabbing at her jacket.

"Aw, what's the matter?" I goad. "Don't want to play the battle of wits anymore?"

Sage looks up at me through her eyelashes, and I do my best not to stare, but fuck, those purple eyes catch me off guard every fucking time.

"Not when you're so unfairly unarmed."

It takes my alcohol-hazed brain a moment to understand what she meant. By the time I do she's already brushing past me, more like shoulder checking me, toward the backyard, her leather jacket slipped back on despite it being pretty fucking hot out.

I contemplate getting another drink, but the lightheadedness I feel tells me maybe I need some food first. Setting my glass down on the kitchen island, I make my way outside to see that nearly everyone has dished up and is scattered throughout the various hangout areas in the backyard.

Once I load up my plate, I head for the pool, sitting at the edge just far enough back that my feet don't quite touch the water. I'm eating for a few minutes before I feel her next to me. Her scent permeates the fog I'm swimming in, and I look over with a half a smile to see Erica sit down next to me, staring at me in concern. I frown at that.

"What's wrong? Are you okay? Are the girls?" I ask quickly.

She shakes her head softly. "Are you okay? It's noon. How are you already this drunk?"

I relax a little before I roll my eyes.

"I'm not thhhhat drunks, Little Red," I say slowly, my tongue suddenly feeling heavy.

"You're literally slurring your words, Trev. What is going on with you? I know the move is an adjustment and everything, but I haven't seen you like this in years, not since..." she stops herself, choosing not to go on, but I don't have the same self-restraint right now.

"Since college? When I was fucked up over you, and you were fucking Seb behind my back?"

She gives me a hurt look as she leans away from me a bit.

"Seriously, Trevor? I can't keep making excuses for you. That was a decade ago. You need to let shit lie, or I don't know what's going to happen."

"What's that supposed to mean?" I ask with furrowed brows.

She closes her eyes, taking a deep breath before she looks at me again, her green eyes filled with unshed tears as she speaks.

"It means you need to get your shit together, or I can't have you in my life anymore, or my girls' lives. Do you know that Rosie came up to me and asked what was wrong with you? Why you were stumbling around? This is not fucking fair to them, and it's not fair to you either. I'm trying to be here for you, Trev, but you're making it really hard to love you right now."

She goes to stand, and I reach for her desperately, my hand resting on the small of her waist as I try to pull her back to me.

"Baby, wait. I—"

She smacks my hand away, a look of irritation on her face, one I've never seen pointed at me as she speaks.

"Do not call me that, and do not touch me right now. God, Trevor. You really have no clue how many times your name comes up in my marriage, do you? How many times I've defended you, fought for you. I'm trying here, but you have to try too."

With that, she walks away, back to the corner of the yard where Sebastian is staring at me with a look that could set me on fire. I look around to see Slater and Declan giving me equally disappointed looks while Vi and Scarlett give me sad shakes of their heads. Humiliation crawls into my throat as I go to stand, tossing my still full plate of food into the trash as I make my way to the doorway. I feel eyes on me, and as much as I should ignore them, I can't.

I turn to look over my shoulder, shocked to see that it's not Erica's eyes that I'm feeling on me. It's Sage's. Her eyes aren't full of contempt or disappointment like everyone else. Instead, she's watching me with almost a curious look. Like she's solving a Rubik's Cube.

Solve away, Raven. I've been trying to figure out what the fuck is wrong with me for longer than I can remember.

Chapter 9
Trevor

The next day I woke up hungover as fuck. Like I had straight up partied all night long. Erica's words resonated with me, and I decided that I'm done drinking at least until the season is over. I don't need Rosie or Daphne watching me like that. I don't need anyone watching me like that. The tabloids would have a field day. I can see the headlines now.

Star quarterback fucked up over teammate's wife. Pathetically in love, forever alone.

Shit, that's not bad. Maybe I should sell my own story, make a fortune, and just become a recluse. I'm practically one already.

Today I have practice, and I'm hoping to just fly under the radar since, if I'm being honest, I'm embarrassed about my words and actions at the party. Not just to my friends, maybe former friends at this point, but also the few other teammates who were also there. I need to apologize to, well, almost everyone. But for today, I just want to come in, do my job and go home.

Of course, today has to be one of the only days of the week that Sage is working, right? Each week she has given me nonstop shit, and I'm getting sick of it. She doesn't always start it, I'll admit. Something about that woman just puts me on edge. The smooth silkiness of her voice that I found so attractive that first night is nothing but nails on a chalkboard now.

She's sitting on the floor like a fucking child because at twenty years old compared to me, she basically is one. Her camera is aimed up at us as we walk down the hallway, and I hear her shouting out a question to Roman in front of me.

"What's your favorite Taylor Swift song?" she asks.

up at us as we walk down the hallway, and I hear her shouting out a question to Roman in front of me.

"What's your favorite Taylor Swift song?" she asks.

"Ohhh shit. You're out here exposing me, girl. Uhh, 'Shake It Off.' Because the haters gonna hate, hate, hate, hateeee," he sings as he dances down the hallways past her like an idiot.

I roll my eyes at him as I continue walking.

"What's your favorite Taylor Swift song?" she asks me.

I ignore her, though, continuing my pace without so much as a glance.

"Aw, what's the matter? You too insecure about your masculinity to admit that you can get down with some T-Swift?" she goads.

Clenching my jaw, I spin around, coming back to face her as I lower myself down just in front of the camera. Though I'm glaring at the lens, I hope she can feel the hate I'm shooting straight at her.

"'Bad Blood,'" I snap before standing back up.

As if I don't affect her at all, she keeps filming as more guys come in while she speaks.

"Weird. I definitely would have pegged you for 'Anti-Hero.' It's practically your theme song."

I feel my anger boiling over, and I storm off before I can let her get a full rise out of me as she starts asking the guys behind me the same question. I'm not going to let that little brat get to me. She's just an annoying little girl with a big mouth. She's nothing, no one. But the way I practically punch a hole into the wall beside my locker tells me she may be no one, but she sure as fuck knows how to push all of my buttons.

Practice goes by smoothly. I'm lucky that things clicked into place the way they did. Usually joining a new team comes with growing pains, especially as a quarterback. I need to learn all the offense players to understand what my options are for every play, and sometimes, that's a fucking challenge. But I think from our days at Brighton, things with Sebastian and Slater at least are seamless, even if they aren't my biggest fans. I sure as fuck know Declan isn't too happy with me considering he sacked the fucking shit out of me three times today, hard.

When we are all in the locker room, I'm finishing getting dressed when Slater walks by me. Declan is pulling on a fresh T-shirt beside him while Sebastian is walking over to his locker with a towel around his waist.

"Hey," I say to all of them, figuring I need to just swallow my pride and get this over with. "I'm sorry for the way I acted this weekend. I was drunk, and it's not an excuse, but I wasn't thinking. I fucked up, and I'll apologize to the girls too."

They are silent for several moments, but eventually, Slater is the first to speak. He slaps my back as he shrugs.

"We know, man. You good?" he asks, watching me closely.

"I will be as long as we're good," I say as my eyes come to Declan.

He keeps his hard stare on me for only a few more seconds before he nods and slides his palm across my own before fist bumping me.

"We're good. But you talk about my wife like that again, and I'll knock your two front teeth out," he promises simply.

I let out a forced laugh because I have no doubt in my mind that if I ever say anything demeaning or degrading about Vi again, it won't just be my two front teeth. I'll probably be eating through a straw for the rest of my life.

When my eyes come to Sebastian, the lightness I was beginning to feel is immediately weighed down once again. I'm not stupid enough to think Sebastian and I could be as close as we were before everything went down. Some may be able to get over the past but not him. He's a stubborn fucker, and I more than know that if it wasn't for Erica, I would have been kicked out of his life a long time ago.

I feel stupid admitting it, but when she told me that my name gets brought up in their marriage a lot, it hurt. Mainly because one look at her face, and I knew it hurt her. My friendship with Erica is hurting her, hurting them. And even if the tiny, totally selfish prick side of me loves that Erica isn't willing to let me go for anything, I know the reality is that if it did truly come down to things, she'd pick Sebastian, every time. It's always been Sebastian. I was just the placeholder.

"I'll be better," I say, knowing an apology from me won't do nearly as much for Sebastian as a promise will.

His narrowed glare softens only slightly to allow a disbelieving look to cover his features.

"I doubt it."

I try not to show that his words cut deep, instead standing a little taller as I speak.

"What do I have to do to prove it then?"

Sebastian crosses his arms over his chest, standing up to his full 6'6" height as he looks down at me.

"You want my forgiveness? Want us to be good?"

I nod.

"Stay the fuck away from my wife then."

I blink at the pure hatred that his tone holds.

"What?"

"You heard me, stay the fuck away from her. Stay away from Erica, stay away from my girls. Get the hell out of my life, and we will be good. We can be teammates, play our game, and then go our separate ways."

"But," I start. "Erica is my best friend. I can't just walk away from her. And I love those girls more than anything."

Sebastian lets out a scoff, shaking his head almost in disbelief.

"Fine, then we aren't good. Don't speak to me unless absolutely necessary. Don't come near me unless it's life or death, and if you so much as put one finger on my wife again, I'll fucking break it off."

With that, Sebastian gets changed angrily, throwing his wet towel onto the ground before slipping into his shoes and storming off. I watch him go before turning back to see Declan and Slater giving me helpless shrugs, like they think I've made my bed, and now I have to lay in it.

Without another word, I grab my shit and make my way out of the locker room.

It's decided, coming to Seattle was the worst decision I've ever made. Well, second worst.

As if the day couldn't get any shittier, my phone begins ringing, and it's a number that has my irritation ratcheting up in an instant.

"Hey, Dad," I say into the phone as I continue walking down the hallway.

"Trevor, I need you back in Brighton this Friday," he says, getting right to the point.

I roll my eyes at his brashness as I speak.

"I can't. I have a job, remember?"

"Watch your tone, son. You have a sport that for some unbeknownst reason you get paid to play. This is actually important, though. We are having a board meeting about the merger with Kryon, Inc. Remember?"

Fuck no, I don't. When my dad starts rattling on about business, that's where my attention heads out. He's been shoving the family business down my throat since I could practically walk, and I've never wanted to be involved. When I got hurt back in college, I was resigned to it. I thought I'd never get a chance to play professional ball. But here I am, and there is no way I'm missing practice, pissing off Coach, and putting my job on the line for a stuffy board meeting.

His shitty comments about how what I do isn't really working, that I'm just screwing around, that I'll never be successful if I keep up this pace, usually roll off my back, but he called me on the wrong day.

"Well, what can I say? You know how it is. Tardiness is personified laziness, right?" I snap, throwing back his old saying that he used to use on me anytime I was half a minute late anywhere in my life.

"Trevor, goddamn it," he grumbles as he lowers his tone. "The other board members are concerned about your lack of interest in the company. They want you to sell your shares. You need to be here and show that you're invested in the company that will one day be yours."

"I don't want the company to be mine. It's your baby. Keep it, pass it on to whoever is sucking on your asshole this week. I don't care. I have a job to do, and I'm not abandoning it for a board meeting about a merger I could give two shits about, for a company I want no part in," I practically shout now that I've stepped outside.

The phone is silent for several seconds, the heat from the sun beating down on my neck before my dad's voice comes through the phone.

"You'll be joining us via Zoom. I'll push it to an evening meeting to accommodate your 'job,'" he sneers, heavy emphasis on the word job like I'm a child playing pretend. Like I don't make millions a year and am a household name throughout the nation. "In return for my generous accommodations, you will be punctual, and you will at least pretend to give a damn. Football won't always be there for you, but this will. You need to stop being a child and grow the fuck up," he says before he hangs up.

My fingers wrap around my phone tightly, jaw clenched before rage fills every ounce of me. I wind my arm back and throw my phone against the wall, taking a small amount of pleasure as I watch it splinter apart into literal pieces.

"Now what did that phone ever do to you?" Sage draws out slowly, a vape pen sitting between her fingers as she raises it to her mouth and inhales.

"Mind your own fucking business," I snap.

"God, are you always this much of a prick? Or am I just special?"

"Oh you're fucking special alright. I've never met a brat more fucking annoying and infuriating than you in my life."

She pushes off the wall she was resting against, flying in front of me and bumping her chest against mine. If she wasn't well over half a foot shorter than me and as heavy as a sack of flour, I'd say the girl was actually a little intimidating.

"Call me a brat again and see what happens, Michaels."

I scoff at her, rolling my eyes when she grabs a fist full of my shirt, yanking me down a few inches before I right myself.

"Just because your daddy doesn't love you, your friends hate you, and you're desperately in love with a woman that doesn't love you back, doesn't mean you get to treat everyone around you like dirt. Get the fuck over yourself."

With that, she turns, practically stomping her way over to a newer looking Camry. It fires up almost instantly and is practically peeling out of the parking lot and onto the street. For some reason, my temper has ebbed just a bit, and I'm able to blow out a deep breath before I look down at the broken fragments of my phone. Funny, it almost looks like the broken fragments of my life.

Chapter 10
Sage

The following weeks leading up to the preseason, Trevor Michaels stays out of my way, and I stay out of his. It's not all that hard, though the marketing team did ask that I get more content with him so I guess all good things must come to an end. I'm on the sidelines, the crowd practically deafening as all the players line up on the field.

It's the first preseason game of the year, and you can practically feel the energy buzzing in the air. We have home field advantage, which is always a nice way to start a season off. My dad is tense, scowling at the field like it's personally offended him while ignoring nearly everyone around him. Typical.

I already did some pregame content. Some locker-room-pump-up stuff and a few Q&A bits that marketing should have a field day editing. If I hadn't grown up as the coach's daughter, I probably would have been embarrassed by how much naked ass I've seen today alone. But guys would take the opportunity to ogle women, were the situations reversed, so yes, I got some footage of some of the nicest asses in the league. One of the top ones being Jackson Donatello, to no surprise.

The sexy bad boy cornerback has been practically salivating over me for weeks, and I've enjoyed every second of our flirtations. He's so desperate at this point, I have no doubt he'd walk off the field right here and now just so that he could bend me over the bleachers and fuck me raw. To be honest, I'm getting a little over my games myself. I won't be able to hold off with him for as long as I was initially planning, which will make for a longer period of him bugging the fuck out of me, but there are plenty of great looking players I can move on to when I'm done with him.

As if he can feel my eyes on him, his head turns in my direction, those sharp eyes practically slicing over my body through his helmet before he gives me a wink that makes my pussy throb. Yep. I won't be lasting long at all.

Both teams line up as Trevor begins his little quarterback rambling. Obviously I know all of the correct terminology, I just don't really give a shit, though. The ball is hiked and slides right into Trevor's grasp where he quickly reads the field, throwing the football to Slater who is already a solid ten yards in front of his defenseman.

The throw is perfect, spiraling through the air with the speed of a bullet and precision of a thread slipping through a needle. It lands right in Slater's outstretched hands as he takes off like a bat out of hell. He makes it about twenty yards before he's finally tackled.

Everyone on the sidelines claps excitedly as my dad smacks his hands together in what I think is supposed to be a clap, but the aggressive way he does it looks more like a punishment to his palms. All of the guys come together in celebration, several of whom pat both Slater and Trevor on the backs before lining up again.

We are playing the Georgia Beavers, and though they didn't do amazing last season, they weren't the worst team in the league. You wouldn't know it by this game, though. Before I know it, it's already the fourth quarter, and we are up 36-7. Obviously our defense has done a great job of holding off their offense, but we didn't get those big points on the board from just our defense.

The Crusaders have been one of the top teams in the league for years, but they were always missing that little bit extra, that something to put them over the edge and make them unstoppable. As much as it pains me to admit it, the change is obvious. They needed a superstar QB, and as much of a self-absorbed prick as he is, Trevor Michaels is in fact a superstar.

The clock runs out with the Beavers attempting a Hail Mary, though I don't know why they even bothered considering the twenty-nine-point lead we had on them. Probably that delicate male ego trying to save at least a little face.

I capture some footage of the Crusaders celebration as I rush up to several of the more enthusiastic players who are shouting and bouncing around. A few of them told me they rehearsed some dance thing that is sure to go viral, and sure enough three defensive linemen line up in front of me and basically begin twerking, badly. I can't help but let out a laugh as I toss my head back.

In the rush of players and family coming onto the field, I'm shoulder checked and lose my balance. I make sure to tuck the camera to my chest, hoping my body will take the brunt of the crash since I seriously don't want to even know how much this thing costs, when a thick pair of arms smoothly catch me at the last minute. Blinking my eyes open, I look up to see the lightest blue pair of eyes I'd ever seen. I mean, I've seen them before, but I never realized how blue they are, like the crystal-clear waters of the Maldives.

For a moment, I'm caught in his gaze, speechless, hardly able to wrap my brain around the reason why I can't look away beside the obvious reason that he's a beautiful man. The pretty boy vibe really isn't my thing, but I think Trevor could be everyone's exception, at least once. And he was mine already, and despite my blatant lies, he was fucking good too.

Trevor hasn't looked away from me either, like he physically can't. Something must shake him out of this weird hazy bubble we inadvertently found ourselves in though, because in the next minute, he is practically shoving me to my feet. He looks down at me with a disgusted scowl, his helmet abandoned at his feet as he quickly bends down to pick it up.

"Watch where you're fucking going."

And just like that, any physical appreciation I had for the man dissipates into thin air.

Motherfucker.

I feel a set of hands cupping my hips from behind before a soft warm breath tickles the back of my neck.

"Did you see that touchdown I made just for you?" Jackson says in a low voice, his lips just barely brushing against the nape of my neck as he speaks.

My sour mood lifts just a bit as I turn to face him, making sure to step out of his reach just a touch.

Always keep them wanting more.

"I saw you made a touchdown. Didn't know it was for anything more than your paycheck, though," I say with a tilt of my head.

He chuckles quietly as he runs his tongue along his lower lip.

"Fuck you're such a ball buster. You ever gonna give me a break, girl?"

"Why would I do that? Everyone knows that if a man wanted to, he would."

Jackson shakes his head but smiles.

"Yeah? Well tell me what I gotta do to convince you to let me take ya out sometime."

I let out a faux sigh of disappointment.

"If you have to ask, I guess you don't have what it takes."

Turning on my heel, I walk away without a backward glance. I hear him laugh again and shout out something to me, but I don't acknowledge it. Partially because he seems to love this cat-and-mouse game almost more than me. The other part though is that Trevor seriously put me in a shit mood, and when I finally ride the dick I've been flirting with for the last three weeks or so, I don't want to be in a sour mood because of Trevor fucking Michaels.

Chapter 11
Sage

Erica called me and asked if I wanted to get my nails done with Scarlett and Vi today. I guess they were having a girls' day and wanted me to tag along. I've never had a lot of girlfriends before, so my automatic response was going to be no thanks. I think Erica is starting to get to know me too well, though. Before I could even respond she was cutting me off, asking for my address and saying she was already on her way.

We all got manicures, Erica going with a deep green, Vi a cobalt blue, and Scarlett a hot pink. I was going to go with black since it's my go-to, but a fire-engine red was calling my name, and I have no regrets. They fucking slap.

After nails, the girls were hungry, and Scarlett practically begged and pleaded for Dick's Burgers. If you're not from Seattle, you'd probably think that the place was made up, or a hole in the wall. Instead, it's practically a Washington staple. Personally, it's not my favorite place to go, but I'm not too picky.

Since it's a drive-in, we decided to take it somewhere to eat instead of eating in the parking lot. I suggested my place, since I'm the only one who lives alone. Scarlett and Erica grab the food, as a very pregnant Vi and I get out of the car and make our way inside where thankfully there is an elevator to my floor.

"Ow, little girl." Vi winces as she backs up against the cool metal wall holding her stomach.

My eyes widen in panic as I step closer to her.

"Are you okay? Are you having the baby or something?"

Vi gives me a small smile and a laugh before shaking her head.

"No, believe it or not, I still have a little over a month left. She just decided to use my bladder as her own personal kickboxing bag."

I wrinkle my nose up at that and frown.

"Rude."

"Right?" Vi laughs.

Scarlett watches Vi with a sad smile before absentmindedly running a hand over her flat stomach. I don't know a ton, but Erica told me that Scarlett was diagnosed with cancer last year. Ovarian cancer, and she ended up having to get a full hysterectomy. Apparently she was devastated over it, but they did freeze her eggs, so she still has a chance to have biological children of her own one day, just maybe through different methods.

When the elevator doors slide open, I step out first, leading everyone down the hallway. However once we are a few steps outside my apartment door, I freeze. I locked my door. I know I did. I double-checked that I locked it just like I do every single time. So, why the fuck is it wide open?

My breathing begins to quicken as I take a step closer, now noticing the frame is completely splintered apart. Like someone broke in.

When I crest the corner, my heart sinks as fear takes hold of me. My place is trashed, absolutely ransacked. The couch is tipped over, dining room table chairs are broken, and there is a slash through the new painting I bought at the flea market last week.

"Holy shit!" Erica exclaims. "What happened?"

I don't respond, though. Instead, I reach for the baseball bat tucked behind the bookshelf in the entryway and slowly make my way inside. I hear the girls creeping in behind me when I whip my head over my shoulders, putting my finger to my lips as I do. They all look scared to death, and I instantly feel equal parts humiliated and worried that they are with me right now.

I pop my head into my bathroom first, noticing all of the makeup I had out has been crushed, snapped, or smeared. The bathroom mirror is even shattered, and my straightening iron is laying bent on the floor as the obvious culprit. There is also water covering the floor. The toilet has literally been ripped out and is lying on its side, the pipe slowly leaking water everywhere. My eyes follow the trail that is now soaking into the hardwood floor hallway. Nothing like a fuck ton of water damage on an upper floor.

Letting out a slow breath, I check my bedroom, and I could cry at what I see.

My dresser is tipped over, several clothes literally ripped to pieces. The two windows in the room are broken, pieces of glass litter the perimeter of the room. My bed is also flipped with several long jagged knife slits in it. My safe keeping place...all of my savings...gone.

Panic fills me as Erica comes behind me, touching my shoulder gently.

"Sweetheart, we need to call the police."

I turn to look at her, furrowing my eyebrows. Police? They aren't going to do anything. Whoever did this is long gone, and so is my getaway cash.

"Why?" I ask instead.

Erica's eyes bug out of her head as she looks at me.

"Um, because you were obviously robbed. Did they take anything that you can tell?"

I don't respond to her, my eyes tracing over the destroyed room, tears beginning to build behind my eyes despite how hard I bite them back.

"Yes, hello?" I hear Erica's voice say. "I'd like to report a break-in."

Slowly, Vi leans into my vision, placing a comforting hand on my shoulder.

"Are you okay?"

I look up at her with watery eyes.

"No," I croak.

She gives me a sad look as she squeezes me softly.

"Do you have any idea who could have done this?"

A gut feeling tells me who could potentially be behind this, but I do my best to push the emotion-driven thought away. It couldn't be him, not just because of the reassuring phone call that I had with Calista, but as of a few months ago he had a stylish piece of ankle jewelry, making it impossible for him to leave Santa Fe County.

I just shake my head as silent tears begin rolling down my face. Vi wraps her arms around me while Scarlett and Erica give me sad sympathetic looks. They think I'm crying because my stuff is destroyed. I couldn't give a shit about any of that, though. I'm crying because the small sense of safety I was holding onto, the reassurance that I had a little something to make sure I never ended up in the same situation that I was in again, is gone.

The police show up after an hour or so. They honestly seem like they couldn't give a shit and are shuffling out the door within minutes.

"We will do everything we can, but I don't think there is really anywhere to go from here," one says to me, causing me to scoff and shake my head at his bullshit.

"Are you kidding me? What about DNA? They touched everything in here obviously, or the security cameras in the hallway. Obviously they came in some-how," Erica throws at them with an irritated fold of her arms.

He looks at her and shakes his head.

"It's a lot more complicated than the stuff you see on TV, ma'am. We will open a report, and if we catch the people responsible, we will let you know," he says, finishing his sentence on me.

Oh great. Can't wait to never get that phone call.

With that, he turns and walks out of the apartment to join his other useless buddies.

"Are you fucking kidding me?" Erica practically fumes. "What do they ex-pect you to do? Just replace all of your things? And what about security? They didn't even fix your door!"

"They're police officers, Erica. Not handymen," I snort in a self-deprecating kind of way.

Vi is talking on the phone, but she quickly hangs up as she takes a step over to us.

"I just made some calls. I have a guy coming over to repair what damage he can."

I run a hand through my hair, only imagining the type of phone call my father will get when he is notified about this. I mean, it's his name on the lease. Not sure he'd care outside of losing his security deposit. He practically cut me off when I skipped town two years ago and sang 'I told you so's' until the cows came home when I got back. He didn't even bother to ask why I left him, why I had to come crawling back to Seattle. He just tossed a job, car, and apartment at me and has barely spoken to me since.

"Where are you going to stay tonight?" Scarlett asks. "I mean, you can't stay here. Your door doesn't even lock."

I grab the bat to my left, cradling it in my hand as I look at the open doorway. "Don't need a lock at this point."

Erica rolls her eyes like I'm being ridiculous. Like I could never handle myself in a situation like that. Oh how wrong she would be.

"I'm not even going to respond to that. If you don't have a place to stay, you'll come stay with Seb and me until your place is fixed."

My eyebrows sink at that, and I shake my head before she can even finish her sentence.

"No. Thank you, Erica, but no. I'm not bringing my shitty problems to your doorstep. You have a family to look out for."

"You think they targeted you on purpose? That they could do it again?" Scarlett asks with a small gasp.

I glance at her and shrug, letting things lie in the air before Erica speaks. I honestly don't know what to think. The cynic in me tells me it's too coincidental, but the small piece of me that is trying to stay positive, hopes to fucking god that isn't the case.

"Fine, not any of our places. I know somewhere, though. Best security system money can buy and plenty of room."

I raise an eyebrow at her in question. I can't deny a place with a solid security system sounds more than appealing right now. I'm trying not to let my fear overtake me, but I'm two seconds away from trembling out of my skin.

"Where?"

Chapter 12
Trevor

"**N**o," I say for probably the tenth time since Erica showed up on my doorstep.

"Please," she begs again.

"No, absolutely fucking not."

"Why not?" she huffs as she crosses her arms over her chest.

"Why not?" I laugh. "How about because she's a raging bitch, and I don't want her anywhere near me, let alone in my fucking house."

"First off, don't call my friend a bitch. Second, this isn't a house, Trev. It's a fucking mansion. You could give her the entire east wing, and you'd never even see her."

I shake my head, refusing to budge on this.

"I'm sorry. You know I'd do anything for you, but it's a no."

She rolls her eyes at me like I'm the one being difficult. Glancing to the empty doorway, she lowers her voice as she takes a step closer, like Sage could hear her all the way outside from the car if she's not careful.

"She's really scared, Trev. You should have seen the place. I think she knows who did it, and she won't tell anyone, not even the police. Her door doesn't even shut. Please, just until Vi's handyman makes the place safe.

I clench my jaw, hating how I can already feel myself wavering. Goddamn it. I hate that this woman is my fucking weakness. All it does is fucking hurt. Hurts me, hurts her. I know it hurts Seb. He just masks it with anger.

I need to get over her. I need to let her go. I just...can't. Erica's big green eyes look up at me, begging, pleading, and just like that, I fucking fold.

"Fine," I bite out. "But if she's in my way, she's out on her ass. I don't give a fuck if she sleeps on the street."

Erica looks at me like I'm an alien as she cocks her head to the side.

"Why do you hate her *so* much?"

"She's fucking rude. She gets under my skin and *enjoys* it. I've never met anyone more obnoxious in my life, and of course she has to be Aberton's daughter. Of course she has to work for the Crusaders, and absolutely of course you of all people had to make friends with her."

She shakes her head at me.

"Can you drop the shitty attitude at least for a minute? It was like trying to bathe a cat just to get her in the car to come over here."

I can't help but let out a dry chuckle at that. I could picture Sage like a feral cat experiencing water for the first time. Maybe if I dump a bucket of water on her while she sleeps she'll voluntarily leave, and Erica won't be mad at me. At least not too mad.

Not a bad idea.

"Fine, but I mean it, Erica. If she pisses me off, she's out of here, your friend or not."

"Thank you," she says as she pulls me in for a quick hug before scurrying off toward the driveway.

I grab my protein shake and make my way into the living room, sitting down on the couch as I look out the floor-to-ceiling window where Erica is standing at the passenger side of her car, practically yelling. I can vaguely see Sage crossing her arms and shaking her head like a petulant toddler.

Scoffing to myself, I roll my eyes. At least she won't be here long. She hates me as much as I hate her. Us in the same house for more than twenty-four hours is either going to end up with her moved out or one of us dead, preferably her.

When she steps inside, a sad single backpack slung over her shoulder, I expect her usual brand of snark to come immediately. But one look at her, and I know something is off. The air in the house suddenly shifts. Instead of the big, bold confidence she struts around with like it's her second skin, she's timid, her shoulders slumped down, her long sleek hair falling into her face as her eyes look around the room uncomfortably.

Something about it has me standing and crossing the room. The closer I get, the more I realize how off she looks. She's shaking. You can't really tell at first glance, but I see it in her fingertips. They are quaking uncontrollably, and when she meets my gaze, her normally bright and fiery purple eyes are left dim, deflated and practically emotionless.

"It won't be for long. I'll stay out of your way," she says softly, like her throat is too tight to squeeze much more sound out of it.

I find my eyebrows knitting together as I watch her, crossing my arms over my chest so I don't do something stupid like comfort her.

"You're fine. C'mon, I'll show you what room you can stay in."

She glances back to Erica, an uneasiness radiating from her. For once since meeting her, she truly looks her age. A scared twenty-year-old who doesn't know what to do or who to trust. I mean, she really shouldn't trust anyone but herself with much, but the one thing she can trust is that while she's here, she will be safe.

Erica nods at her with a kind smile that has Sage looking at me and nodding. I lead the way, letting the girls trail after me as we step up the glass staircase, walking across the hallway that overlooks the living room as I turn right and lead them to one of the spare rooms. There are plenty I could stick her in but this one is one of the only ones that doesn't have a balcony attached, and something tells me she'd probably appreciate the security of not having one right now.

When I open the door, I step to the side and allow the girls to step in. Sage's eyes look around the room carefully, appraisingly. I wonder what she sees when she looks at the place. Does she know I haven't done a thing to it? That I bought it this way and haven't cared to change anything. It's just a house I plan on sleeping in and working out in when I'm not traveling or at practice. It's not anywhere I'm rushing to get back to. I bought it because of the gated community, private driveway, and extensive security system. Some fans are fucking crazy. It also has a state of the art gym which I liked, though I won't lie,

I was sticker shocked when I saw how little money gets you up here compared to my house in San Antonio.

Sage doesn't comment on the room, though. She doesn't speak for a while. Instead, she just stares at me, embarrassment clear in her features along with a million different emotions that I can't even begin to name. I can feel the questions I have for her practically bubbling on the tip of my tongue. Like why didn't she go to her dad for a place to stay? Or a friend? Who broke into her house? What kind of enemies does she have, and why the hell is she trying to protect them if they ruined her place? It feels too out of place to voice any of those things, but the discomfort at having her in my space has me clearing my throat.

"Erica can write down the gate code for you, and I'll get your fingerprint added to the biometric scanner for the door."

Sage nods as I turn to head out.

"Thanks," she says softly, so softly I barely register it.

I choose to act like I didn't hear it, because what else do I say to it? Despite this being a clear violation of rule number three, I'm not as irritated as I probably should be. She's scared and doesn't feel safe. Erica has taken her under her wing, which means she obviously cares about her, and if Erica cares about her, then I guess I care enough to make sure she can sleep in a house where the doors lock. At least for a little while.

Later that night, I push the door open, surprised to see Sage in the kitchen. I would have thought she would have holed up in the room for the rest of the night. Instead, she's bobbing her head to Bad Omens as she stirs the mixing bowl that she's holding in her hands.

Her usual spunk looks to have returned as her body gyrates to the music, giving me flashes of her in that club. Fuck, the girl knows how to move her body and is unapologetic about it. She's currently wearing a slouchy black sweatshirt that is slipping off one shoulder and a pair of black yoga shorts. I'm not sure if the woman has a single color in her closet, outside of the Crusaders gear she wears, and even those clothes are black and Crusader green.

My eyes run down her body, stopping on that perfect peach-shaped ass as it moves around in my kitchen. She may be a pain in the ass, but she's definitely a hot pain in the ass. Too bad I don't do repeats, I wouldn't mind killing some time with her again. As long as I could tape her mouth shut or something.

When she turns to face me, she nearly jumps out of her skin, letting out a high-pitched shriek that has me wincing as she reaches over for her phone, turning the music almost all the way down as she glares at me.

"You couldn't have announced yourself?" she snaps.

I raise my eyebrows at her in surprise.

"In my own house? Oh, my mistake. I'll be sure to let you know. Hey, I gotta take a piss, is that okay with you?" I snark.

She doesn't skip a beat as she sets the bowl down.

"As a matter of fact, it's not. Don't you know dogs go outside? I saw a lovely bush with your name written all over it out front." She smiles so sweetly it's venomous.

"I see you're back to being your bratty self," I say pointedly.

"And you're back to your 'I'm hot shit' attitude."

"Raven, you were at the game. I *am* hot shit."

"Oh, like you played every position by yourself in that game? Must have missed that part. God, you're such an egotistical narcissist."

"At least I'm not a jaded little girl with daddy issues," I toss out, almost regretting it when I see the flinch that passes through her body at my words.

It doesn't take a genius to realize that Aberton doesn't have a great relationship with his daughter. All of the times I've seen them in the same room, they hardly look at each other and something tells me that the same lack of interaction extends off the field.

I expect her to lash out, to shout at me, call me an asshole or something, but she doesn't. Instead, she seems to shed the hurt off like an unwanted coat, setting the bowl in her hands down onto the counter, as she smooths out her hair and points a daggered look my way.

"You're right, Trevor. I do have daddy issues. Do you enjoy throwing people's obvious trauma in their face? Is that why Erica doesn't love you? Is that why she left you for Sebastian? Because she saw the real you? The one you try to hide behind that golden boy façade? She realized that you were less than what she deserved, and she found what she had wanted all along in your friend?"

Blinding rage rips through me at her words, and my stomach turns. My pulse is thundering, my breathing labored. I'm ready to wrap my hand around her fucking hair and drag her ass out of the house when she scoffs at me, throwing the bowl of whatever the fuck she was mixing into the fridge before stomping away.

I want to drag her ass back here, but I do my best to stay rooted in place because I'm definitely not in control of my emotions right now. My eyes look around to see several other bowls and dishes scattered around the kitchen and what looks like flour smeared across the marble counter.

"Hey! Come clean up your fucking mess!" I shout out to her.

I watch as she leans her head over the banister to look down at me as she rolls her eyes.

"Get your maid to do it."

Two seconds later, I hear a loud slam of her bedroom door shutting before I mutter out a string of curse words and begin cleaning up after her.

Fucking. Brat.

I literally opened my house up to her, begrudgingly so, and not three hours later, she's already crossed the fucking line. I don't care how much she means to Erica. I'm not putting up with this shit.

My hands angrily scrub at the dishes in the sink, rinsing them off before putting them into the dishwasher. I used to be a slob when I was a teenager, always having someone to pick up after me, and I do have a maid that comes twice a week, but that's to do the deep cleaning stuff like the bathrooms and mopping the floors. Clutter didn't used to bother me, but as I've gotten older, it has become a huge pet peeve of mine.

I'll let her stay the night, mainly because I don't want to see her fucking face right now, but tomorrow she's gone.

Chapter 13
Sage

The grease from the bacon snaps at me, searing my skin and causing me to drop the tongs in defense.

"Ow! Fuck," I grumble as I quickly reach for a paper towel near me, wiping away the searing hot liquid before turning to check on the lemon blueberry scones I made this morning.

I've always liked cooking, mainly because I've always liked eating. A lot of people think that because I'm fit, I starve myself or watch what I eat, when in reality I eat like a fifteen-year-old boy.

No one really taught me how to cook—no one was really around to take the time to show me. But one day when my dad was working late, a cooking show came on the TV, and I was hooked. I've gotten pretty good over the years, and I always like coming up with new combinations of flavors.

Another thing food is good for is apologizing. I don't do it often, but when I do, I mean it. I was a bitch yesterday, more so than usual. More so than what is acceptable. I was on edge, in my emotions, and if I'm honest, pretty fucking scared.

I snapped. Trevor, despite hating me, opened his door to me when he could have easily slammed it in my face. Despite the fact that I know Erica had everything to do with his sudden generosity, I still didn't have to hit him below the belt like that.

I don't know the full story, but from what I can tell, there is more than I could probably even guess. I know that Erica and Trevor used to date, and I know they broke up when he went to college. I also know she met Sebastian a few years later, and that he was Trevor's best friend at the time. Key word on was.

If Erica hadn't told me that part, I would have known anyway. Anyone can step into the room with Sebastian and Trevor and feel the temperature practically plummet. You can tell there is some tension from Trevor toward Sebastian, but the icy glares, the stiff body language, and aggressive energy is all Sebastian. The nosy part of me is so curious.

Did Sebastian steal Erica from Trevor? Was she dating both of them until she wasn't? Were they a throuple?

I doubt the last one based on the two alpha-male personalities alone, but you never know.

Still, despite how obvious Trevor makes his feelings for Erica, it's not my business. I was being a bitch, so now I'm here trying to undo my bitchiness with some refined sugar and processed pig fat.

I hear footsteps pad down the stairs before a shirtless Trevor emerges. His hair is sleep-mussed, his black boxers practically skintight. I do my best to keep my eyes on his, but they skim down his exposed skin, greedily taking in every inch. I didn't really get a good look at him during our back-of-the-club romp, and now I'm kind of sad for past Sage because fuck. Trevor Michaels is hot. Like really hot.

His body is lean but firm, all hard lines and smooth skin with the softest tan, probably thanks to those Texas summers. As far as a quarterback's physique, his body is perfection, and the way his boxers are leaving practically nothing to the imagination has pussy butterflies running through me. Yup. Pussy butterflies. If you didn't know that was a thing, you obviously aren't fucking the right people.

A soft noise leaves him, and my eyes jump back up to his, catching the curious, albeit guarded, look on his face as he watches me. Not knowing what to say, I grab one of the cooling scones and offer it to him.

"Eat," I say as he continues staring at me.

He lifts a dubious eyebrow.

"Why? You trying to poison me?"

I roll my eyes and set the scone onto an empty plate before scooping a pile of bacon beside it.

"Please. I'd never ruin my cooking with poison. If I wanted you dead, I would have suffocated you in your sleep or something."

Trevor doesn't look amused as he looks around the kitchen.

"Charming. Did you not wreck my kitchen enough last night? Figured you'd have another go at it?"

I grit my teeth as the smart-ass response rests right on the tip of my tongue as I speak.

"I'm trying to apologize. This is how I apologize. Take it or leave it."

Trevor's standoffish attitude ebbs a bit, but he still wears a disbelieving look as he assesses me.

"Really? That's the best apology you are capable of?"

"Yup."

Trevor scoffs but glances down to the scone for a moment before grabbing it. He rolls it around in his hand a few times before his blue eyes come to mine, not budging an inch as he lifts the pastry to his mouth. Surprises flashes in those crystal eyes, followed by what looks like appreciation.

He takes another bite and another before reaching for more. I can't help but bite back my satisfied smile. Ask any cook, there is nothing quite like watching someone enjoy your food. Even better if they weren't expecting it to be much in the first place.

"Didn't know you could cook," he mutters as he swallows a bite.

"You don't know much about me," I shrug.

"Weird, right? You're so approachable."

An unexpected laugh bursts from me before I can stop it, causing me to tilt my head to the ceiling and shake it. When I face Trevor again, his posture is more relaxed, happily shoving his face full with my scones.

"True. Thank you for letting me crash here, though. I understand if you want me out of here. I was an asshole."

He watches me for several seconds before setting the half-eaten scone onto the plate as he walks past me to the fridge.

"Your shit is already here, and Erica will have my balls if I kick you out. You can stay if you make more stuff like that, and you keep the snarky comments to a minimum," he says as he pulls out what looks like a pre-made protein shake.

"I'll try," I say, knowing that until my apartment is at least secure again it's not safe for me to go back there. Not that they now know where I live. Hopefully I'll only be here a day or two tops, though. Then I can figure out whatever the hell I'm gonna do next...

Trevor nods as he takes a seat at the island while I dish up a plate of my own. I hesitate for a moment, contemplating if I should take it back to the room I slept in or not. Obviously sensing my indecisiveness, Trevor hooks his foot underneath the seat beside him, kicking it out in offering to me. I don't think much of it as I slide into the seat and begin eating.

Several moments of silence pass by before Trevor's phone dings on the countertop, and he reaches for it, a small smile curving his full lips upward as he taps out a response to whatever message he got.

"Who is that?" I ask, earning a sharp look from Trevor.

"None of your business."

"Hey. If I have to watch the attitude, so do you."

"My house, my rules, Raven."

I roll my eyes at the stupid nickname as he continues typing. It doesn't take a genius to figure out who put a smile on that surly face this early in the morning.

"How did Erica sleep?"

Trevor's eyes flick to mine as he gives me a look full of suspicion.

"Fine. Why?"

I shrug. "Just wondering."

"Bullshit," he scoffs.

"I just can't imagine a man like Caldwell being good with his wife sending another man good morning texts. He seems a little too...possessive."

Trevor snorts in a way that sounds like he definitely agrees before he runs a hand through his disheveled hair.

"For your nosy information, she was just texting to make sure I didn't murder your bratty ass. I told her I came close."

"I'm shaking," I say with my hands held up in mock fear. "What's the deal with all of that, though?"

"With what?"

"You, her, him," I say as I punctuate my words with a piece of bacon.

"I thought this whole breakfast was an apology for being nosy," he says with a tired sigh.

"Nah, this was an apology for crossing the line from kinda bitchy to straight-up cunty. I'll never apologize for being nosy. Knowing your opponent is half the battle."

"We're opponents?" he asks dubiously.

I nod at that with a slight furrow to my brows.

"You're right. You aren't even in the same league as me."

He shakes his head and rolls his eyes, but I see him forcibly bite back a smile as I speak again.

"So, what's the deal? Spill the tea."

"The tea?" Trevor asks.

"Oh my god. I knew you were old, but I didn't realize you were that old," I say on a sigh.

"Fuck off. Thirty-one is hardly old."

"Eleven years older than me. Sounds pretty fucking old."

He narrows his eyes at me, taking an overly aggressive bite of the bacon in his hand that oddly does something to me. I like pushing his buttons like this, watching the all-American, pretty boy thing he has going on drop for a minute before that darker, jaded side comes out. It's the side of him I saw first, the side that had me getting tongue fucked by a stranger bent over the side of a couch in the back of a club.

We're silent for a little while, and I think that's the end of it until he speaks.

"She was mine first. We were together for years, and then I...I fucked up."

"Cheated?" I guess.

"Fuck no," he snaps as his head whips up to me, a look of outrage splashed across his face. "I'd never. But I did break us. Thought we needed it when I went off to college. Only took her being on campus for five minutes to realize how royally I fucked up. Unfortunately, five minutes was long enough for her to meet Seb."

I grimace at that, feeling surprised at his honesty and also pity for the obvious heartbreak in his tone.

Poor guy is really fucked up over her.

"And now?" I question gently.

Trevor blows out a deep breath as he folds his arms over his chest, leaning back in his chair as he stares at the wall in front of him.

"Now...they're married with kids and the whole white picket fence thing, and I'm just...me, I guess."

"Do you want that? The ring, the kids, the whole shebang?"

He shrugs, still refusing to look at me.

"Well, you have to move on then. No offense, but they seem pretty happy as is, and no matter how well you fuck, I don't think they'll be opening up their marriage for you to join anytime soon."

Trevor's eyes narrow, and it looks like he's about to tear into me, so I raise my hand to stop him.

"I said no offense. I just meant, why don't you try to take your eyes off the 'one that got away,' for now and focus on the future? You're a professional NFL player. I'm fairly certain you could have anyone you want."

"Yeah," he says absentmindedly, his palm outstretched against the cool countertop as silence slowly creeps in around us.

Poor love sick fool.

"Give me your phone," I say with an outstretched hand.

He gives me a 'yeah right' look, but I just continue to wait.

Slowly, he hands it to me, and I hold the screen up to his face to unlock it before I begin my mission.

"What are you doing?" he asks.

"Helping," I say.

"How?"

The app finishes downloading, and I spin it around to face him before I start filling in the sign-up info.

"Luxe in Love? What the fuck does that mean?" Trevor asks.

"An ad came up for it the other day. It's like Bumble but for wealthy people. If you want that whole all-American dream thing, you're gonna need to find someone who is on your same level. Not a social-climbing gold digger. This dating app has a minimum annual salary requirement of $250,000 for all applicants. Any chance you have a paystub laying around?" I ask, to which Trevor just blinks.

"Fine. I'll just screenshot the last article that stated your $49.2 million dollar annual contract with the Crusaders."

"What the fuck are you doing?"

"Signing you up for a rich people dating app. Keep up, old man."

"I'm not fucking old," he grits between his teeth.

I ignore him though and continue putting in his information as I start filling in his bio.

"A star NFL quarterback looking for my forever teammate?" he scoffs as he reads over my shoulder. "What, do you write greeting cards for Hallmark in your spare time?"

"Fuck off," I say simply as I pull up the screen and pass it to him.

"Alright. What do you think of her?" I ask, showcasing a beautiful brunette with dark brown eyes who is the CEO of a pharmaceutical company.

Trevor shrugs and wrinkles his nose slightly. So I scroll again, to which he's even less enthusiastic than before. He rejects almost everyone, blonde, brunette, even the redheads. No one is good enough. Until we finally come across a pretty blonde who is a divorce lawyer. Her striking blue eyes are very similar to Trevor's. They are the kind of eyes that catch you off guard and take your breath away.

"She's hot," Trevor says as he points at the screen.

"Definitely. And she's obviously smart and will have no problem putting you into your place when you need it. I like her."

I swipe on her, and the app announces that they've made a connection. I type out a quick, but smooth, message to her like I'm Trevor. It's obvious that his infatuation with Erica is hurting everyone involved, and I don't think he's trying to be a bad guy. I think he's just a little selfish and doesn't want to live a life without her. Which is fine, but he doesn't have boundaries, and he clearly needs them. They say the only way to get over someone is to get under someone else, but based on Trevor's playboy reputation, I'm thinking he needs something with a little more substance if he has a chance of moving on.

I know, look at me being all saintly.

The girl's response to my message comes almost instantly.

"Hope you have something semi-decent to wear. You have a date tonight."

Chapter 14
Trevor

The dark liquid in front of me swirls in its smooth glass. The liquor is near mesmerizing, or maybe it just is in comparison to the woman across from me. Don't get me wrong, she's hot. Her long blonde hair, full red lips, and tight body would be a great way to waste the night away.

Unfortunately for both of us, the moment she opened her mouth was the moment my interest faded. Her voice is fucking annoying, like the high-pitched voice from that nanny sitcom my mom used to watch. She immediately started talking about how many kids she wants and where she wants to get married. I get that I have been out of the actual dating scene instead of just the hook-up game for a while, but even I know that's fucking crazy.

Let's be real. I only came because I knew Sage would bug the fuck out of me until I relented. I've got my rules for a reason, and number five is the most important reason of them all. You fall in love, you get hurt. That's just the way it goes. Still, I can't help but see her point even slightly.

I'm in pain every fucking day because no matter how hard I try to stick to my rules, there is one little problem. I'm still in love with Erica, and at this rate, I don't know if I ever won't be. So, maybe trying to see one woman a little more frequently wouldn't be the worst thing in the world. I'm not saying I want to fall in love and undoubtedly get my heart smashed to smithereens again, but maybe something consistent could help distract me from the redhead who never leaves my mind.

Except this woman. She is definitely not consistent casual hookup material.

"Are you even listening to me?" her nasally voice whines, causing me to lift my eyes from the glass for the first time in easily ten minutes as I look at her.

"Truthfully, no."

Her mouth parts like she's shocked by my honesty. I may be an asshole, but I vowed to myself almost ten years ago to being an honest asshole, no matter what, no lies. She doesn't say anything. Instead, she shoves her phone into her purse, slings it over her shoulder, and slides out of the booth of Blackwoods where Sage chose for our 'date.'

My eyes roam around the room before landing on the little raven-haired devil. Sliding into the booth, Sage stays quiet with a smile playing on her lips as she takes a drink out of her dark-colored glass.

"Enjoy the show?" I scoff.

"Yeah, kinda. I thought you'd be all smooth pickup lines, dropping her panties to the floor within two minutes. You looked like you were more interested in taking that Pappy home than her."

"Did you hear her voice?" I say with a lift of my brow.

She rolls her lavender-colored eyes in annoyance, but I see the smile playing at the corner of her mouth.

"The whole bar heard her voice. Still, you could have tried."

"And you could have stayed home," I grumble as I drain my glass, gesturing for the bartender to get me another.

"And miss the opportunity to watch you crash and burn? Not on your life, Michaels."

"Well, what now? You gonna admit this was a stupid idea and let me be miserable in peace?"

"God no. I'm too meddlesome for that, but for now," she pauses as a waiter about my age sets down another round of drinks for both of us, earning a smile and a wink from Sage before she lifts her glass. "We drink," she continues as she raises her glass, clinking it against mine before downing it in one go.

"This isn't a college bar serving well bourbon, you know? This is meant to be savored, enjoyed."

"No, it's meant to get me fucked up and nursing the same glass all night isn't going to get the job done," she says as she calls over the waiter again.

"Can we just get the whole bottle? Put it on his tab," she says as she gestures to me.

I roll my eyes but don't refuse as he goes to the bar coming back moments later with practically a full bottle of Pappy. Sage takes the bottle, filling both of our glasses halfway before looking at me. Her dark hair falls in her face a little, but one run of her hand through the silky tresses has them pushed out of her face in a way that reminds me of just-had-sex hair.

Does everything this woman does just exude sex appeal? She's not even old enough to be in this bar, and yet she's been charming every waiter, bartender, and man who walked in here like the temptress she clearly is.

I don't think she saw me watching her as she sat at the bar. My head was facing forward, but my eyes were tracking her every movement, fascinated with the confidence she radiated, the way she carried herself, and the obvious draw she had over every man and woman in this bar.

"Question for a question, yeah? If you don't want to answer, you drink," she asks as she lifts her glass slightly.

"Why?"

Those vibrant eyes roll as usual, I swear to God they'll get stuck like that one day with how often she does it.

"Because it's fun, jackass. Just shut up and agree."

I bristle at her demanding attitude as I sit up in my seat a little more.

"Why are you so prickly?"

"Is that your question?" she asks.

"Sure, why the fuck not."

"Daddy issues, mommy issues, and ex-boyfriend issues," she fires off passively as she lifts the glass to her lips and sips.

"I thought you said you only drink if you don't want to answer?"

She shrugs. "I was thirsty. My turn."

Sage pauses for a moment, tapping her red-painted nail against her chin.

"What's your favorite color?"

I frown at that.

"Who cares?"

"I do," she says, "hence why I asked."

She stares at me unyieldingly, like this is actually an important question.

"Green." *Like those eyes that live rent free in my head.*

Her face lifts with what looks like intrigue as she leans closer.

"Any particular reason?"

I lift my glass to my mouth, taking a healthy sip of my drink as I do. I know why. She knows why. The words don't have to be uttered and make me out to be more pathetic than I already am.

"Where did you go to college?" I ask.

"Didn't."

"Why not?"

She gives me a smile, a beautiful one, showcasing her perfect teeth and full lips, but the sarcasm and maybe even a little bit of pain in her eyes taints the sight.

"Thought it would be better to follow a boy instead."

I nod at that—guess that's where those ex-boyfriend issues come from.

"Bet your dad loved that," I muse as I take another drink, quickly abandoning the game as I wait for her response.

She snorts and nods as she sips her drink.

"Oh, totally," she drawls. "I'm not sure I remember what a conversation with a parent is supposed to consist of when the words disappointment or screw up aren't intertwined in every other sentence."

"I know the feeling," I say on a dry huff, flashes of my last conversation with my father coming to the forefront of my mind.

Her head tilts to the side slightly as she stares at me, those bright eyes practically burrowing into my soul.

"What's up with that? Your parents don't think being a superstar NFL quarterback is enough of an accomplishment? Wouldn't any parent be thrilled for their kid to achieve that?"

"You'd think. My parents always thought I was destined for the boardroom, not the field. My father, more so than my mother."

"That's pretty first-world problems there, bud," she says simply.

My god, she's so fucking blunt. If you just met her, you'd probably be thrown off by her abrasive personality. For some reason, I'm starting to get used to her attitude, though.

I'm not sure that I like that.

Before either of us can say more, she pours another glass for both of us, and we tip back our glasses before repeating the gesture. We sit there in comfortable silence for several moments, allowing the soft fuzzy haze of our buzz and the background music to take up the empty space of the room.

I watch as Sage's bare shoulders sway in the booth, the skintight black cocktail dress she slipped on when she said she was coming to spy on my date hugging her every curve. Goddamn. She's fucking hot when she isn't mouthing off.

The song changes, morphing into a smooth rhythmic beat. Sage's closed eyes fly open at the sound of it, damn near taking my breath away at the intensity of them just for a moment before she scrambles to her feet and reaches for my hand.

"C'mon," she says with a small smile playing on her lips.

Chapter 15
Trevor

Hazily, I follow after her, lacing our hands together as I stand. She twirls in the middle of the room, and I lift my arm to accommodate her spin before she comes back, softly chuckling as she softly rolls her hips against me.

My hands drop down to her waist, gripping her tightly as she does it again.

"What are you doing, Raven? This isn't the club. The world isn't your dance floor."

She turns to look at me over her shoulder, a challenging look in her eye accompanied by that playful smile I'm not used to seeing on her.

"Shouldn't it be?" she asks as she grinds her ass against me again.

Fucking hell. I should probably give a shit that we are literally dry humping in the middle of this bar. Should probably care that I've already had her, or maybe I should care that I can't fucking stand her. No one has ever infuriated me so consistently in life than this woman right here. Something about the way her shoulders relax, the way her body sinks into my touch as if it's the first time she's truly relaxed in years has me holding her tighter, ready to lay out anyone who tries to dim the rare sight of her light.

My hands have a mind of their own. I'll blame the obscene amount of bourbon we've drunk as they seek out her silky skin. It doesn't take long for me to feel her satin bare thighs, gently lifting her dress with each move. I allow my fingers to dance over her, tracing random patterns against her smoothness until my fingers graze just under her hemline.

She startles at that, spinning around in my arms in a flash. Her eyes come up to mine, gently lidded no doubt from the effects of the alcohol running through her veins. I'm about to apologize for obviously crossing a line when she reaches a hand up behind my head, pulling me down for a kiss.

I haven't kissed a woman on the mouth in almost a decade. It complicates things. It's too personal, too emotional, but as soon as I feel her gentle pull, I'm sucked in, closing the distance between us until my lips are crushed against hers. Her soft tongue slips into my mouth, tangling with my own as I reach up to grip her face. The kiss isn't sweet or gentle. I'm not sure you could ever use those words to describe Sage Aberton. It's passion, desperation, an intrinsic biological *need*.

When I feel her teeth nip at my lower lip, it does something to me, causing me to push her away. She looks up at me dazed, disappointment beginning to cloud her features as I reach into my wallet, drop more hundred dollar bills than I care to count onto the table before I take a step closer to her, cupping her face again to get one more taste of her, stealing this one right off her lips.

She arches into me, softly gasping into my mouth as I return the favor, biting down on her lower lip before sucking it into my mouth. Quickly, I pull away, grabbing her hand with my own as we stumble out of the bar and out onto the street. My eyes flick around the streets of Belltown, too in a rush to make some mistakes with the dark-haired beauty by my side to order a ride or call my usual service.

A yellow cab catches my attention down the road. Shit, I didn't even know those things ran out here anymore. I lift up an arm to hail it, and thankfully, the guy seems to see me. I usher Sage in first, closing the door as I drop a stack of bills into the money transfer bowl in the divider as I drag her over into my lap.

"Just drop us at the corner of Fourteenth and Avenue E. There's a grand there to keep your eyes forward."

The guy doesn't respond before the car takes off. Or maybe he does, and I don't hear him. I don't know, I'm too busy devouring Sage as she straddles me. Her dress has risen, all that's left between us is a thin piece of lace and my pants. Shouldn't have spoken so soon, though, because her hands make quick work of my slacks, undoing my belt before reaching inside and pulling out my cock.

"Fuck," I hiss as I lean my head against the back of the seat.

Most women would be shy, nervous. They'd fumble or try to be sexy by asking what I want them to do next. Sage does none of those things because to her this isn't about pleasing me, it's not about winning my affections hoping she can snag the NFL quarterback. She hates me, and the feeling is mutual. Right now all she is focused on is her pleasure, and I can honestly say I've never seen something so goddamn sexy.

She rises up on her knees, lining herself up over me before sinking down. Her pussy feels like fucking heaven as she grips me, slowly lowering herself until I'm fully seated inside her. A soft mewling noise escapes her mouth, and I thrust up instantly, desperate to hear it again. She doesn't disappoint, her mouth falling open as her hands come to my shoulders to stabilize herself.

"Fuck, yes. Ride me, Raven," I encourage as I cup the back of her ass and help guide her movements.

Her eyes flutter open softly to look at me as she nods, her hips beginning to gyrate in a hypnotic rhythm that has my balls tightening already.

"Fuck, Trevor. I forgot how good this dick is, for an old man at least," she teases with a wink.

"Does this feel old to you, baby?" I ask as I push up deeper than before, causing her mouth to drop open as I begin pounding into her from underneath.

"Did you take your little blue pill this morning or what?" she moans.

Is it possible for her to ever not be a smart-ass? Even when my cock is practically inside her cervix? I'm thinking no.

"Shut the fuck up, Raven, or I'll stuff your mouth full."

The amusement in her eyes twinkles as she looks at me.

"Promise?"

I feel her hand reach behind, cupping my balls as she continues bouncing on me, her tits practically spilling out of her dress as she does.

"Such a dirty little girl," I grit through clenched teeth as I try to hold my release at bay.

"You have no idea, Michaels," she groans as her movements pick up, becoming less coordinated and more desperate.

"Can't wait to find out," I mutter as I slip my hand in front of her, brushing my thumb against her clit.

"Come on my cock, baby. Show me how much you love getting fucked in this taxi like the little slut you are."

"Out of the two of us, you're the slut, Trevor," she argues, but the way her pussy clenches at my words contradicts herself.

"Let me feel you fall apart on me," I say as I bring her head closer, running my lips against the soft shell of her ear. "Let go for me, baby. Come."

As if my single word was a command she could never refuse, she screams, her orgasm tearing through her as she gasps and moans and curses. I feel her pussy squeeze me so tight, it sends me spiraling. My balls draw up and empty inside her as she continues riding my cock like a goddamn goddess.

"Fuck, fuck, fuck. God. Yes!" she rambles as her movements slowly ease, her breathing labored, and her hair all over the place. She runs a hand through it, looking freshly fucked and kinda perfect as the car stops.

"Uh, we're here." The driver coughs uncomfortably.

I expect Sage to get embarrassed. Had this been Erica, she would have been mortified. Scratch that. Erica would have never done something like that in the first place. She's too shy, too soft. Sage, however, laughs. Fucking laughs as she pops open my door, smoothly sliding off my dick and out of the car.

"Hope you enjoyed the show, big boy." Sage smiles.

I let out a surprised laugh at that, tucking my cock back into my pants as I slide out of the car and slam the door shut. Looking ahead, I see Sage walking ahead of me down the sidewalk just a bit before entering the security code for the gate. When it opens, she turns to look over her shoulder at me, a daring look in her eye as she takes off running, and something in me takes over as I chase after her.

Chapter 16
Sage

My legs stretch out as long and as fast as they can in these heels, which I'll admit isn't very fast. The pounding of Trevor's feet from behind me sounds closer and closer until I get to the front door. I go for the handle when disappointment sinks into my stomach. Locked, duh. I try to press my finger against the scanner, but it's too late.

In the next moment, Trevor is behind me, his front against my back, caging me against the large wooden door.

"Caught ya, Little Raven. What do I win?" he asks as he runs his nose up the length of my neck before his teeth nip at the flesh of my ear.

"A pat on the back?" I guess.

His rough laugh rumbles in my ear, sending goose bumps running up and down my skin.

"So fucking sassy. I told you to shut up, or I'd stuff your mouth full."

One of his large hands drops to my waist, spinning me to face him before he reaches into his pants and pulls his already hardening cock back out. Fuck. Talk about a reboot rate.

I think about refusing him, about torturing him with some more banter or something, but I'm too fucking turned on for any of that right now, and I drop to my knees right there on his front porch. Not because he told me to, but because I *want* to.

The cement slab bites at my bare knees, and I shuffle a bit to adjust when I feel something soft sliding underneath me. I look down to see Trevor's designer suit jacket laying just in front of me as he gestures for me to move onto it.

"How chivalrous of you," I say with feigned delight and a million bats of my eyelashes.

"Figured it was the least I could do since I'm gonna fuck the hell out of your mouth."

My eyes narrow at him, but I don't have time to say a word before his cock is pressing against my lips, pushing his way inside my mouth. I take him until he hits the back of my throat before he draws out and does it again. He keeps pushing deeper and deeper until his cock is fully down my throat.

"Fucking hell, how are you not gagging?" Trevor curses as his hands cup the back of my head, encouraging my movements.

I want to tell him that his cock really isn't that big, but that would be a lie. Trevor has hands down the biggest cock I've ever taken, and if I had a gag reflex, I'd be struggling right now. Thankfully for both of us, I don't, and I'm enjoying this too much to give him shit.

Some women don't enjoy sucking dick, and that's okay. I, on the other hand, love it. The actual act of it is okay. Not overly pleasing per se, but it's the power. No matter how big and strong or powerful a man is, when a woman is on her knees for him, she's the one who is in control.

I tilt my head up to find Trevor is already staring at me, his hips thrusting against me as he fucks my mouth. My tongue runs up and down the length of him, the taste of myself still lingering against him. Again, probably not a common response, but I actually don't mind the taste of myself. And the fact that I'm tasting it because I just rode his dick not five minutes ago in a moving car with a little audience, yeah, that shit is hot.

"Fuck, you take me so good, baby. You like sucking my dick, don't you?" he asks as I nod.

"Of course you do. You're so good at it. At least this mouth is good for more than just being a smart-ass."

I nip at the side of his cock in warning, causing him to let out a half yelp, half chuckle. His hand pushes against my head, forcing me to take him deeper as I slip my hand beneath my dress and begin rubbing myself. Not two seconds pass, though, before Trevor is pushing away from me and stepping toward the door. He unlocks it in record time before lifting me up and throwing me over his shoulder.

He heads straight for the stairs, taking the steps two at a time. My head bounces with each step, and I punch his back when he takes the last step jerkily.

"Asshole! Put me down!" I say, to which he ignores me as he continues jogging down the hallway before getting to his room.

Kicking his bedroom door open, he wastes no time before he drops me onto a plush bed that I practically sink into. I push away the down comforter beneath me just before Trevor reaches down, spreading my thighs wide apart, burying his face between them.

"Shit!" I gasp as my hand goes to the back of his head, my fingers pushing through his thick blond hair as his tongue begins to attack me.

He licks, sucks, and tongue fucks me, all while his hands run up and down my bare skin, pushing my dress up further and further. It's an overload of sensations that has me practically shaking, and with two flicks of his tongue over my clit, I'm falling over the edge, *again*, screaming out my pleasure as I come all over his pretty boy face.

When my orgasm eases, he slowly rises from between my legs, a predatory look on his face that tells me he's not nearly done with me yet. Not sure I've ever met a man so ready to go back-to-back rounds like this, but I'm fucking here for it.

Shoving down his pants and kicking them to the side, he makes quick work of unbuttoning his shirt as I pull my dress up and over my head. As soon as the soft fabric passes my face, he's on me again. Our mouths are a wild battle of tongues, lips and teeth. It's nothing short of ravenous, and at this moment, it's all I crave.

Trevor grips my thighs tightly, spreading them wide before pushing them back. His eyebrows raise in surprise as they continue to go and go until they are almost parallel to my head.

"Bendy little thing, aren't you?" he says almost to himself before he pushes inside me once again.

"Reckless little thing fucking me not once, but twice, with no protection, aren't you?" I sass back as his thrust rubs the head of his cock against my G-spot.

He pauses for a moment, like the lust haze has eased back for a moment and allowed him a moment of clarity.

"You're covered, right?"

"Lucky for me, yes. You clean?"

He rolls his eyes. "You know we get tested regularly."

"I also know your reputation, though with the game I saw tonight, I can't imagine where those rumors stem from."

That comment earns a sharp snap of his hips that damn near has me crawling up the wall.

"Yeah, Raven? I don't have game? Is that why I'm buried in your tight cunt right now? Filling you up until my cum is dripping out of you?"

"Yep," I gasp, barely able to form a coherent thought, let alone a sassy come-back.

"Thought so," he chuckles as he rests his hands on my thighs and continues fucking me. My body jerks as he thrusts into my G-spot again and again.

"Fuck, fuck, fuck," I grit through clenched teeth as I hold onto my legs, closing my eyes tight to try to hold off my third orgasm of the night.

"I don't think so, Little Raven. Show me those pretty eyes. Look at me while I fill you up."

My eyes fly open, and as if that's all he needed, he loses it, his cock twitching just before he comes, sending me shattering apart right along with him. I thrust against him, trying to wring every ounce of pleasure I can out of this until my body collapses.

Trevor flops down on top of me, barely allowing my legs to come back down before he practically squishes me. We lay there in silence, existing in this blissful little post-orgasmic bliss before reality sets in, and Trevor takes a deep breath before rolling onto his back on the bed.

Blowing out a calming breath I try to gain my wits. That was stupid. I hate Trevor. He's a self-absorbed prick. Albeit a self-absorbed prick with a wicked tongue and a huge dick, but that's neither here nor there.

Besides, I'm stuck in his house for at least a few more days. I mean, not technically, I guess. It's not like Erica is my mom. I don't have to stay here. At the time, I was just too anxious and scared to fight her. The weight of my current situation has a chill running up my spine, and my distaste for Trevor Michaels is waning. Talk about the definition of the lesser of two evils.

Slowly, I go to stand, doing the awkward hobble to the bathroom before cleaning myself up. When I come out, I see Trevor sitting up on his bed now wearing a pair of boxers and an uncomfortable look. I raise an eyebrow at him as I make my way over to the discarded dress on the floor.

"Look," he says. "That was great, but you obviously know I'm not in a place for feelings or relationships or—"

I can't help but laugh, quickly cutting him off as I shake my head and smile. He frowns at me as he crosses his arms.

"Dude, we fucked. It's not like we are picking out engagement rings. Don't think about it too hard. I don't usually do repeats, but I've been stressed lately, and at least I don't have to pay for an Uber to get back home for the night, so win-win."

He blinks, his face full of confusion but his mouth tightly shut.

Okayyy? Gripping my discarded clothes, I give him an awkward wave before I walk out the bedroom door and down the hall back to the spare room that is temporarily mine. The biggest reason I don't do repeats is because the first guy I did do a repeat with ended up being the literal devil himself. I'm sure that I wouldn't come across the same situation twice, but I'm not willing to take that chance.

Even if I've slept with Trevor before, it's not like it really matters. He can hardly pay attention for longer than two minutes to a woman who isn't Erica, and even if he says he wants to get over her, I think we both know that's bullshit.

So, until I leave I guess, I wouldn't be opposed to breaking my repeat rule a few times, especially if there isn't anything good on TV, or I just feel like having my pussy eaten by a man who acts like it's his last meal.

Chapter 17
Trevor

A sweet smell wakes me up the next morning. I blink my eyes, looking around to find myself alone in my room. It smells like something is baking. My mind runs with possibilities before it lands on the most reasonable scenario. Sage. She must be downstairs making something.

I shake my head as I push out of bed. I fucked up last night. It was one thing to break rule number three and let her crash with me for a little while until her apartment is put back together. It's another to break rule number four and number one on top of that. She's trouble, and the fact that my rules keep seeming to fall by the wayside anytime she's around isn't good for anyone.

I have no doubt she's downstairs right now, trying to play it cool while also simultaneously hoping this is the start of something. As much as it may surprise people, I actually don't like hurting people. I don't enjoy having to let women down, explaining to them that they'll never get more than I offer because I just don't have anything else to give. These women want my heart, but the thing is, I don't have it, haven't for years. It's still with *her* and not even a walking wet dream like Sage could change that.

As I open my door and make my way down the stairs, I mentally prepare myself for the tears, maybe even for some shit to get thrown. Sage doesn't strike me as a crier, more of a throw a toaster at your head kind of woman.

When I round the corner, I expect her to be done up in that 'I just woke up this way' but you know she got up a good twenty minutes earlier to do her hair and makeup in a natural way. Instead, I find her in an oversized Metallica T-shirt that more resembles a shapeless dress, her hair up in a greasy looking messy bun, and her face free of any traces of makeup, the dark circles under her eyes attesting to that.

She's nodding her head to some heavy metal song as she pulls a pan out of the oven, setting it onto the stovetop before turning to face me. I anticipate the doe-eyed smile to come into play because obviously she didn't realize I was awake yet. Maybe she was trying to surprise me with food in bed or something?

Instead though, she gives me a casual head nod as she reaches for a bowl of what looks like icing. I blink several times, a little confused why she hasn't said anything to me yet. What is she doing? I've had more than my fair share of women try to 'play it cool.' It's all the same song and dance. In the end, they all are after one thing. Only Sage isn't showing the usual tells. She's not making the same moves. Honestly, I'm not even sure what game we're playing at this point. There has to be a game, right?

Her eyes come up to me as she wrinkles her nose in what looks like confusion. "What?"

I stare at her for a few seconds before I shake my head.

"What are you doing?"

She looks down at the bowl before looking back at me.

"Uh, making breakfast? I do it every morning, believe it or not."

"And there just so happens to be enough for me?" I ask dubiously. She can't think I'm this naïve.

Sage sets the bowl down, leaning against the counter as she tilts her head to the side, her eyebrows dipping as she seems to almost bite back a smile.

"What? If you think you're getting a single one of my pumpkin cinnamon rolls, think again. The very least you could do is say please." She laughs in a way that doesn't sound very amused.

"Wait, what? Fuck this, Sage. What are you playing at?"

She looks from side to side as she shakes her head.

"Dude, I don't know what you're going on about, but it's too early for this shit."

Grabbing the bowl in front of her, she turns to face what I now know are cinnamon rolls before she begins icing them.

"So you didn't wake up early to bake for me? Try to, I don't know, win me over or something?"

A choked laugh escapes her as she looks over her shoulder at me.

"Michaels, I know we haven't known each other for long, but does any of that sound like something I would ever do?"

I frown at that. "No, you seem like the type of woman who would make something delicious and eat every bite right in front of me, just so I couldn't have any."

Turning to lean against the counter, she raises a cinnamon roll to her mouth before taking a bite, giving me a teasing wink as she does.

"Not a bad idea," she says over her mouthful of food in the most unladylike fashion possible. God, my mother would have a heart attack if I ever brought a woman like her home. One look at those tattoos, and she'd be in an ambulance. One smart-ass remark and my father would probably be right beside Mom.

Feeling like a tool, I run a hand through my hair as I look over at her.

"So, last night?" I hedge hesitantly.

Sage rolls her eyes as she shakes her head.

"I told you, we fucked. It was fun, but you definitely don't have to worry about me going all gooey heart eyed for you or anything."

"Why's that?" I ask, purely out of curiosity.

She presses her tongue to the side of her cheek as she softly shakes her head.

"Besides the fact that you're head over heels for a woman you can never have?" she asks.

I nod as I do my best to ignore the pang that spreads across my chest at her words. They suck, but they're true.

"You're not my type, not really at least. I'm definitely not looking for anything more than some fucking around, but if I was, you wouldn't be my first choice," she says with a small shrug as if her statement is no longer offensive because of that.

"Who is?" I ask, not knowing why I give a shit. It's not like she's my type. Far from it. I've always been drawn more to softer women, delicate, definitely not as abrasive and snarky as her.

Sage waivers for a moment like she's running through a roster in her head before she grabs another cinnamon roll.

"Jackson."

"Donatello?" I ask dubiously, not able to hide my disgust.

She nods as she takes a bite.

"Why haven't you hooked up with him then?" I ask when she doesn't say anything.

"I will," she says with a nod as she swallows and walks over to the sink to wash her hands.

I don't like that. I don't know why, but it doesn't sit well with me. Before I even know what I'm doing, I'm making my way around the kitchen island, caging her in against the sink as her ass presses against my already hardening dick.

"He couldn't handle you," I say in a low voice in her ear.

"No?" she questions, keeping her eyes forward as she does.

I reach down and grip her hips with my hands to keep her in place. My lips run over the shell of her ear before biting down.

"Nope. Not like I can," I say as one of my hands moves from her shirt to her thigh, slowly snaking underneath her shirt.

"Are you trying to proposition me, Michaels?"

"Maybe. Is it working?"

"Maybe." She laughs as my hand cups her bare pussy. Fucking hell. If I'd have known she wasn't wearing panties, things would have gone a little different from the start this morning.

My other hand releases her hip, running up to her chin before tilting her head up to look at me. The minute those bright purple eyes land on me, my pulse thuds in anticipation of having her again.

"I don't want you to think this is more than it is," I say.

She smiles up at me but not in a sweet way, more like an exhausted way.

"Trevor, it's like you've never had casual sex before, I swear."

"Oh trust me, I have. But it's different. You're Erica's friend, you're staying at my house, and you're my coach's daughter."

"Don't forget I'm over ten years younger. Quite the forbidden little fruit you got here," she smirks.

"Fucking smart-ass," I say as I crush my lips to hers.

Chapter 18
Sage

"So, Declan talked to your leasing manager and got him to okay a more secure door. It's steel, not wood, and it has three locks just in case," Vi says through the speakers of my car.

"Jesus. You guys didn't have to go that hard. It's not that big of a deal."

"Someone broke into your home, destroyed all of your personal items. It's a huge deal. You're like the baby sister I always wanted, and we aren't letting you stay there until we know you're completely safe. Any word from the police?"

"Nope," I say shortly as I turn into the training center parking lot. Not like I was expecting to hear back.

"That's absolutely ridiculous. I'll have Declan make some calls and—"

"And what? Lay out the chief of police?" I tease.

"If that's what it takes," Vi sasses, a slight southern twang tinging her words. They were only down in Knoxville for a year or so, but apparently that's all it took for her to pick up the barest hint of an accent.

"I appreciate it, but you guys have done too much already. I'll be fine, promise."

"I know you will, because we are all going to make sure of it. Almost all of the repairs are done on the inside, just waiting for a new countertop for the bathroom to come in and the glass for your windows. How are you surviving at Trevor's? I know you two don't get along the best. You know you're more than welcome at any one of our houses."

"It's fine. We've come to an understanding."

"Really?"

"Mhmm," I smirk, thinking about how we *understood* each other all over the kitchen island this morning.

"Well, good. Hopefully you'll be back in your place by next week."

"It's cool. We have away games for the next two weekends, so I'll be traveling so much it won't matter."

"Ugh, I forgot. I hate that there are travel restrictions in the third trimester."

"For good reason. No one wants to watch you give birth thirty thousand feet in the air, no offense," I laugh.

"Yeah, well if I have to give birth when he's gone, I'll make him grovel for a year at least."

"With the way that man worships the ground you walk on, I have no doubt he'd do so willingly."

She sighs dreamily into the phone, a sound that may be cute to some, but has me feeling nauseous almost instantly.

"Alright, lover girl, I have to get to work. Thank you guys again. I know we haven't known each other for long, but I appreciate everything you all have done for me."

"Time is irrelevant. You're one of us, babe. Have a good day!" she says before hanging up.

I smile softly before pocketing my phone as I grab my camera and purse. After locking my car, I make my way up to the front doors where I see a few of the coaching staff. I nod to all of them as I snake my way down the halls before taking up my spot where I'll be filming today. The last video I did about everyone's favorite Taylor Swift song went viral, so I decided to do some similar content to keep the momentum going.

I'm just getting my camera turned on and ready when I hear a voice guaranteed to put me into a shit mood.

"Sage, get in here!" Dad barks from outside his office down the hall.

My hands tighten to fists as I slowly set my things down and make my way to his office. When I step inside, he's leaning against the desk with his arms folded across his chest and that same disappointed glare I've become so accustomed to, especially since I came back to Seattle.

"What's up, Coach?" I ask as I hang back in the doorway, hoping he'll make whatever it is quick so I can get the fuck away from him.

It's easy to forget how deep your daddy issues are when you are hundreds of miles away. When you're less than a hundred feet away is another story.

"What's up?" he scoffs. "I just got off the phone with the landlord of your apartment building. Said you've been having a ton of work done to the place because of a break-in?"

I shrug and look down at my already chipping nail polish. "Yeah, they trashed my place."

"Why the fuck didn't you tell me?" he asks, the barest amount of hurt bleeding through his words.

Looking up, I frown at him as I cross my arms over my chest.

"I didn't think you'd care."

He rolls his eyes. "Of course I care. I'm the one who put the security deposit down on the place."

I let out a bitter laugh as I shake my head.

"God forbid the millionaire NFL coach loses out on a two thousand dollar security deposit when thugs break into his daughter's apartment and stab, smash, and destroy every single possession she ever had."

Dad frowns at that, pausing for a minute before he speaks.

"They ruined everything? Do you need money to replace some of it?"

"No, I don't. Thanks, though," I huff.

"Well maybe you'll learn your lesson about locking your door. You have to start taking some responsibility for your life, Sage."

I can't help but scoff in disgust before I turn on my heel, storming out of his office. He calls out to me, but I don't give a fuck what he has to say. He's a self-righteous prick who was a shit dad and an even shittier person.

A few of the players start walking down the hall, and I do my best to shake off my pissy attitude, though even I can hear that I don't do a good job.

"What other sport could you go pro in besides football?" I ask Slater and Declan as they walk in.

"Baseball for sure. My wife says I have the butt for it," Slater winks at the camera before turning around and shaking his ass.

That earns a half laugh from me as Declan answers.

"Same."

A few of the other guys come in saying things like basketball and soccer. Johnson even says ballet. Trevor walks in next, giving me a devilish grin as he swaggers down the hall.

"What's the question of the day, Little Raven?"

"What other sport could you go pro in besides football?"

"Can't imagine there isn't anything I couldn't do. I've been told I'm really good with my hands," he winks, causing me to bite back my growing smile.

"Alright, move it along, Michaels," I say as a few others come down the hallway.

When I get a few more players recorded, I pack up my things and get ready to go back to Trevor's so I can work on it there. As I go to stand, I turn, walking straight into the wall. Or at least I thought it was a wall. Instead, I look up to see Jackson's blinding white smile as his tattooed cover hand grips my hip to right my balance.

"Easy, babygirl. Didn't mean to startle you," he says with a wolfish smile.

"Mhmm, I'm sure not," I say as I take a step out of his reach, smirking at him as I do.

His lip ring is still in, and I watch as his tongue plays with it almost deliberately like he's trying to capture my attention before he closes the distance between us again, cupping my hip with one hand as he leans forward.

"Let me take you out tonight. I've been patient enough, haven't I?"

I let out a laugh as I tip my head back.

"Patient? You? Never. Bro, you're basically the definition of a simp," I tease.

He grins as he shrugs his shoulders.

"With an ass like yours, how could I not be?"

I twist up my mouth as I nod.

"Got a point there."

Jackson laughs as I smirk.

"Fine. Where am I meeting you?" I relent.

Excitement fills his eyes as his smile widens.

"I can pick you up."

"Nah, I like to keep my options open in case I want to ditch you."

"Ouch," he laughs. "Meet me at Blackwoods. Nine o' clock."

Flashes of the last time I went to Blackwoods dance in my head. That was a good night, despite the company. Let's hope it'll be even better with someone that's a little more aligned with my usual type. Besides, it's about time I catch and release him anyway.

"Mmm, make it eight. You're gonna have to at least buy me dinner before I put out, Donatello."

"Whatever you want," he smiles with a husky lilt to his voice as his face comes closer to mine, so close I feel the cool metal of his lip ring brush against my skin.

Knowing that it's better to make him wait, I pull away, giving him a Cheshire-level smile before turning without a word and heading to my car.

Always keep them wanting more.

Chapter 19
Trevor

After practice I take a quick shower before heading home. My arm is already starting to twinge, and the fact that it's so early on in the season has me more than a little worried. Maybe I'll see if Scar is up to working with me for a bit in her downtime. She used to be the team's Athletic Trainer before she got sick. She worked miracles when Slater got hurt, and everyone thought his career was all but over. He said she's been doing a lot better since she hit her six-month, cancer-free mark, so maybe she'll be interested.

As I make my way home, I can't help but smirk when I see Sage's car in the driveway. I wasn't sure how I felt about this little thing this morning. But if she really thinks she can keep any and all feelings in check, and this can be a casual thing while she's crashing with me, then I'd have to be a fucking idiot to turn it down.

My cock is already stiffening in anticipation as I shut down the purring engine of my Corvette that *finally* got here before I head inside. Maybe Sage will suck my cock like she did last night if I eat her pussy. Couldn't tell you which I'd enjoy more. They're both pretty fucking great.

Erica has already texted me twice since yesterday, making sure that Sage and I are getting along okay. I don't know why she feels so protective of her, but I know she means something to her, so even if we wouldn't have come to our little truce, I'd have figured out a way to tolerate her attitude. Turns out it's a lot easier to tolerate Sage when she's face down, ass up, or that smart fucking mouth is wrapped around my cock.

When I push the front door open, my stiffening cock hardens to a solid pole as I see Sage in a slinky burgundy dress similar to the little black one she wore last night. I smirk as I make my way over to her, only faltering when I see her reach for her purse.

"You going somewhere?" I ask, causing her to turn to face me, a carefree smile on her face as she nods.

"Yep. See you later."

She goes to walk past me, like I'd actually just leave it at that. I catch her by the crook of her arm, holding her back a second as I turn to face her.

"Where are you going?"

She lifts a disbelieving eyebrow as she looks at me.

"What, are you my parole officer or something?"

"Are you on probation?" I ask.

Honestly, I could see it. Sage shrugs with a tilt of her head.

"Not in this state."

I can't fully tell if she's joking or not when she pulls out of my grasp.

"Seriously. Where are you going?"

"Well, not that it's any of your business, but I'm grabbing dinner with Jackson."

"You can't be serious," I deadpan, irritation instantly taking over me.

"Why not?" she laughs. *Fucking laughs.*

"Because he's a douchebag," I spit.

"And you're not?" she says with a cocky smile.

I roll my eyes at her as I cross my arms over my chest.

"Where is he taking you?"

"Doesn't matter. I gotta go."

Sage turns on her heel, opening the front door as I call out to her.

"What time you gonna be back?"

Looking over her shoulder, those vibrant eyes lock on to mine, a slow smirk spreading across her face as she winks.

"Late."

With that, she shuts the door and heads out. I hear her car start up several seconds later before the front gate opens. I'm left standing in the middle of my living room, fucking fuming. Fuming about what exactly, I'm not one hundred percent sure. All I know is that I'm pissed.

My mind whirls for several seconds as I contemplate what to do. Then, I'm pulling out my phone, scrolling over to my requested folder of my DMs and picking the first good-looking woman's message. I ignore her words, tapping out a quick message to meet me downtown before I jog upstairs to change.

It didn't take long for me to figure out where Donatello would have taken her. There are only a handful of places that offer the anonymity that a lot of us crave when we are going out for the night. I don't know much about him since we are early in the season, but I can tell that he's not one of the fame seekers. He's confident in his skin, albeit a little cocky. Who isn't though, right?

I grab the door for my date, allowing the giggly blonde influencer to step inside Blackwood's first. My eyes drop to her practically photoshopped ass in her bright red bodycon dress. I picked her up downtown before we headed this way. I don't give out my address for obvious reasons, and I didn't want to wait around in some apartment lobby for her to finish getting ready. Her name is Sarah or Sierra. I couldn't really tell because of her squeaky voice, and I honestly don't care enough to check our messages.

As soon as I step inside, my eyes begin scanning the room. It's not an overly big place so you can see almost every table and booth as soon as you walk through the door. However, when my eyes do a full sweep of the restaurant, I come up short of the people I'm looking for. I contemplate leaving but decide to check one more spot.

The doe-eyed hostess greets us instantly, smiling wide as she turns her attention to me.

"Good evening, Mr. Michaels. Just two?"

I nod. "Do you have anything in the back?"

She nods eagerly as she gathers up two menus and gestures for us to follow her. I step in front of my date as I do, not the most gentlemanly thing to do, I know, but I'm on a mission right now. When we crest the corner, she pushes open the doors that lead to the private room in the back. Instantly, I notice several high profile locals sitting in the scattered seating area. It only takes me two seconds to find who I'm looking for, though.

Sage is sitting in a plush seat, sipping what looks like bourbon as Donatello leans his elbows against the table, a salacious grin across his face as he begins wiggling that ugly ass lip ring of his. I see an empty table directly behind them and point to it wordlessly. Thankfully our hostess takes us right to it without an ounce of hesitation.

Sharon sits down across from me as I take the seat facing Sage. As soon as my ass hits the seat, her eyes are on me. Those unique watercolor eyes narrowing at me as she shakes her head and turns her attention back to her *date*.

A waitress comes over to the table almost instantly, taking our drink order and bringing them over in record time. Some fruity pink drink for my date and a bourbon for me.

"So," Shirley says. "It must be so fun playing football. I've been watching you for years. You are, like, so good at scoring goals." She smiles enthusiastically.

I hear a scoff come from behind her, my eyes landing on an annoyed-looking Sage rolling her eyes as she lifts her glass to her lips. I can't help but smirk as I lean forward, feigning interest in Sheryl as I give her my full attention.

"Touchdowns, baby, and yeah. I'm fucking good at everything I do."

"Can't wait to find out all about that later." She giggles in a laugh that grates my skin.

I'm about to lean into her insinuation and play it up a bit when I hear Donatello speak.

"So, what do you say I grab the bill, and we head back to my place? I just got a movie theater installed. We can throw a movie on, get a little more comfortable," he rumbles deeply, the obvious suggestion in his tone causing my jaw to clench in irritation.

What is it about this guy that has me wanting to take him down a peg or ten?

Sage laughs lightly like he just told a ridiculous joke.

"Nice try. You promised me food. I'm not one of those women who skips meals. You gotta work to keep me interested."

"I can tell." He laughs. "I like that about you, though."

"Hmm," she hums with a soft smile, shooting him a wink that has me inhaling deeply through my nose.

I do my best to tune them out, focusing on the drink in front of me and occasionally my date. Though with the amount of selfies she's taking, I don't think she minds me ignoring her too much. Looks like she's having a fine time on her own.

Throughout dinner, every laugh falling from Sage's lips and brush of Donatello's hand against hers sets me on edge more and more. I can practically feel the crystal glass ready to snap in my hand as I lift my third drink of the night to my mouth. Movement out of the corner of my eye snags my attention as Sage stands from the table, making her way out the door to the main dining area.

I don't even hesitate, pushing away from the table as I stand, following her step for step. My hands push open the door she slipped through, turning my head to the left to see her stepping through the bathroom door. I chase after her, my fist banging through the women's door before closing it behind me. I find the deadbolt lock and flip it into place. Hopefully there is no one else in here already.

Sage startles as she pauses outside the bathroom stalls.

"Trevor? What the fuck are you doing in here?"

I don't answer her, instead I continue walking toward her until our chests brush against one another. My breathing is labored, too labored for me to just be walking. I can practically feel adrenaline coursing through my body similar to when I hear the sound of that first whistle blow. I can't for the life of me figure out why the fuck my body is acting like this.

"Hello? Anyone home?" Sage snarks.

I snap, reaching down and gripping her hips to turn her away from me, pulling her to the bathroom counter. She gasps but doesn't fight me, her eyes coming to mine in the mirror as my hand pushes against her lower back, forcing her chest flush against the countertop.

"Spread your legs, baby," I say, nudging my knee between her thighs.

She obeys almost immediately and something primal inside me beats its chest at her obedience.

"Good girl. Show me that pussy," I encourage.

Her lower back arches, those violet eyes never leaving mine as she does. My hands come to the hem of her dress, raising it up to rest around her hips, only leaving her black silk thong in sight. I wrap my hands around the thin fabric, ripping it in two before tucking the damp material into my slacks pocket.

"Fucker!" Sage hisses. "Those were my favorite."

"I'll buy you more," I say with a roll of my eyes as I pull out my cock, rubbing the drop of pre-cum across my tip as I line up with her.

"You better," she grumbles, though the heat in her eyes tells me she isn't as mad as she's trying to make herself out to be.

"Shut up and take my cock," I say before thrusting into her.

Her back arches sharply, a moan tearing out of her throat as her hands grip the edge of the counter.

"Fuckkk," she groans as I bottom out inside her.

"Goddamn. You have got to be the tightest pussy I've had in years," I rasp.

"Doesn't surprise me," she pants as I pull out before slamming back into her. "You haven't fucked since World War II, right?"

My hand comes down to the side of her ass, causing her pussy to squeeze me on impact.

"Will I ever be able to fuck you without you running your fucking mouth?"

"Probably not," she says, her eyes fluttering closed as my thrusts become more frantic.

"Eyes on me, Raven. I want to look into those cosmic eyes when you come on my cock."

They fly open at that through the mirror, holding my gaze as she reaches between her legs, her hand moving in quick movements over her clit.

"That feel good, baby? You like touching your pretty pussy while I fuck you from behind?"

"Mhmm," she says as her eyes flutter closed again.

"Eyes," I command, forcing her to spring them open yet again.

Just like every time, as soon as she does, my pulse jackhammers in my veins. Fucking hell, they're like magic or some shit.

"Just like that," I praise. "Good girl."

"Trev," her voice gasps as I adjust my angle, rubbing the head of my cock against her G-spot.

"That's right. Say my name. Let everyone know who is buried deep inside you right now. Who has you bent over, bare and raw, fucking the shit out of you while your date is waiting at the table for you to come back?"

"Douchebag award goes to you," she laughs as it shifts to a moan.

"Dirty bitch award goes to you then, I guess," I smirk as I smack the side of her ass again.

She grinds against me, nodding her head as she meets my movements thrust for thrust. I feel my balls begin to tighten as that familiar tingling sensation at the base of my spine builds. My pace increases, desperate with the need to fill her up.

"I want you to remember this. When he's trying to slide between these sweet thighs tonight, just remember who made you feel this full, this good. No one can fuck you like I can, Raven. You know it, and so do I. So when you're done playing with your little toy out there, come on home, and I'll give you another round," I say before pushing her hand out of the way and rubbing her clit, my forefinger and thumb pinching it just right and causing her to scream out her release.

The walls of the bathroom practically shake as she squirms and screams, wiggling beneath me as my cock pulses before emptying inside her. I give her every fucking drop, letting my cum fill her to the brim before my movements eventually slow.

Our breathing is heavy, foreheads dotted with sweat, as I slowly pull away. I push my cock into my pants, but before Sage can pull her dress down, I'm bending down behind her, running my hand between her slick thighs. I feel my cum leaking down her legs and flatten my tongue before licking her from behind, pushing my cum right back where it belongs.

A breathy moan escapes her as I continue licking her before I add a couple fingers, massaging her G-spot as I do. When I go to stand, Sage is watching me with intense intrigue, and I can't help but feel like a fucking king for somehow temporarily silencing this loudmouth woman.

Lifting my cum coated fingers to her lips, I nudge against them as I look down at her.

"Open."

Her mouth parts slightly, just enough for me to push my fingers inside. Her tongue meets me greedily, wrapping around my digits as she licks and sucks every drop of our combined release.

Goddamn it. She may be fucking infuriating, but she is so fucking sexy.

"Good girl," I say before running my other hand along the side of her jaw, outlining the length of her throat as she swallows.

Without another word, I pull away from her, turning toward the bathroom door before unlocking it and slipping out. She doesn't try to stop me, and I wouldn't even if she called out to me. I did what I came to do, I think at least. I'm still not exactly sure what led me here to begin with. I'm sure Donatello will take her home tonight. She may even fuck him. But I have no doubt it will be my cock she's thinking about, and *our* cum she'll be tasting.

Chapter 20
Sage

When I finally am able to shake off the orgasm-induced haze, I stumble out of the bathroom and back to my table. I tried to clean myself up as best as I could, but I can still feel Trevor's cum inside me, and I fucking hate how turned on that makes me.

As I sit down, Jackson smiles up at me. Not in a sweet doting way, more like a wolfish 'I'm going to devour you' way. A way that before Trevor and his airheaded bimbo walked in, had me more than ready to ride his cock until the sun came up. Now, despite the fact Jackson is definitely more my typical speed, I can't get those bright blue eyes out of my head. That clean un-inked skin. The almost threat in his voice as he told me all I'd be able to think about was him. And I'm pissed that the motherfucker was right.

We finish up our dinner, and Jackson pays the check quickly before placing his hand on my lower back as he ushers us out of the restaurant. When we get to the street, he starts guiding me toward his Mercedes G-Wagon parked in the corner lot. I do my best to push the annoying, privileged, entitled, blond quarterback out of my head and focus on this tall, dark, and tattooed sex-on-a-stick of a man in front of me.

Instead of opening my door, Jackson backs me up against the door, caging me in with his thick corded arms. I smirk up at him, knowing what comes next and more than ready to get this night rolling. His lips come down to my own, a little softer than I had anticipated for him. Like, a lot softer. Like almost too pillowy, soft, and squishy. This kiss is like we are in a bad rom-com movie or something.

The feeling of his full lips is actually a little disgusting. Like two wet marshmallows sticking to me against my will. Oh my god. I don't think I've ever had such a horrific kiss before. Pulling away from my mouth, he begins kissing down my neck, leaving a sloppy wet trail in his wake. Oh god. This is fucking gross. How can this guy have been alive for twenty-four years, and no one has told him what a terrible kisser he is? Nope, nope. Can't do it. As much as I'd love to fuck Trevor's little stunt right out of my system, I'm not willing to sacrifice myself in the process.

I slide out from under his caged in arms, giving him what I hope is a sympathetic smile.

"Thanks for dinner. I had a great time."

He blinks his eyes slowly, as if he's clearing his lust-fueled haze.

"Wait, what?"

"I have to get going. Travel day and all for the game tomorrow, right?"

Jackson frowns as he takes a step closer to me.

"I thought you were coming over. Spend the night or something?"

I feel bad at the true disappointment on his face, but then I remember the feeling of his almost slimy lips on me, and my sympathy wanes.

"Rain check? I'll see you tomorrow on the plane," I smile as I turn on my heels and high tail it out of there.

Once I round the corner, I wipe the back of my hand across my mouth. God, that's just not even fair. The way that man oozes sex appeal, he should be a lot more skilled than that. I think I should just be thanking my lucky stars he didn't try to use his tongue.

I shiver at the thought, unlocking my car quickly before sliding in. It doesn't take me too long to get back to Trevor's house, and when I step inside, I notice almost all the lights are off apart from the glow of his bedroom light under his door. I'm not stupid, I know why he's up so late despite the fact that our plane leaves at six in the morning tomorrow.

He wants me to go in there. He wants to know that I couldn't continue my date because of our little romp in the bathroom. What he doesn't know is that isn't at all the case. That I had every intention of screwing that memory right out of my head. Unfortunately for me, I chose the wrong guy to do that with.

Though I'm more than a little sexually frustrated and would love nothing more than to finish this night off with an orgasm or two, I know I shouldn't. If the balance of power tips, he will be the one in control, and I don't play like that. I'll never let a man have control over me again.

Reigning in my self-control, I turn in the opposite direction and head toward the room I'm staying in, locking the door for good measure. Whether to keep Trevor out or me in, they are both good options. After I go through my nighttime routine, I climb into bed and close my eyes, irritated when the first image that pops into my head is that familiar handsome face staring at me in a bathroom mirror.

My alarm goes off too fucking early, and as much as I want to turn it off and roll over, I know I have to be at the game to get some more content, and if I miss the team plane, my ass will be paying for my own later flight. That's not happening.

So, I slide out of bed, take a quick shower and do a bare minimum blow dry before deciding to just throw my hair up into a messy bun. Maybe I can get a few more hours of sleep on the plane since we're flying all the way out to Philadelphia today.

I grab the bag that I had the good sense to pack before my date last night and my purse before heading downstairs. When I come to the bottom of the steps, I hear the blender going off and see Trevor manning it in the kitchen. He's in street clothes. Just a pair of gray sweatpants and a Seattle Crusaders T-shirt that is wrapped around his body like a second skin. I try not to let my eyes drop but c'mon, gray sweatpants. It's like he's trying to get the attention of every woman within a twenty-mile radius.

And he would too. Trevor Michaels fills out anything well, but gray sweatpants are my new favorite thing to see him in. He sees me staring at him, which sucks because a cocky grin falls across his face as he winks at me.

"Morning, Raven. How'd your date go?"

"Great," I lie. "Sorry if I woke you. Got in kinda late," I say with a yawn that's not all that fake. It's just not from a night of being fucked against the headboard like I had originally planned.

Trevor stops the blender, pouring two smoothies before sliding one to me. I frown at the gesture before nodding my head in thanks. Trevor lifts his own cup to his mouth as he takes several gulps before running his tongue across his lower lip, though I don't know why. It's not like there's anything spilled on them.

"Really? Would you consider eleven late for a date?"

I go to argue and more so lie that I got in much later when he raises his phone and waggles it at me.

"High-tech security system, remember, baby? I watched you pull in last night."

Cheeky fucker.

"What, were you sitting by your phone, just counting down the minutes until I pulled up?" I fire back, causing his cocky grin to slip away, as irritation flashes to the forefront of his features.

"I definitely have more important things to be doing than waiting around for you to get done with a subpar fuck."

God, if only he knew how true his statement no doubt is. Not that I'd ever give him the satisfaction.

"Like track down where I'm at and bring a fake date to keep an eye on me?" I say with a raised eyebrow.

Trevor scoffs and rolls his eyes as he takes another drink of his smoothie.

"That's ridiculous."

"No, what's ridiculous is that every time I laughed or smiled in Jackson's direction, you looked like you were ready to have a coronary."

I set down my smoothie and take a step toward him as I continue speaking.

"What's ridiculous is that when I get up to go to the bathroom, you follow me like a territorial dog."

Another step.

"The most ridiculous thing is how you bent me over that bathroom counter, nothing but pure jealousy and irritation on your face as you fucked me."

"Jealousy?" he scoffs like it's the most insane statement he's ever heard. But he doesn't deny it which makes me take a final step to him, pressing my chest against his as I tilt my head up and smirk.

"You were jealous last night. Jealous I went out on a date instead of staying in and riding your cock. You were jealous I was giving my attention elsewhere, and you needed to steal it back in the most petty way possible."

I expect him to deny it, to push me away or scoff at me like he loves to do. Instead though, he pushes his body even closer to me, lifting his hand to cup my chin as he tilts up just slightly, those bright blue eyes boring into me as he speaks.

"It got you home, didn't it? You didn't sleep in Donatello's bed. You were in mine, not the bed I would have preferred you in, but one of mine all the same. If you didn't already know this, you do now. When I want something, I take it, and I make no apologies for how I get it."

I don't know what to say to that. Mainly because I feel like there is more being said than what his words convey, but I'm not too sure that I want to know what they mean. So instead, I swallow and nod.

"I could tell." I laugh, though it doesn't come out as smooth and confident as I was hoping.

His eyes flare, but the rest of his expression doesn't change as he speaks.

"Good."

As if the building tension between us suddenly dissipates, he takes an easy step away from me, grabbing his smoothie and the packed duffle bags at his feet before nodding toward the car.

"Let's go, Raven."

I grab my smoothie and bag before following him out as we load our things into his Range Rover and make the quick drive to the airport. We don't say a word on the car ride there, and barely acknowledge each other when we get inside the plane. Trevor is ahead of me and walks straight to the back where Slater, Declan, and Sebastian are sitting. All who smile at him, well, except for Sebastian.

My eyes scan over the rows before landing on Jackson who gives me a disinterested sneer. Okayyy, looks like someone is a little salty about last night. If I was a bigger bitch, I'd tell him the real reason why I couldn't get away from him fast enough. Lucky for him, though, I'm tired and a little disoriented from this morning's encounter so instead, I take an empty window seat near the coaching staff and roll up a sweatshirt against the window before closing my eyes.

Chapter 21
Sage

The boys just got back from halftime, and the score is sitting pretty close at 13-7. The Philadelphia Cougars are one of the best teams in the league. They made it to the playoffs last year where the Crusaders fell short. Things seem to be different this year though if preseason is anything to go off.

I watch with rapt attention as the ball is snapped, tossed easily into Trevor's hands before he scans the field like the professional he is. There are several options for him, but the Cougars seem to be blocking off nearly every offensive man. Trevor's eyes cut to the right to see Sebastian create some distance from his defender.

Trevor pitches the ball, sending a perfect spiral through the air. It looks high, though, too high. He overshot it. There is no way Sebastian can—

With a catch so solid you can practically hear it from the other side of the field, Sebastian reaches his arms up high, snatching the ball right out of the air before tucking it to his chest. Fucking alright then. I guess that's what having a 6'6" tight end is good for.

Sebastian's legs stretch out far, eating up the distance to the endzone. He's definitely not our fastest guy, I think that title is reserved for Slater, but he is by far the tallest and definitely has the longest legs so he can still cover some distance.

Several guys chase after him, but it's no use, he makes an easy touchdown, slowing down only once he's crossed over that white line. All the guys come together in celebration, jumping and patting each other on the back. I can't help but watch as Trevor comes up to Sebastian, reaching out to pat him on the back to which Sebastian quickly steps out of his reach and jogs over to the ref, leaving

Trevor standing there frankly like an idiot as the rest of their team line back up into formation.

A pang of sympathy runs through me as I watch Trevor's disappointment. He tries to shrug it off, jogging back, but I can see it in his body language. The strained relationship between him and Sebastian hurts him. He knows what he'd have to do to fix it. He can't let her go, though. Even when he knows she'll never be his again. Even when he knows Sebastian has every right to hate his guts for wanting his wife. I still can't help but feel that there is more to the story. I mean, it's very possible that Sebastian wants nothing to do with him because he's still in love with Erica, but at the same time it feels like something actually happened. A line was crossed or something, something bigger than some angsty love triangle drama.

I shake my nosy thoughts out of my head, scooting to the side for a better angle as I squat down and begin filming the next play. You never know when you'll catch something legendary, and though we could always grab some stuff from the streaming of the game, fans seem to be responding well to the first person perspective of the game, like they are here on the sidelines experiencing it.

Two more touchdowns from our team, one by Slater and the other by Jackson and three brutal sacks by Declan, and the game ends. I start packing away the camera and get everything ready to head back to the hotel. Normally the team would head back home after a game, but since this was a later game the team decided to stay in the hotel one more night.

I'm more than okay with it because my back is killing me, and my tits are sore. Unfortunately, that combination can only mean one thing. When I get back to the hotel, I take a long hot shower, change into some comfy clothes only to find out, yep, I was right. The red sea is running, which means it's officially bitch season for the next three to five days. Thank God I had a few tampons floating around in my purse for emergencies.

Why is it that as soon as you recognize you're on your period, all the symptoms seem to hit you at once like a freight train? Is it a mental thing? Like your brain allows you to feel it all now. Or does it force you to? Like a placebo thing? Either way, I don't give a fuck. I just want it gone.

I curl up into a ball in bed, holding my stomach tightly as I mindlessly stare at my comfort show. I swear my vagina is trying to punish me for not giving her a child. Like the dramatic psycho bitch she is apparently, no child means an endless painful blood bath.

Just as my eyes begin to flutter shut, a knock comes from the hotel room door, causing me to groan.

"Go away!" I shout, not giving a fuck who is on the other side.

"It's me," Trevor says.

"Hi, you're the problem, it's you," I shout in tune with Taylor Swift's "Anti-Hero."

I hear Trevor's chuckle as he tries the door handle again.

"C'mon, let me in, Little Raven. I'm bored and want to fuck."

"Well I don't," I snap.

"I'm not going anywhere until you open up," he says as I hear what I assume is his back leaning against the door.

Grumbling to myself, I toss the blankets to the side, stomping my way across the room like a petulant child. I throw the door open, not giving a fuck what a swamp monster I must look like with wet hair, baggy sweatpants, and a T-shirt three sizes too big for me.

I watch surprise pass across Trevor's face as he looks me over. I don't wait around for the insults to roll in before I stomp back over to the bed and crawl under the covers, resuming my fetal position.

"What's wrong?" Trevor asks as he steps inside, letting the door shut from behind him.

"Nothing," I huff as I face the TV.

"Obviously it's something. I've never seen you soooo…"

"Choose your words carefully, Michaels," I say, shooting him a narrowed look as a particularly painful cramp tears through me.

I squint my eyes tightly and groan in pain as he frowns and takes another step closer.

"Are you okay?"

"No," I grit. "I'm not. Can you just go? Please?"

He shakes his head and crosses his arms.

"Not until you tell me what's going on."

"Why?" I laugh hollowly. "You gonna fix it for me?"

"Maybe, if you'd stop being a pain in the ass, and tell me what to fix."

"My vagina is bleeding profusely, and my stomach is cramping as my uterus sheds its lining. Can you help with that?" I say with a sickly sweet smile.

Those bright blue eyes round, his face paling as he swallows and shakes his head. What is it with men being squeamish over a little bit of blood? It's not like they have to deal with it for days every single month.

"Your period?" he asks.

"No shit, detective. Just get out of here. I've no doubt you have groupies in every state at the ready. I'm extra pissy when I'm on my period, and I can't even get comfortable in this stupid hotel room so just leave me alone. Please."

He's silent for a moment, and I think he's about to leave when he surprises me.

"What do you need?"

"What?" I ask.

"What do you need? To feel comfortable?"

I debate on telling him to fuck off, but you know what, if he's offering help I won't turn him down.

"I need a heating pad and pain relievers. I want chocolate, buttery popcorn, ice cream, and the softest blanket you can find. Can you do all of that?" I laugh pathetically as another intense cramp cuts me off.

When it subsides, I glance up to see Trevor tapping away on his phone.

"I'll be back soon."

"Wait, really?" I ask as he walks over to my dresser, swiping the room key as he goes.

He doesn't respond, though. Just opens the door, slipping out before letting it shut behind him. Huh. I wasn't really expecting that. Then again we will see if he even comes back.

I don't remember closing my eyes, but the next thing I know, I feel a hand gently brushing hair away from my face. My eyes fly open, my heart instantly thundering with fear before I register that it's only Trevor. I let out a soft, relieved breath before sitting up slowly.

"What time is it?" I ask with a yawn.

"A little after eleven. What do you want first?"

"Of what?"

He takes a few steps to the coffee table to the left of the bed where three overstuffed grocery bags are sitting.

"I didn't know what kind of ice cream you wanted so I got chocolate peanut butter, mint chip, and cookie dough. Also none of these fucking hotel rooms have a microwave, and you can't just buy pre-popped popcorn at the store, so I hope you like it from the movie theater," he says, pulling out a small bag of popcorn that looks like the kind you buy at the concession stand before going to the movies.

"Wait, you went to the movie theater? Just to get me popcorn?"

His brows furrow as he shrugs his shoulders.

"You said it would help."

I shake my head in disbelief as I run a hand through my hair.

"No, I mean, it's one of my top five comfort foods. I just can't believe you actually went out of your way like that, for me."

Trevor stares at me for a few moments, as if he's censoring himself before he shrugs nonchalantly.

"I have a lot of least favorite people in this world. You aren't one of them."

Aw. I think that's Trevor speak for he likes me. I'm about to give him shit for it, but then he's walking over with a tall, fancy water bottle and a bottle of pain relievers, so I decide to keep my mouth shut.

Twenty minutes later, and I have snacks covering nearly every inch of the bed, the most ridiculously soft blanket wrapped around me with a heating pad strapped to my lower stomach as Trevor reaches over and steals a bite of my ice cream while we watch bad 90's sitcom reruns.

"Thank you," I say after several silent moments.

Trevor plops the spoon back into the chocolate peanut butter container as he shrugs.

"It was nothing."

"No, it was actually something. You could have left me to be miserable. Got into some fun with a nameless woman for the night, but instead you chose to be my personal errand boy and that was...cool of you."

"Cool?" he asks with a chuckle, raising an amused eyebrow at me as does.

I roll my eyes as I shove his shoulder.

"You know what I mean. Stop being a dick, and take the fucking compliment."

Trevor laughs and shakes his head, nudging me back as he does.

"Anytime, Raven."

My eyes begin to flutter, as exhaustion from the day begins to take over me. I don't even know how Trevor is still awake. He's the one who had a game today. I just took some videos and pictures.

"You crashing?" he asks as he begins gathering up my abandoned snacks and bringing them to the table.

"Yeah," I say as I snuggle deeper into the bed until I'm fully laying down.

Once the bed is cleared off, I watch as Trevor hesitates, just for a moment before he kicks off his shoes, shucking off his pants and shirt before climbing into the other side of the bed. I don't say anything and neither does he. I don't do sleepovers. He's made it clear he doesn't either. But does it really break either of our rules if we don't fuck beforehand? I'm gonna say no because it's the answer that doesn't make my brain confused as fuck as to why I don't mind the idea of sharing a bed with Trevor Michaels tonight.

I shut my eyes, rolling over to face the other direction as the fake audience laughing of the show playing in the background begins to lull me to sleep. I'm almost out completely when I feel the bed shift slightly, and a pair of arms loosely wrap around me. I want to ask him what he's doing, but when I feel his hand gently rub against my lower stomach, exactly where I'm cramping, I sink into his touch and pass out.

Chapter 22
Trevor

I woke up first the next morning. It took me a minute to figure out exactly where I was. Obviously I'm no stranger to waking up in random hotel rooms. A solid five months of my year is spent traveling nearly constantly.

The hotel part didn't throw me. It was the woman who was beside me. The fact that there was a woman beside me, period. That's rule number six. The usual awkward good mornings, the false expectations. It always sounded like a fucking nightmare. But last night I knew this morning would be different, that Sage is different. She's just as adverse to that shit as I am, maybe even more so.

If I hadn't broken rule number two as well, I probably wouldn't have high-tailed it out of there like I did. It's not like I was worried she was gonna make things weird. If I'm honest, I was worried I was gonna make things weird. She's the one staying consistent. I'm the one who's out of fucking sorts.

Last night was completely out of character for me, at least for the me I've been for the last decade. Erica used to get really bad cramps, and she always loved it when I rubbed her stomach. She said it helped a lot. She was also a huge snacker like Sage and…I don't know. I felt bad, I guess.

Fuck. I felt bad? What is going on with me?

I face forward in the seat on the plane, trying to focus on the music playing through my ear buds, hoping they will drown out the fucking monotony of thoughts running through my head that have no business there.

I don't even have to look up to know when she steps inside the plane—it's like I can feel her, and I don't like it one fucking bit. Despite my inner voice coaching me to continue facing forward, my eyes disobey, glancing as she makes her way down the aisle. My eyes flick to the empty seat beside me and part of me kinda hopes that she sits next to me. It's better than someone who isn't gonna shut up the whole flight back or something.

To my surprise, she doesn't even look my way. I watch as Donatello reaches a hand out to stop her, saying something I can't hear before she looks down at him. I quickly pause my music, but it's too late to hear him. All I see is her giving him a small smile and a nod before scooting in to take the window seat beside him.

What the fuck?

My eyes narrow at her. Despite her being three rows in front of me and on the other side of the plane, I expect her to feel my glare on her. I thought she was done with him. She never told me how the date went, but the fact that she was willing to bend over in the bathroom in the middle of it tells me she isn't all that interested in him. Then again, I'm not sure Sage is the type of woman to be interested in anyone. Not for more than a night at least, and that's not a dig at her at all. I get it. The appeal, the ease. No strings, just pleasure for all involved. It's clean, simple. Pain free. At least for me.

Suddenly, my view of her is blocked when Slater plops down in the seat beside me. I push his chest, forcing him against his seat as I lean over.

C'mon, Raven. Look at me.

As if my thoughts were enough to get through to her, her eyes come to mine. A light flipping feeling hits my stomach the second her gaze is on me. It's something I haven't felt in a damn long time, and I'm wondering why the fuck I'm getting like this all of the sudden. With her eyes on my own, my mind goes blank. What the fuck am I doing? Trying to get her attention? For what reason? If I was interested in her, wouldn't I have at least stuck around this morning? Said what's up or something before I went back to my room? I didn't, though. And that was for a reason. We are barely temporary roommates. Most days, it's a miracle if we don't kill each other.

What do I care if she hooks up with Donatello? She's a grown woman, barely, who can handle herself. She doesn't need my permission or approval. She's got a daddy for that shit, though obviously Coach isn't too interested in that title.

I watch Donatello steal her attention once again, a soft smile curving her face as she looks at him. Softer than any smile she gives me, that's for sure. And it pisses me off. My fists curl in my lap in irritation as Slater speaks.

"If you don't want people to play with your toys, then you gotta put your name on them."

"What?" I sneer.

Slater gives me a dry 'don't be dumb' look before he glances over to Sage and Donatello.

"You got a thing for the coach's daughter. Whether you just wanna fuck her, or you actually dig her, doesn't matter. Seeing Jackson just talk to her has you ready to throttle his ass. It's all over your face."

"Fuck off," I huff lazily as I settle back into my seat and pull out my phone to start my music up again.

"Someone's in denialllllll," Slater sings, causing Dec to laugh as Seb comes up behind him, both of them taking the two seats across the aisle from us.

"About what?" Dec asks.

"Nothing," I say lazily, hoping Slater will drop it.

Of course, ever the little gossip and shit stirrer that he is, he doesn't.

"A certain grumpy quarterback wants to fuck a grumpier team social media girl."

"That's a hell of a title," Seb says with a lift of his brow.

Slater rolls his eyes and flips Seb off.

"Whatever. You guys knew who I was talking about. Let's be real. I know it's not just my wife who's been whispering this shit into my ear at night. Everyone can see how bad they want each other. That's why they hate each other so hard."

"According to Erica, they're already fucking," Seb says easily as he scrolls through his phone.

"Who told her?" I ask.

I haven't told Erica anything about Sage and I hooking up. I didn't know Sage was telling people. Out of all the people in the world, too, did she have to tell Erica? I mean, I guess it doesn't really matter. They are friends, but it feels weird that she's talking to my ex about us.

"That's just her assumption, but looks like you just confirmed it, though," Seb says with a less heated look than normal before he's back to his phone.

"No way? Already? Fuck you move quick," Slater laughs. "You did get her to show some ID, right? Baby girl doesn't even look old enough to drink."

"She's not," I mutter as my eyes swing back to her.

Slater laughs at that before he starts rambling on to Declan about some plans Vi and Scar are putting together and just now telling them about. I guess it wasn't Sage who let it slip, not that we were trying to keep it quiet or anything. I mean, maybe besides keeping it from Coach. Something comforting settles in me at that, maybe it's trust? I don't know, but whatever it is, the thought relaxes me and sets me on edge all at the same time.

The ride home is a quiet one. I have plenty I want to say, plenty I want to ask, but I know all of those things will only be followed up by questions that I'm not prepared to answer. So, instead, I stay silent.

Sage stares out the window, like she's somewhere else entirely, lost inside her mind. As much as I try to keep my own blank, I can't help but wonder what has that look on her face. Is she happy? Upset? Confused? She's so fucking hard to read sometimes, and for some reason, I'm fucking desperate to figure her out. Maybe because every time that I think I have her pegged, she flips the script on me, and I'm left speechless and back to square one.

Her phone buzzes as we turn on our street. I do my best to covertly look over, but I can't see who messaged her. Being the fucking asshole I am, I can't stop my mouth before it opens.

"That Donatello?"

She looks away from her phone to glance up to me with her brows down-turned.

"Why would it be Jackson?"

I shrug, doing my best to keep my eyes on the road and not on her.

"You guys seemed cozy on the plane ride. You guys are dating. I just—"

"We aren't dating," she quickly corrects.

Good. I was bluffing on that last part.

"Well, you guys went on a date. He's still flirting, and all googly-eyed at you. I just assumed," I shrug.

"Yeah, well, it would never work."

"Why?" I ask a little too eagerly.

Goddamnit, Trevor. Get it together.

"Honestly?" she asks before pausing for a moment. "He's the fucking worst kisser I've ever experienced in my life."

My head whips over to her so fast, the car swerves for a moment before I correct it. My hands tighten around the leather wheel as my jaw ticks.

"You kissed him?" I grit out.

"Uh yeah?" she laughs as if that was a given. "And it was terrible. All wet and slimy and ugh," she shivers in her seat as she shakes her head. "Don't tell anyone, though. He's a nice guy. I don't want him to feel like shit."

I pull up to the driveway, entering the code to the gate quickly before pulling through and parking. When I shut the car off, I turn in my seat to see Sage is already watching me. Like she expected me to say more. Why is she so fucking intuitive?

"Good," I say simply.

She raises an eyebrow at me. "Good?"

I nod. "I'm glad he was a shit kisser. He wasn't good enough for you anyway."

"He wasn't?" she asks lightly, though it doesn't sound much like a question.

"Nope."

"Well, I'll make sure to set my standards a little higher next time. Maybe I'll kiss the next guy before I flirt with him. Save me a little bit of time," she says as she goes to get out of the car.

I stop her in her tracks, though. My fingers dig into her thigh as I pin her to the seat. My teeth are clenched so tightly I hear them crack as I do my best to control my breathing.

"No."

"No?" she questions.

"Yeah, no. There isn't a next time. There won't be any kissing other guys. This pussy is mine until I say so," I say, sliding my hand away from her thigh before cupping her.

She gasps softly at the motion but does a fantastic job of keeping her tone even as she speaks.

"And if I tell you that isn't going to work for me?"

"Then I'll make you come on my face over and over again until it will work for you," I say deeply, brushing my thumb against the soft leggings where I know her clit is.

Sage shudders in her seat, her hips slightly arching into my touch as her eyes close softly.

"Open your eyes, Raven. Look at me."

She does as I tell her, those full pouty lips practically all I can focus on as I speak.

"I don't ever want to see you on a date or watch you flirt with another man until we're done. Is that understood?"

"So bossy," she teases as I increase my pressure, causing her to let out a soft whimper of desire.

"Is that understood?" I repeat.

"Fuck, fine. But the same goes for you. I don't want to catch any diseases from your bimbo of the day collection."

I fight not to let my mouth turn up in amusement at that one. For such a brat, she's funny.

Sometimes.

"Deal."

"Okay, well, if you'll excuse me, me and my horny, but bleeding, vagina want a long hot shower and bed."

"I can't stop the bleeding part, but I can help with something else," I say as my cock begins to harden.

Fuck it. It's just a little blood. We could fuck in the shower for easy clean up as long as it won't hurt her.

She screws her face up at me like the very idea is disgusting as she shakes her head.

"No thanks. Your cock could massacre my pussy on a normal day. I don't need to see it actually covered in my blood."

I can't help but bark out a laugh at that as she gets out of the car and heads inside while I grab our bags.

Chapter 23
Sage

The following day I get a text from Vi letting me know that my apartment is all put back together. It feels like it's been forever since everything happened, when in reality it's been about a week. Time flies when you're getting fucked by one of the most famous NFL quarterbacks, I guess.

When we get to my door, a very pregnant Vi lets out a deep breath as she holds her stomach.

"You good?" I ask.

"Yeah." She smiles. "I'm just kinda over being pregnant. I can hardly walk to the kitchen without getting out of breath."

"I'll bet. You literally have a little succubus attached to you," I say with a wrinkled nose.

Vi laughs. "Don't you want kids one day?"

"I mean, maybe. In like thirty years or something."

She lets out another laugh like I'm hilarious, which I am but like also not super joking. Kids kinda scare me. Like other people's kids are great but that's because I get to give them back. Being responsible for another life? Teaching them right from wrong, building their morals, being responsible for their generational trauma? No thanks. I'm good for now.

When we step inside, my mouth parts. This doesn't look like my apartment at all. I mean, the bones of it are all the same, better looking actually, but the décor is completely different. Gone is my broken forty-five inch TV, now replaced with one so big it barely fits on the wall. A fancy marble coffee table takes up the space in the middle of the room accompanied by a brand new gray sectional.

My eyes continue throughout the apartment, catching on each new detail. The bedroom is by far the most drastic difference. The windows are fixed, which is great, but a large wooden bed frame now holds what must be a brand new king sized bed, replacing the torn-to-shreds queen that I had before. Matching side tables on either side, appearing to have come in a set with the coffee table from the living room.

The comforter set is a light lilac color, and the room is decorated with black accents. It's feminine without being too girly. I love it all, but I can't even imagine how much all of this is going to cost me. Especially with my emergency cash gone.

"Vi, this is amazing, but you guys spent too much money. It's gonna take a while to pay you back."

She waves me off as she shakes her head.

"Don't worry about it, really. Declan already paid the contractor, so we are square there, and as for all of the new furniture and things, we didn't pay for it."

I frown at that. "Who did?"

She turns her head to the side with a confused smile like I should know this.

"Trevor. He gave me his credit card and told me to buy whatever you needed for the place. To be fair, I may have gone a little overboard, but he's kind of a jerk sometimes, so I think it's okay," she laughs lightly.

I try to chuckle with her, but my brain is still trying to play catch up. Trevor paid for all of this? He gave her his credit card to replace my things...what the fuck? We've just barely started tolerating each other. Why would he do that?

Shit. I'm gonna have to push my pride to the side and thank him. That's gonna suck.

I guess this means I get to move out of Trevor's house. Finally. I've been there long enough. We're already developing little routines, and it's getting too stuffy. To be honest, it's kinda nice not being alone all the time. It's nice to be protected in a sense behind that big iron gate and all the ridiculously over the top cameras surrounding the property. If I have to really think about it, staying with Trevor wasn't the worst thing in the world. I got some great sex out of it, a few laughs, and he even paid to have my whole apartment redecorated. Maybe I should give him, like, a thank you/goodbye blowjob or something.

I'm chuckling to myself at that thought when I hear Vi swear from the living room. It takes me a moment to realize she isn't in the bedroom with me anymore. Furrowing my brows, I step out of the room to see her standing in the middle of the hallway, her feet on either side of some spilled water.

"If you'll hand me a towel, I'll clean that up," Vi says, her hands cupping her lower stomach.

"Sure," I say as I walk over to the paper towels. "Spill some water?" I ask.

"Something like that," she says as her face tightens in what looks like pain while her knees bend slightly.

Realization dawns on me suddenly, and I feel like a dipshit for not realizing it faster.

"Holy fuck! You're in labor! Your water broke!" I shout.

Vi nods her head, her face still pinched in pain.

"Fuck. What do I do? Who do I call? An ambulance? Declan? Definitely Declan. What else!" I ramble frantically.

Vi lets out a deep breath as she seems to stand a little bit taller.

"Sage, calm the hell down. My god, you're worse than Dec. Please call him, and if you wouldn't mind giving me a ride to Seattle Memorial, I'd appreciate it."

"Of course. Oh my god! You're having a baby! We need a wheelchair or something. Do you want to, like, sit on my chair, and I'll push you?" I ask, walking over to the swivel office chair in the corner.

Vi laughs and shakes her head. "I can walk for now. Let's just hurry if it's okay?"

"Yeah, hurry. Duh. C'mon," I say, gently ushering her out the door, only grabbing my purse at the last minute before quickly locking the door.

The elevator takes forever, and once I get Vi into the car and buckled up, she hands me her phone. I call Declan, but it goes straight to voicemail. The boys are in practice for another hour at least. He won't even be near his phone until then. I call him again and again, my own panic seeming to rise more than Vi's despite the increasing pain she seems to be in.

Pulling out my own phone, I call Trevor a few times. If anyone is going to be on their phone during practice, it would probably be him. Unfortunately, he doesn't answer the numerous calls I make in rapid succession.

"Shit, shit, shit," I mutter.

"No luck?" Vi asks, a hint of fear tinting her words for the first time.

"I got this. Don't worry. Just keep that baby in your uterus until we get to the hospital."

Vi laughs through what looks like another contraction.

"I'll do my best."

"Good," I mutter as I dial another number. One I usually hate using.

It rings and rings, and for a moment I don't think it's going to go through. Until I get a terse, "What?"

"Dad. You need to let Daniels go for the day. His wife is in labor, and I think the baby is coming fast. She looks like she's in a lot of pain."

"Fucking hell," he grumbles into the phone before he pulls it away slightly. "Daniels!" he shouts, the sound slightly muffled. "Your wife is in labor. Might want to get to the hospital."

I hear Declan's distant, "WHAT!" before Dad is back on the phone.

"He's on his way. That all?"

"Yeah," I say before I hear the disconnecting sound.

Cool. Love you too.

We pull up to the emergency parking of the hospital at the next moment, a person jogging out to meet us.

"She's having a baby!" I shout, the hysteria in voice evident even to my own ears. I take a calming breath as I run around the car to help Vi into the wheelchair they pull out for her. She nods her head in thanks to them as they begin wheeling her inside.

"We will get you to triage in just a second and find a room for you."

"Thank you," she says on a wince.

They wheel her off into basically a corner of a waiting room while the nurse lackadaisically walks over to the desk, chatting with her friends and laughing as they thumb through paperwork. We sit there for several minutes, not a single person coming over yet before I've had enough.

I storm up to the counter, my irritated glare pinned on both the nurses. They cast me an equally irritated look covered by a plastic smile.

"Can we help you?"

"Me? No. Her? Yes," I say as I gesture to Vi. "Why has no one taken her up yet? She should be on the VIP wing, right, Vi?" I ask as I turn around to face her. "Trevor told me Declan spent a ridiculous amount of money to make sure that you'll have your own suite."

She waves me off as her hands white knuckle the wheelchair arms.

"It's fine, Sage. No matter what room I'm in, a baby is coming out of my body. It doesn't really matter."

"Wait, Declan Daniels?" the nurse asks. "You're his wife?"

Vi nods as both of the nurses suddenly scramble toward her. "Oh god. Sorry. VIP wing it is, Mrs. Daniels."

From there, things move a little quicker. A nurse has just finished checking to see how dilated Vi is when Declan barges through the door, Trevor hot on his heels.

"Baby!" Declan shouts as he runs into the room, rushing to her side of the bed as he presses a kiss to her lips.

"Are you okay? I'm so sorry I didn't get your calls."

"It's fine." Vi smiles. "Sage has been amazing."

Declan's eyes come to mine, thankfulness practically overflowing them as he nods to me.

I smile at him as he presses his forehead to hers, whispering soft words that I can't quite hear. They calm her in a way that I clearly couldn't, and she even gives him a dopey smile before another contraction takes over.

"Trev? Can you call Scar, have her pick the kids up from school and daycare?" Declan asks Trevor.

"Of course," he nods. Trevor makes his way out into the hallway as I follow after him. When I pass through the threshold, he surprises the hell out of me. Without saying a word, he wraps his arms around me in a tight hug before pulling back, brushing a piece of hair away from my face as those bright blue eyes look down at me.

"You good?"

"I'm fine, mild panic attack. I haven't even seen the worst of it, and I can already tell I don't have what it takes to do all of that," I say with a shake of my head.

Trevor's fingers continue running through my hair, pushing it out of my face even though it's no longer in the way. Almost like he's just enjoying running his fingers through my hair. I know I'm enjoying it, so I don't bother to ask him to stop.

"You never know. I don't think there's a thing in this world that could stop you from anything."

The confidence in his words takes me by surprise, and my eyes raise to meet his. They're softer than normal, bluer, if that were even possible. His almost featherlight touch against my skin causes a wake of goose bumps to run up and down my arm as he seems to be almost lost in thought. It's only for a second though before he's shaking himself out of it and dropping his hand to his side.

"You know," he continues. "Because you're such a pain in the ass. I don't think you would ever allow anything to beat you out."

I chuckle at that, pushing away the disappointment at the loss of his touch.

Definitely not exploring that feeling right now.

"Maybe so. I am pretty badass," I agree.

Trevor laughs as we turn to head out of the hospital.

"So modest."

"Nope," I grin. "Are you sure you want to leave? Should we stay, and I don't know...wait?" I ask as we near the exit.

Trevor shakes his head. "Nah. Who knows how long it'll be, and they need their little family bonding time when it does happen."

I nod as we get out to the parking lot where I notice Trevor's Mercedes is parked next to my Toyota.

"Why did you come anyway?" I ask.

He hesitates for a moment and shrugs his shoulders.

"Dec was pretty worked up when you called Coach. I figured he couldn't drive, and I wanted to make sure you were good."

"Me?" I ask with furrowed brows.

Instead of answering me, he climbs into his car and fires it up. I, however, continue staring at the dark silhouetted man in the car. Why the hell would he be worried about me? I'm not the one who was in labor. Sure, I was freaking the hell out, but he had no way of knowing that. Eventually, I shake my head and unlock my car before starting it up. I back out of the spot I'm in, and Trevor pulls out to follow behind me the whole way home.

When we got back to the house I told Trevor that I was going to make myself some dinner. He nodded his head and was about to go upstairs when I stopped him and asked if he wanted some too. If I didn't know better, I'd say his mood seemed to almost lift at that offer before he came over to the bar top and watched me work.

Don't get me wrong, baking is my passion, but I like to cook too. It's fun and honestly being a cook has been a really delicious hobby of mine so it's a win, win.

Trevor has a housekeeper who comes a few times a week, and she also gets all of the groceries. Since I've been here I've always bought my own stuff and brought it back, but yesterday he told me it was dumb for me and her to both go grocery shopping just to bring it back to the same house. I wanted to argue since the difference was that I was buying my groceries, and she was buying them on his little black card. But I decided not to because he's loaded, and I'm not. Plus I look at it like retribution for all the times he was an asshole to me.

As I'm prepping the stuffed bell peppers, I pause mid motion. He hasn't just bought groceries for me today, and as weird as it is to me that he would go out of his way to try to replace my things, honestly upgrade my things, it was really nice.

"Vi told me about my apartment," I say as I resume my task at hand, cutting the tops off the peppers, scraping them out for the sole purpose of keeping my eyes off his cerulean blues for as long as possible.

"What about it?" he asks.

I pause for a moment, sparing a glance to see that he's already watching me intently.

"About how you paid for all of the stuff. You practically redecorated the entire place, and the stuff definitely wasn't from Bargain-Mart."

"I fucking hope not. The dent Vi put in my card tells me it should be really nice stuff."

I let out a short laugh at that as I nod and turn to face the stove and start cooking the meat.

"It was. Thank you," I say, rushing out those last words.

Trevor doesn't say anything for a moment. Instead, all I hear is the soft creaking of the bar stool before his slow but purposeful footsteps make their way over to me. Anticipation thrums in my veins, my heartbeat thumping steadily against my ribcage. In the next second, his hands appear on either side of me, gripping the countertop as I stir the beef.

I feel him before I hear him next, his lips brushing against the shell of my ear as he speaks.

"How did those words taste coming out of your mouth?" he asks, a smirk blatant in his tone as he does.

I turn to look over my shoulder at him, narrowing my eyes at his mocking smile.

"Like acid."

His smile grows as one of his hands comes down to grip the front of my hip, pulling me back until my ass is flush against him. I feel his other hand wrap around my throat gently, forcing my head to tilt up even farther as he looks down at me.

"You're welcome, Raven."

Without another word, his lips are on mine. They move slowly, softly. It's a complete contrast from every other kiss we've had. They are usually so rushed and frantic. We're typically too busy fighting for dominance to do much more than lash against each other. This time, though, just this once, I let him take control. Because fuck, he's so good at it.

His tongue comes out, stroking against my own in a steady rhythm that has my body practically sinking into him. I can't help but push back softly, waiting for the tempo to change. For him to abandon this slow sweet kiss that shouldn't be shared between us.

This isn't a kiss for a couple of friends with benefits. Or in our case, enemies turned acquaintances with benefits. No. This is a kiss for lovers. True actual lovers who crave each other, who savor every last drop of one another. This is a kiss that leaves your body weak and your soul alive. It doesn't belong to us.

Slowly, he breaks the kiss, not pulling away fully as he looks down at me, his eyes flicking back and forth between my wide eyes. I expect him to react, to freak out, push me away, or maybe for us to start fucking. He doesn't do any of those things, though. Instead, he presses another kiss to the crown of my head before releasing my throat and mirroring his grip on my other hip, his head just barely tucking into the crook of my neck as he holds me.

It takes me a second to grasp my composure before I focus back to the practically burning meat.

Whoops.

Again, I'm readying for us to descend into some awkward silence or something, both of us too wrapped up in whatever the fuck is going on in our heads, but per usual lately, Trevor Michaels takes me by surprise.

"You don't have to go," he murmurs against the bare skin of my neck.

"What?"

"You don't have to go," he repeats, his lips brushing against me with every word spoken. "If you aren't ready to go back there, you're welcome here."

I can't stop myself from smiling at that, hating that my stomach does backflips in response to his words.

"Yeah?" I question coolly.

Trevor adopts my same tone, and I feel his shoulders shrug slightly, but he doesn't move away or release his hold on me as he does.

"I mean, it just makes sense. We both go to the same place for work most days. We travel together, and you make me food."

"All true. And you make me come," I point out.

He grins at that as he places a gentle kiss against my skin.

"That I do."

"Well, sounds like a pretty decent setup," I say as if I was weighing my options.

"Yeah?" he questions, a soft lilt to his voice.

I do my best to bite back my smile. I'm showing too much emotion. I'm feeling too much emotion. I need to lock shit down. Get out of here and run like hell. I'm not safe here, not long term, and anyone around me won't be safe. It's best that I leave soon, keep moving, keep hiding.

But as Trevor's grip on me tightens, like he can practically hear my thoughts, the fear inside of me dims out until it's nothing but soft burning embers. It's stupid to say that I feel safe with him. We can barely tolerate each other most days, but something inside me tells me that if anyone was going to protect me, in more ways than one, it would be him.

Chapter 24
Sage

The next two weeks practically fly by. Between games, practices and pretty much nonstop sex, we've been busy. Not that I'm complaining or anything. The Crusaders were undefeated up until last night's game. We played the Philadelphia Cougars again, and unfortunately, this time they bested us. I think the guys went in a little too cocky and got dealt a nasty piece of humble pie.

The Cougars are one of the best teams in the NFL for a reason. Their defense is practically unmatched. Trevor was taken down again and again, and unfortunately, we weren't able to get very many points on the board before we ran out of time. Despite losing yesterday's game, things are looking good for the Crusaders' postseason, but we'll see for sure soon enough, I guess.

I've reached out to Calista a few times over the last few weeks, and I've gotten radio silence. It's typical for us to go a week or two without talking, but it's been closer to three weeks with no communication, and it's making me uneasy. If I had a way to reach out to Hammer I would, but for now I guess I just have to wait.

I send another text to Calista asking her to send me some kind of message indicating she's okay before I slip into the shower. Once my hair is combed and my face is washed, I decide to just wrap a towel around myself before heading downstairs. Practice is canceled for today, apparently there is some rat infestation at the training center, which means a day off for Trevor and me.

Days off and no plans usually translates to a naked day full of fun, so I don't really see the point in getting dressed when Trevor would no doubt rip it to shreds the second I step foot in the same room as him.

Smirking to myself, I saunter downstairs, noticing that he isn't up yet. Lazy bum. I could be nice and make him breakfast in bed or something. Then again, I could just grab us a couple of protein shakes, and we could stay in bed.

Yep. I like that plan better.

I open the fridge, grabbing two of the chocolate shakes before I hear the front door open and shut. Huh, maybe he did already get up. Not unlike him to cheat on his meal plan and get some biscuits and gravy from this little dive diner across town.

"Where have you been?" I ask with a smile that drops as soon as I turn.

An older blonde woman dripping in designer clothes is standing in the foyer with a well-dressed bald man in his late fifties by her side, both donning disapproving sneers toward me.

"Who exactly are you?" the woman asks, her obviously fake nose practically pointed to the sky as she somehow still maintains eye contact.

A weaker woman would probably wither under her glare, but I'm way too desensitized to a rich asshole's disparaging looks and remarks.

Thanks, Daddy.

"I'm Sage," I say with something that is closer to a snarl than a smile as I very plainly let this rich bitch know I'm not intimidated.

Her eyes narrow on me, and she opens her mouth to speak when a voice comes from the stairs.

"Mom? Dad?"

Trevor comes down, only wearing a pair of boxers as he runs a hand through his very obvious sex hair. Just because we don't sleep in the same bed doesn't mean we don't fuck right before bed and first thing in the morning if we can swing it.

"Trev," the bitchy blonde who is apparently his mom says, her eyes tracing over him in the same distasteful way that she did to me.

Well, at least I'm not special. That just appears to be her lovely personality.

"What are you guys doing here? How did you get in?" he asks as he makes it to the bottom of the stairs, his eyes coming to me for a split second. I watch as he catalogs what I'm wearing, or more so what I'm not wearing before he comes to stand in front of me, almost like he's trying to shield me. It's sweet but totally unnecessary. I'm more than covered, and I have no issue standing butt-ass naked in front of his snooty parents.

"Like the date of your first Super Bowl is such a complicated security code," his father draws out with a roll of his eyes.

I watch as Trevor's back muscles tense instantly as his father takes a step forward.

"The gala is tonight, remember? I assume you still plan on attending."

Trevor pauses for a moment before his voice comes out a little more strained than before.

"Of course, sir."

"Good." His father nods, his eyes coming to me, his own version of a judgmental lookover scraping against my bare skin before his face pulls into a distasteful frown. I wonder what is so repulsive about me. Is it the tattoos? The nose ring? Or maybe the fact that I'm just some younger naked girl standing in the middle of their son's kitchen.

"Sweetie, who are you bringing as your plus one?" his mom asks. She casts me the fastest glance before facing Trevor again. "I was thinking Erica. She's always such fantastic company. I'll call her and make sure she's free," she says as she pulls out her phone.

"No," Trevor says.

His mom's head lifts, staring at him with a perplexed look.

"Why on earth not?"

Trevor blows out an aggravated breath as he shakes his head.

"Because she's married, Mom. With two little girls. She doesn't have time to drop her family and come be my date at a gala for your company. It's inappropriate, and neither her nor her husband would appreciate her being put in that situation."

I'm surprised at how outraged Trevor seems to be. With how obviously in love with Erica he is, you'd think he'd jump all over a chance to have her on his arm for the night. Then again, maybe that's the sadder part. He's resigned to the fact that doing something like that would only hurt everyone involved, so instead he suffers in silence. Honestly, though, I expected them to talk more. I thought they did at least. Maybe they do when I'm not around, but I feel like before I moved in Erica was always getting lunch with Trevor or texting him. Now whether I'm with her or him, I never really see any communication between them, and it has my nosy ass all the more curious.

"Her husband," Trevor's mom laughs. "If you can even call that degenerate such a name. The fact that she had children with someone like that still makes me sick to my stomach. She was such a good girl."

Sebastian? A degenerate? What the fuck is this lady talking about. Caldwell is one of the most stand up guys on the team. He's never in the tabloids, he's not caught partying, doing drugs, or getting speeding tickets. He shows up, kicks ass on the field, and races home to his family. If that's so disgraceful, I'd love to know what she thinks about me or honestly her own son.

"Mother, enough," Trevor says curtly. "I will not be bringing Erica. Sage will be my plus one for the night," he says, pulling me more to the side of him as he wraps his arm around my shoulders.

Her eyes narrow into slits as she takes a closer look at me, scraping over me from head to toe as if she was looking to find anything salvageable in me. Well, whatever she was looking for, I don't think she finds it because she shakes her head and crosses her arms.

"I don't think so, sweetheart. You need to set a good image with the board and the media. We don't want you getting mistakenly attached to...her type."

"And what, pray tell, is my type exactly?" I ask sweetly, stepping out of Trevor's grasp just enough to come toe to toe with the blonde viper in front of me.

She gives me a sneer that could curdle dairy.

"Sweetheart, I don't think you should ask questions you don't want to hear the answers to," she says haughtily.

"Hm," I smile so hard, my cheeks hurt. "And I don't think you should keep shooting your face up with Botox. Can you even feel anything anymore? Blink twice if you can understand me." I shrug unaffected as I continue.

"I guess we both have opinions the other doesn't give a fuck about," I shrug.

Her mouth drops open in outrage, smoke practically billowing out of her ears as a pair of arms quickly slip around me, practically lifting me into the air as I'm moved through the kitchen and up the stairs.

"See you tonight. Please let yourselves out."

"Are you seriously going to let your little plaything talk to me like that?" his mom shouts from downstairs, but Trevor ignores her, taking the steps two at a time before carrying me into his bedroom. He kicks the door shut before tossing me onto his bed.

My towel almost comes off at that, but I right it in time when I sit up.

"Well, that was fun," I smile.

Trevor just looks down at me, an unimpressed look on his face.

"Do you have a cordial bone in your body?"

"I think that's number 207, and I only have 206, sorry."

To my surprise he laughs, running a hand through his hair.

"I'm sorry about her, both of them really. They are..."

"Snobby, entitled, arrogant, pretentious?" I guess for him.

He cuts me a sad smile and nods.

"All of the above, but they're my parents," he shrugs.

I nod at that, settling back onto my hands on the bed.

"Parents suck."

A dry chuckle escapes him as he scrapes his hand over his jaw.

"Yeah. Sorry about dragging you into this. You don't have to come. I just wanted her to drop the whole Erica thing."

"Why?" I ask with a tilt of my head.

"Why what?"

"Why didn't you just agree to have her come? Or at least try to have her come?"

He crosses his arms over his chest, clearly trying to close himself off. I've spent too much time with him, though. I know all of his tells, and this is the one that he uses when he gets uncomfortable about being vulnerable.

"I'm tired. Tired of putting her through shit, putting Seb through it. Fuck, putting me through it. I'll always love her, but I can't live my life like this, you know?"

My eyebrows raise in surprise as I nod in agreement.

"Well, good. There are plenty of other women in the world that can hold your interest. Ones who are a lot less married and a lot less off limits," I tease lightly.

He smirks at me in amusement as he cocks his head slightly.

"Yeah? Like a smart-mouthed, raven-haired pain in the ass?"

My smile drops as his words catch me off guard. Trevor's smile disappears seconds later as we just stare at each other for several seconds. I don't know why it takes me so long to react. We can just chalk it up to it being early because I don't know what the fuck I'd say otherwise. I quickly roll my eyes and give a sarcastic laugh as I stand.

"Definitely not. I like to be the girl who has your attention for the night, not your whole life."

"Why though?" he pushes.

A face I haven't seen in months flashes to the forefront of my mind, sending a shiver down my spine.

"Being someone's obsession can only end in disaster."

Trevor's blue eyes are drilling into me, practically prying my defenses back to read more into that statement. Or at least, he's trying to. Fuck, why did I even open my mouth?

Horribly switching topics, I brush past him as I go to open the door.

"Do I have to wear a dress to this thing?"

I don't turn around to look at him, but I can feel his eyes on me.

"Well, yeah. It's fine, though, Sage. I can call someone or—"

"Nope," I cut in a little quicker than I need to. "I'll go. Any chance to irritate some old rich pricks," I say with what I hope is a mischievous smirk over my shoulder at him.

I still see the curiosity in his eyes, and also maybe something close to concern before he shakes his head and gives me half a smile.

"Fucking hell. My mother will have you thrown out before the night is over, won't she?"

"Probably," I shrug. "Will there be booze?"

"As much as you can drink," he says as I turn to face him a little more.

"How long do we have to go?"

He shrugs. "Probably a few hours at least."

I groan at that. "Alright, well can we at least sneak into the coat closet and have some hot, almost-gonna-get-caught, public sex or something?"

Trevor's smile spreads into a wicked grin as he nods. "Fuck yes."

"Fine. I have to go get a dress, though," I say as I turn away from him and step out the bedroom door.

"Send me the bill," he says.

"You know it!" I call out.

Chapter 25
Sage

How I find myself in a fancy-ass dress store, playing dress up while Erica drinks champagne and laughs, I'll never know.

"You can't be serious," I say with a scrunched nose as I come out in the one she insisted would look perfect on me.

"Oh my god, you look amazing," she squeals as she looks over the baby pink gown.

"I look like a pack of Hubba Bubba bubble gum," I say dryly.

Erica tosses her long hair back as she laughs. I, however, am not amused as I continue to give her a deadpan look. She tries to get it together, smothering her laughter as she runs her fingers over the material.

"It's not that bad. It—"

"It is," I scowl. "I told you. I'm wearing black."

She rolls her eyes at me. "Fine, whatever. Black is so boring, though."

I wave her off as I slip into the changing room, taking off the pink monstrosity and tossing it to the side like it will attack me any moment. I pull on the silky robe they left in the room for me before I'm back out on the sales floor and scouring through the black section of dresses. A sales lady was trying to help us, but one flash of Erica's smile and a couple hundred dollars, and they all took an early lunch, closing the store down for our own private shopping.

Even though I come from a pretty wealthy family, my dad sure as hell never did shit like this for me, and I haven't lived a lifestyle like that in years. Obviously Erica was born into this life, though, and it's just what is done.

"What about this one?" I ask as I pull out a simple satin black sheath dress.

Erica wrinkles her nose up as she looks at me.

"Sweetie, you have a gorgeous body, why the hell are you not trying to show off those curves?"

I roll my eyes as I put it back and keep looking.

"I don't mind showing off curves, I just don't want to look like a barbie doll."

She shakes her head as she begins thumbing through the dresses as well.

"So, you met Trevor's parents," she says, her eyes still on the dresses.

"Oh yeah. They just loved me," I laugh.

Erica smirks. "They are a little much, but they do love Trevor. They are a lot like my parents. Very...particular."

"Yeah, and they particularly don't like me," I snark.

Her eyes come to mine, curiosity practically drowning her bright green eyes.

"Does that bother you?"

I shake my head and scoff. "Hardly. I've been disappointing rich assholes since before I could say my first word. I could give a flying fuck about his parents."

Erica nods as she keeps her eyes on me.

"So, why are you going tonight?"

"What do you mean? I told you. Trevor volunteered me," I say with a roll of my eyes.

"You also said he offered to find someone else."

I narrow my eyes slightly. "So?"

"Sooo, just curious what made you want to come down here, bitching and moaning about wearing a dress to spend an evening with two people who you obviously will not align with."

"I'm just being nice, and it'll be funny to fuck with his mom," I say as I pull out another dress, showing it to her and causing her to shake her head once more.

Fucking hell this woman is picky.

I'm aggressively flipping through the dresses now, Erica's incessant questions beginning to grate me as she speaks again.

"Or you got jealous."

"What?" I laugh.

She shrugs. "It's okay to admit that you like him, Sage. No one is going to blame you for it. He's a great guy. He's obviously gorgeous and funny and has the softest sweet side of almost anyone I've ever met."

"And he's madly in love with *you*," I point out.

Her head moves from side to side as her mouth twists up in thought.

"Maybe not as much as you think he is."

"Why do you say that?"

"I can't tell you how many times he's asked me to be his date to one of these things just over the last few years. It's been a lot. Obviously out of respect to Sebastian, I never go with him, even as friends, because I know there is that blurry line. But this time, it's actually local, last minute, and he didn't even entertain the idea of asking me. Instead he assumed you would go with him. It's just...different. And then you volunteering to go after he says he will find someone else—"

"Alright, Dr. Caldwell, thank you very much, but I think I've had enough of your half-baked psycho analysis."

"I'm just saying, if you and Trevor wanted to give things a try past the little fuck buddy thing you guys have going on, I think you two would actually be really great for each other."

I scoff at her words before grabbing a handful of dresses and stomping off toward the dressing room. She's ridiculous. Trevor and I are like gasoline and fire. Sure we can burn hot and heavy for a little bit, right before we burn the world around us to the ground. We would be so destructive together, a disaster in the making. He would never be able to give himself to me the way he needs because he will always love someone else, and I would never be able to give myself to him because I'm petrified to fall in love ever again. As history proves, I don't have a great picker.

A knock comes from the door before Erica pushes inside. Jesus, does this woman have no personal boundaries?

"Try this one," she says as she practically shoves a dress into my chest.

I look down at it and don't hate it right off the bat, which is more than I can say for all the other dresses that Erica has picked out.

Holding the dress up, I nod softly before pushing her out of the room. She laughs as she goes.

"You're welcomeeee!" she sings.

It doesn't take long to slip into it, but I can barely move in this room because the skirt is so big.

"I said I didn't want poofy—" I complain as I step out to the mirror-surrounded showroom floor area.

Erica is looking at me with an excited gleam as my words trail off.

For a moment, I'm speechless. Holy fucking shit. This dress is next level.

The skirt is poofy but not in a bridal circus dress way. It's just a lot of material that fans out to compliment the A-line dress with a thigh-high slit on my left side that is sure to give Trevor's mom a heart attack. The sweetheart neckline has sharper lines than your classic circular shape with a nice deep slit for the cleavage. It's accompanied by a single flat-laid cap sleeve that brings your eyes up to the collarbone. It's practically ethereal, in a dark angel kind of way. I fucking love it.

I glance down at the price tag, my eyes practically bugging out of my head when I see the zeros continue. For a single dress? They are joking, right? For a moment, I kinda feel bad, but then I glance over to my purse where I know Trevor's shiny black credit card is, and I feel a little better. He's an asshole more days than not, and he's dragging me to this thing. He owes me. Besides, our hate sex is some of the best.

"You look amazing!" Erica gushes. "Please tell me you're getting that one!"

I nod as I look at myself in the mirror. "Definitely. Let me change and pay for this, and then let's get some food. Lunch is on Trevor."

After Erica and I got lunch, we went our separate ways and headed back home. When I got to Trevor's house, he wasn't there. So I took my ridiculously expensive dress and decided to start getting ready for this evening. I would never identify myself as a girly girl but that doesn't mean I don't know how to get dolled up every once in a while.

After my body is shaved and lotioned, and my hair and makeup are finished, I look in the mirror. I decided to go with some big barrel curls pushed over one shoulder as opposed to my typical pin-straight hair. I don't think I've worn this much makeup in years, and honestly, I only had the bare essentials until Erica and I stopped at the store earlier today.

I paired the dress with a deep red lip and a pair of black stilettos that I also bought at the dress shop. I wonder how pissed Trevor will be when he sees his credit card bill.

When I'm done, I decide to go downstairs and grab a snack. God knows you pay an obscene amount per plate at things like this and walk away with a fifty-cent piece serving of food. The clicking of my heels echoes through the house, and when I get to the bottom of the stairs I see Trevor walking toward me in a crisp black tux. I've seen him in suits for gameday and press conferences, but there is something about a tux that just hits differently.

His broad shoulders take up every inch of the suit without making it look too tight. Obviously it's tailored to him perfectly, and the material looks like a dream. His hair is styled perfectly, taming the little bit of wildness his hair can take on and instead, presenting him as the put-together golden boy he is, or at least the persona that he tries to display.

I watch as his bright blue eyes round slightly, his mouth just barely separating as he looks at me.

"Sage," he says in a whisper, almost like a prayer against his lips.

The sound sends a trail of goose bumps across my skin and causes my heart to stall just for a moment.

"You clean up pretty well," I say, doing my best to ignore the emotion building inside me.

"You look..." he trails off for a moment, shaking his head as his eyes bounce from mine to my lips.

"Exquisite," he breathes out, so many emotions playing heavily in his eyes.

I feel my pulse begin to thunder, practically hearing the loud thump of my heartbeat.

"You like?" I say with a soft smile, doing my best to come across teasingly, but it sounds more breathy than anything.

I do a turn, and Trevor instantly grabs my hand, lifting it above my head as he guides the spin, slowing down the pace like he's memorizing everything in this moment. When I make it full circle, I notice that I'm closer to him than before. His hand is still gripping mine as he lowers it to rest between our chests. His other hand reaches out and finds the thigh slit in the dress, brushing against the exposed skin in slow, methodical circles. There is no sexual intent behind his touch, no ulterior motive. It's like he's touching me just to feel my skin against his, and I don't really know what to do with that kind of information.

"I love," he says softly, my brain stalling for a moment before I realize he's responding to my previous question of whether he liked it.

Fuck, get it together, Sage.

"Should we go?" I ask, horribly transitioning topics as I do.

Trevor stares at me for another second or two before he blinks and nods.

"Yeah, yes. Let's go," he says as he walks over to the island where his phone and wallet are.

I grab my clutch I left down here earlier before reaching inside and handing him his credit card.

"What's the damage?" he asks as he slips it back into his wallet.

I laugh in a way that I hope is as devious as I feel.

"You don't want to know."

His eyes scrape over me like a set of hot coals, a smirk spreading across his face as he gives me a quick wink.

"Worth it," he says before smacking my ass and leading the way to the car.

Chapter 26
Sage

When we get to the art museum where the gala is being held, Trevor can barely stop the car before the valet is rushing out to us. Trevor slips him a few bills before coming around to my side of the car and opening the door.

"Thanks," I say with a small smile.

He nods as he rests his hand against my lower back and doesn't move it as we walk up the front stairs and into the glass-walled building. When we step inside, the party is in full swing. There is what looks like a silent auction going on around the perimeter of the room and dozens and dozens of tables donned with white tablecloths as well as white centerpieces, chairs and décor scattered around the room.

My eyes skim over the various attendees who are either dancing, getting a drink from one of the bars, or schmoozing, all of whom are dressed in white. What. The. Fuck.

I look to find Trevor watching me with an amused smirk.

"Trevor, what the hell? Is this like a white-out party or something?"

"Something like that."

"Well why the fuck did you tell me I could wear black?"

He shrugs. "Because you wanted to."

"Yeah, but why did you wear black if you knew?"

His words pause for a moment as he looks at me with a soft look.

"I wanted us to be the same."

I am still trying to process why the idiot didn't just tell me that we should us. His dad is the first to approach as he grabs Trevor's arm and attempts to yank him toward him like a disobedient child.

"Are you serious? Do you think you're funny? The invitation stated white attire only. Are you insolent or thick?"

"Both according to you," Trevor says, easily pulling out of his father's grip as he takes a half of a step closer to me, wrapping his arm loosely around my waist.

His dad's jaw is clenching repeatedly, grinding his teeth together when his mother starts up.

"Honestly, Trevor. I'm so disappointed in you. I thought you were teasing when you said you were going to bring this...girl," she says with a sneer as she spares me the sharpest of glances before continuing.

"And this is the exact reason her type doesn't come to places like this. Honestly, a black whorish dress like this? Tell me, do you just enjoy the attention of being a cheap trollop, or are you purposefully trying to ruin my son's life? Because I can tell you that you are doing famously well in both aspects at this moment."

I'm about to make this self-absorbed twat feel two inches tall, but I'm not able to because Trevor steps, quite literally, between us, practically shielding me from his mother's sight as he lowers his tone to an eerie sound.

"You will never speak to Sage that way again. She is my girlfriend, and she will be treated with the respect that title deserves. Any less from either of you, and I will cut ties and obtain restraining orders so fast, your heads will spin. Do you understand?"

"You can't be serious, Trevor! I'm your mother!" she practically shouts, earning a few cursory glances from their peers and causing her husband to pinch her side in warning.

"I understand that, and I love you very much, but I won't allow the woman that I choose to care for to be treated poorly just because you gave birth to me. I watched Grandmother Marilyn treat you horribly my entire life, and Dad never stepped in to defend you. I will not make that same mistake. If you will excuse us," Trevor says before stepping to the side, reaching back for my hand and lacing our fingers together, before pulling me toward the dance floor.

We fall into a waltz almost immediately as the band plays on stage. There aren't many people dancing at the moment, but it's not like Trevor or I have ever cared about causing a scene. We don't say anything, and we honestly don't even look at each other as we both go through the motions seamlessly. I guess thanks are in order for those dance lessons I took when I was seven.

My mind is whirling with so many questions I don't even know where to begin. It was surprising enough to have Trevor step in to defend me to begin with. I can't tell you the last time anyone has ever done that for me. But he went farther than that. He didn't just stand up for me. He tore his own mother to pieces for the disrespect, threatened to eradicate them from his life, for me. Oh, and can't forget that other part.

"So, girlfriend?" I question, an amused lilt to my tone as Trevor's stormy blue eyes snap down to mine.

His jaw is clenched in irritation, and his breathing is heavy.

"Yes," he says tersely.

"I don't remember being notified of this change in relationship status."

"Now you have been," he says, his eyes still on me.

I let out a dry laugh as I shake my head.

"Yeah, well, shouldn't I get a say in this?"

His eyes narrow slightly as he looks into mine, like he's searching for something before he shakes his head.

"No."

"What? Why the hell not."

His eyelids close for a moment as he lets out a huff of a breath before opening them again.

"Because you're too scared to admit that you want this, and I've been too stupid trying to convince myself that I didn't have to have you from the moment I first touched you. So, no, you don't get a say. You are mine, and I am yours."

I'm speechless, staring up at this gorgeous, infuriating, kind man absolutely flabbergasted. You can't just say that you're going to be with someone. Claim them as your girlfriend. Can you? No, fuck. Absolutely not. He can't control me. He can't force me into this. I won't—

My inner monologue is short-lived when I feel Trevor's soft lips come down to mine, crushing against me in a kiss that sends my stomach flipping and my pulse jackhammering. His arms wrap around me like two vines, not allowing a single inch of space between as his tongue comes out to mine, tangling around me as he deepens the kiss. When I try to take control of the kiss, he pulls away, resting his forehead against mine as he lets out a shuddered breath.

"Tell me you don't feel it too, and I'll take it all back. Tell me you don't feel this, and I'll let you go."

His eyes are on me, practically begging. I'm not quite sure which outcome he is begging for, but all I know is that at this moment, I'm terrified. Terrified because I don't want to think this over, because I don't need to. I'm terrified because I shouldn't trust anyone ever again. It's too dangerous, but at this moment, I realize it's already too late.

I lean forward enough to press my lips against his, sealing my fate and his as his hand comes up to cup the side of my face, his touch equally soft and strong. Like I'm a delicate flower that will break in his hand, but he's too afraid to let me go. And I fucking bask in the intoxicating combination.

When Trevor pulls away, a wave of disappointment runs through me as he looks down at me, still cradling my face with perhaps the most gentle, genuine smile I've ever seen on him. I find myself smiling up at him too, just as some old bald guy gets on stage and makes an announcement. Oh, look. The old bald guy is Trevor's dad.

We make our way to our seats, Trevor grabbing my hand and lacing our fingers together, not letting go even when we are settled, and his mother is attempting to catch me on fire with her eyes. I give her a sweet smile before facing the front, watching as Trevor's dad drones on and on. I don't even know what this event is about, honestly. Is it a charity fundraiser? Is the company celebrating something? Are they just a bunch of rich assholes trying to flaunt their wealth in each other's faces?

My gut tells me that's the most likely reason.

The dinner is served shortly after, and the portion size is as big as the palm of my hand. I give Trevor an irritated look, and he only laughs before squeezing my hand and leaning to speak into my ear.

"We will grab more food later, k, baby?"

I try not to let him see the effect his words have on me. Not sure if it's the promise of more food or him calling me baby that has my heart fluttering, but just because I like to fuck Trevor, and could maybe tolerate dating him, doesn't mean I want him to know how easily he can turn me to mush if he wanted to.

I nod as he smiles and gives me a wink before continuing to eat what little is on his plate.

"So, Sarah. I don't think we got the chance to be properly introduced. My son seems very taken with you, so I think it's only proper that introductions are in order. I'm Shannon Michaels."

I bite my tongue not to lash out for the obvious purposeful name misuse. I won't let this woman rattle me for a minute, but ever the shining knight, Trevor rides in and cuts her down at the knees.

"It's Sage, Mother. Don't act like you forgot in the last thirty minutes or even from this morning. If you want her last name so you can run a thorough criminal and background check, just say so."

She looks absolutely taken aback by his bluntness, and I can't help but laugh. Fucking A, this protective Trevor? Yeah, I like this guy.

"Oh for sure." I laugh. "Want my fingerprints too?" I offer, handing her the wine glass I've been drinking out of that has visible smudged fingerprints on it.

She looks down at the glass in disdain before turning her nose up.

"I just like to make sure that my son is in good hands. We don't need what happened to Erica happening to him."

"Yeah, I've been wondering about that. What the hell are you talking about? Sebastian is probably one of the nicest and most family-oriented guys on the team, hell, probably in the state. So why isn't he good enough for Erica? She seems to think he is."

Shannon looks down at me with disbelief.

"You know Erica?"

"I do," I nod. "We are actually great friends."

She scoffs. "And I had such high hopes for her. It seems she likes to associate herself with a certain type."

I feel Trevor begin to fume beside me, but I squeeze his hand in warning to shut up as I lean across the table.

"Mhmm, and how long has it been since you've spoken to her?"

Shannon shifts slightly as she lays her hands in her lap.

"Well, it's been a while."

I nod. "Hmph, seems she definitely likes to associate herself with a type. I guess judgmental bitch doesn't fall under that type."

Her eyes widen in surprise, but the woman has met me twice now. She shouldn't be surprised. I push away from the table, standing before pulling Trevor with me.

"I'm thirsty, let's go get a drink."

Trevor instantly stands, giving his mom a short nod of his head as we step away from the table and walk over to the closest bar. The bartender comes over to us expectantly as I smile at him.

"Two old fashioneds, please."

I feel Trevor's arms snake around my waist as his head dips down to my neck, speaking into my skin.

"First you're telling off my mom, now you're ordering me drinks. Did I forget to mention that I'm gonna be the guy in this relationship?"

A heat wave rushes through me at the feel of his lips on my skin, and I can't wait to make him lick clean the mess he is currently making between my legs.

I give him a confused look as the bartender hands us our drinks.

"No, I know. Pay the man," I say as I step to the side, earning a rough chuckle from Trevor as he digs for his wallet.

The bartender nods his appreciation when Trevor tells him to keep the change before he closes the distance between us.

"Feel all masculine now?"

He scoffs. "Hardly."

"Hmm, well I know you promised me some naughty fun in a coat closet," I say as I take a sip of the dark-colored drink.

Trevor's bright blue eyes darken in color as lust clouds his face. I feel him start to pull me toward the door when some old white dude calls out his name. He curses under his breath before releasing his hold on me and turning to face him with a smile. The two of them walk over to the other side of the bar as they begin schmoozing, and I can't help but huff in irritation. I don't care that he has to mingle. I care that our banter has my panties soaked, and he isn't going to do anything about it right this second. Maybe I'll just have to go finish myself off.

The old man he is talking to has his back to me as he is engaging in a deep conversation with Trevor, involving large hand gestures. Trevor is intently listening, smiling and nodding at apparently all the right times, but I don't miss his eyes occasionally coming to me.

An idea pops into my head, and I can't bite back my smile as I lift the cherry stem from my glass, raising it to my lips before running the plump red fruit over my equally red lips. The next time Trevor does a check-in glance toward me, his eyes stay there.

Perfect.

Slowly, I suck the fruit between my lips, making sure to take my time until the fruit slips into my mouth. Trevor is watching with rapt attention as I pull the stem off, swallowing the cherry before slipping the stem into my mouth. It takes me a few moments, but when I'm finished, I pull the stem out to reveal the double knot I created with my tongue.

Without another word, I throw it into the trash, turn on my heel and head toward the main entrance, knowing Trevor will follow.

I'm actually not sure where I'm going, it's not like I've been here before, but I know the bathroom is this way, and where there are bathrooms, there are usually empty rooms or closets. Maybe I can slip into one before Trevor, and—

My thought is cut off by a rough grip on my arm, pulling me into a dark closet before slamming the door shut on me. My first instinct is panic until I smell the clean scent of Trevor's cologne. Ease instantly overwhelms me before excitement takes over as his arms wrap around me, plastering my ass against him.

"Now where do you think you're going, Little Raven?" he rumbles quietly.

"Well, you left me to talk to some old rich dude, so I was going to take matters into my own hands," I bluff.

"Mmmm and what 'matters' are you referring to?" he asks as one of his hands slips between the high slit of my dress, brushing over the silky material of my panties.

I can't help but gasp as his finger traces a perfect line down the front of me, but I do my best to make my tone even as I speak.

"I was gonna finger fuck myself until I came."

"Fuck!" Trevor practically growls as he sinks his teeth into the sensitive flesh of my neck before shoving past my panties and burying two fingers inside me.

The pain of his bite and pleasure of his fingers causes me to let out a yelp. Trevor pulls back slightly as his fingers begin moving inside me, while he kisses the aching skin.

"What are you? A fucking vampire?" I grumble as he pushes deeper, rubbing against my G-spot and causing my head to fall back against his shoulder.

"Nah, baby. Out of the two of us, you're the one that does the sucking."

"Hell yeah, I do," I say proudly, earning a rough chuckle to come rumbling from his chest, as his thumb begins circling my clit.

"You like that, Little Raven?"

"Yes," I gasp, not having enough brain power to say anything else as the height of my orgasm begins to creep up on me.

"Such a naughty little girl sneaking away in the middle of a party to play with yourself. You should know better. If you need to be touched, you come get me, babygirl."

"I don't need you," I throw out, causing him to laugh and stop all his movements. I whimper at the loss, my climax so close my body is practically shaking.

"No? So I should just head out then?"

"I'll fucking cut your balls off while you sleep if you do."

"All I heard was you'll be near my balls when I sleep. Sounds like a win to me," Trevor teases.

"Goddamn it, Trevor. Make me come, now," I demand.

I can't really see him, even with my eyes now adjusted to the dark coat closet, but that doesn't mean I can't feel the Cheshire smile on his face as he whispers in my ear.

"Anything you desire, Little Raven."

He begins moving his fingers again, curling inside me in just the right spot before rubbing. It only takes seconds for me to see stars as my mouth drops open, and I let out a shout. I feel Trevor's hand wrap around my mouth to muffle me as he finger fucks me from behind, but honestly, I don't give a damn how loud I am.

Before I can even properly come down from my high, Trevor is spinning me around until I'm facing the door before pushing on my lower back, effectively folding me like a lawn chair and hiking up my dress. I feel his cock press against me as he pulls my panties to the side before thrusting in.

"Goddamn, you feel so fucking good," he grits through what sounds like clenched teeth as he stills.

I wiggle my hips, trying to encourage him to start fucking me, but the grip that he has on my hips tightens to an almost painful point.

"Give me a sec," he rasps.

"C'mon, Trev," I whine. "This isn't your first rodeo. You've never had a problem before."

"Things are different now," he says on a labored breath as his grip continues to tighten on me.

I wriggle in discomfort but don't tell him to let go. Some strange part of me kind of likes the bite of his touch. Maybe because I know he'd never use his strength against me for malicious intent. Just the fun sexy kind.

"How so?" I ask as my hips just slightly move.

I feel his palm come down and slap against my bare ass, sending a ripple of pleasure up my spine as he speaks.

"Because you're mine now, and I've never felt anything better in my life."

My stomach flips at his words as I turn my head back to face him. I still haven't had time to properly think things through. I mean, this can only end in disaster. We are terrible for each other. A couple of commitment-phobes who are enemies turned lovers? How completely predictable and cliché can we be?

Still, there is something warm that pools in my chest when he calls me his. Something settling. So despite what a shit show this might turn into, I'm gonna chase that warm glowy feeling for as long as I can.

"Fuck me like I'm yours, Trev," I practically whisper.

Even in the practically pitch-black room, I can see his bright blue eyes flare as he nods, pulling his hips back before slamming into me again. I let out a moan of pleasure as he repeats the motion over and over again.

"Trevor," I gasp.

"Yeah, say my name, babygirl. I love hearing my name on your sweet lips."

He thrusts deeper this time rubbing against my G-spot and causing my legs to almost give out. Trevor makes up for it by practically holding me up as he continues fucking me. I feel his hand come to my ass, massaging me before giving it a light slap.

"You gonna let me take this ass soon, baby? I've been dying to fill you up."

"Yes," I moan. "Fill me up. Fuck me everywhere," I chant as my second orgasm of the night begins building.

"Such a good fucking girl. You'd let me do anything I wanted to this flawless body, wouldn't you?"

"Fuck no," I laugh, causing Trevor to laugh as well.

"Good, I like the challenge," he says before bottoming out inside me, causing a blinding light to flash before my eyes as I shatter apart. This time he doesn't bother trying to cover my scream. Who gives a shit about the party. All that matters in this moment is me, him, and how hard each of us can come.

I feel Trevor's cock swell inside me before his cum begins coating my pussy. He folds his body over my own, his mouth hitting the back of my neck as he peppers it with soft kisses as he rides out his orgasm. The act is so tender, so unlike our usual hump and dump interactions that it has me leaning back into his touch. When he pulls away, though, I can't help but be thankful because my legs are fucking ruined from being bent over for this long in heels no less.

When I stand, I look like a baby giraffe, trying to gain my footing as I stumble. I feel Trevor's cum leaking out of me and down my thigh, and as hot as that shit sounds in books and stuff, it doesn't feel the best. Trevor seems to already be on it, though, because he's sifting through jacket pockets. Looks like we are in the coat check room.

Sorry if your silk wrap smells like sex, Martha.

Trevor seems to know what he's looking for as he pulls what looks like a pocket square out of a jacket pocket. He walks over to me and begins wiping up the dripping cum before giving me a mischievous smile.

"You're the fucking worst," I laugh.

He finishes wiping me clean before tossing it into the corner on the floor. His privileged little shit attitude is showing, but to be fair, all of these people are privileged little shits, so fighting fire with fire, right?"

I push open the closet door, coming face to face with an acne-faced redheaded guy who can't be more than four years younger than me. He looks to be the coat check boy, and based on the reddening tips of his ears, my guess is he has been at his post for a little while. Some women might get embarrassed, but he looks embarrassed enough for the both of us, so I shoot him a wink and blow him a kiss as I reach back and grab Trevor's hand, pulling him through the hall.

He lets out a low chuckle as he slips his arm around my waist and guides me the opposite direction of the ballroom.

"Where are we going?" I ask as I look up to him.

An easy smile is on his face as we step through the front doors.

"Home."

Chapter 27
Sage

After the gala, Trevor made good on his promise, and we stopped at a diner to get some real food. His phone started blowing up as soon as we sat down, and I can only imagine it was his parents wondering where we disappeared to. Eventually, Trevor just turned his phone off and tossed it into the glove box.

That was two nights ago now, and each night, Trevor practically dragged me to his room and pinned me down as he curled himself around me. I act like it's such a burden when honestly, I have never felt more cared for, protected, or safe in my life. We haven't really talked about anything since the gala. I mean, what's to talk about, I guess? We are in kind of a weird transition, but whatever it is, I like it. It feels...comfortable, which is definitely not something thought I'd ever say about Trevor Michaels.

Today is a home game, and it's the third quarter. We are playing the South Carolina Stingers and currently beating the shit out of them. The score is 37-7, so it's more than safe to say we have this one in the bag, and we are one step closer to the Super Bowl.

That's every team's overall goal, right? The Crusaders haven't been in a long time, unlike the San Antonio Cobras or the Knoxville Bucks who are frequently teams in the Super Bowl. I think they have what it takes this year. They are practically untouchable, and that has more than a little to do with the new egotistical, ridiculously talented, in more ways than one, quarterback.

I got more film and pictures than I will even know what to do with and honestly, I'm kind of over the job. What's my dad gonna do? Fire me? Be my fucking guest. I love football, but I don't want to sit on the sidelines every day for the rest of my life. I want to do something for myself. Something I can build for myself, have for myself.

While they were in the tunnel for halftime, I snuck up to the family and friends' section of the stadium bleachers and took an open seat. I could have gone up to the box where Vi, Erica, and Scarlett are but figured this was easier. It took Trevor all of four minutes to find me, and I can't deny that I kind of love that.

The Stingers call timeout, and the jumbotron busts out the good old kiss cam. First it lands on a sweet-looking elderly couple that has the whole stadium awwing. Then it lands on a mom and her teenage son. He looks embarrassed as she grabs his face and kisses his cheek, causing me to chuckle when his face turns beet red. Then I see my face on the big screen, right next to the brother of one of our linebackers beside me.

I turn to look at him with raised eyebrows, but he only grins before he dives in and presses his lips against mine. It's over quickly, and he shoots me a wink before settling back in his chair and focusing on the game that's resuming. I turn to face the field too, but my eyes catch on a very pissed-off-looking quarterback.

Trevor's fists are balled up at his sides, staring directly in our direction. I can't quite see his face from here, and I'm not sure if he's glaring at me or the guy next to me. One thing is for sure, though. He's about to come fucking unhinged.

Trevor

I've never wanted to be on defense more in my life. I have an uncontrollable amount of rage rushing through my veins, and all I can do with it is throw a damn ball. I can barely see straight. Everything is just fucking red. I'm on the sidelines, and instead of watching the game like I technically should, I'm staring up into the stands at the little girl who is about to get her ass spanked raw and the stranger beside her who is going to lose his life.

The game doesn't matter anyway, the Stingers' QB is inexperienced, and he fumbles the ball almost instantly, allowing one of our guys to lay him out just as the clock runs out. *Perfect.*

I point into the stands, my finger landing on Sage before pointing to the tunnel. I can't quite see the look on her face, but I do see her head nod. Guess she can follow directions when she knows she fucked up.

I race through as few interviews as I can get away with before I'm storming past teammates and coaches, on a one-track mission to find her. It doesn't take me long to see that long black hair and those bright purple eyes. To my surprise, they look softer than I was expecting. I thought she'd be ready to go at it, to tell me off, and yell at me for being jealous. Instead, she almost looks nervous.

"Hey, Trev," she says, attempting to sound casual.

I don't bother speaking as I continue walking, reaching out to grab her hand as I pull her with me. We walk a little past the locker room before I drag her into a little alcove to the side, hidden from everyone down the hall.

Pushing her against the wall, I cage her in with my arms above her head, my chest heaving as my pads push into her with each inhale. Those gem-colored eyes look up to me expectantly for several seconds before she speaks.

"Look, Trev. I'm sorry. It was just a kiss cam. I didn't know it was going to upset you so muc—"

I slap my hand against the wall before turning away from her, giving us space as I calm down before I turn and come right back to her.

"Just a kiss cam? Just a kiss cam. Sage, do you not understand that just another man breathing the same air as you sends me fucking spiraling? Do you not get that a single brush of another person's lips against yours is enough to set me on a killing spree. Prison time be damned, it would be worth it."

Her eyes are wide and filled with surprise as I exhale a heavy breath and shake my head.

"You didn't know it was going to upset me?" I laugh hollowly, allowing a little bit of my hurt to bleed through. "Of course I'm fucking upset. I had to watch *my* girl kiss some random guy in front of seventy-five thousand people. I've played the game of chasing after a girl who wasn't fully invested in me. I won't do it again. I can't," I say roughly, my last word breaking slightly as my throat tightens.

Emotion begins to fill her face as she lifts a hand up to cup my cheek, pulling my eyes down to hers.

"I'm so sorry, Trev. I wasn't thinking. This thing between us is new, and I was inconsiderate and a dumbass. I'm not her, though. Our story is different."

Her words are like a balm to my bruised and battered ego. I swallow as I see the absolute devastation on her face, like she can't believe she did this. I know I'm making a bigger deal out of this then it needs to be, but fuck. I'm hurt.

Before I can speak, she's undoing the front of my football pants.

"What are you doing?" I ask as she peels them down before removing my pads and boxers.

She wiggles her yoga pants down and kicks them to the side before looking at me.

"Punish me."

"What?"

"Punish me. Use me. I hurt you, and I want to try to take that hurt away. Use me, Trev."

My eyes fall down to her bare pussy, as my cock starts to harden. This girl is too fucking perfect. A hate fuck sounds like a great idea. Closing the remaining distance between the two of us, I press her against the wall before grabbing her right leg and lifting it up until it wraps around me.

"I'm gonna fuck you until I don't hate you anymore."

"We might be here a while then," she says with the start of a smile.

I don't even give her a second. I immediately push inside her, causing her mouth to drop open into an O. My thrusts are fast and punishing. By the wincing on her face, I can tell I'm not being as gentle as I should be. But then the image of my girlfriend's face on that jumbotron comes to mind, and I lose it all over again, slamming in and out of her with a newfound fury.

Her eyes roll into the back of her head, and she whimpers my name as I thrust deeper. I'm not sure if it's out of pleasure or pain, but I'm so lost in my own head that I know I need to take what she's so willing to give me.

A door opens and shuts just a little ways down the hall that has both of our eyes snapping to each other. No one knows we are together, and this would be a pretty fucking bad way for her dad of all people to find out. Still, I can't stop myself from letting her tight cunt wrap around me, practically pulling the cum out of me.

"We're gonna get caught. This was a stupid fucking idea," I scold her as I continue.

She nods. "So dumb."

"What's daddy dearest gonna think when he sees his star QB balls deep in his little girl? What about one of the other coaches or players walking over here and finding you like this? Don't think I won't gouge out someone's eyes just for looking at what's mine, Sage."

"You're nuts. I don't doubt you," she teases with half a laugh.

"Fuck, yes I am," I grit through clenched teeth as I close my eyes and allow myself to work through all the feelings suffocating me currently. I blow out a heavy breath as my grip on her tightens.

"Tell me you're mine. Tell me I'll never have to see shit like that again. Tell me it's just you and me," I demand with each thrust.

I expect her to babble her agreement, beg for it all to be over. Instead, she looks up at me with a heavy look and gives me a serious nod.

"I'm all yours, Trev. It's just you and me."

The weight that has been bearing down on my shoulders lifts instantly, and I lose it. I feel myself empty inside her as I wrap my arms around her, holding her as tight as my chest and shoulder pads will allow me. Fucking hell. This woman is going to be my undoing. I can feel it. From the moment our eyes met in that club, I knew it. I just didn't fully understand it then.

When my movements slow, I ease back to look at her face, cupping either side before bringing her lips to mine. When I pull away, my thumb rubs soft circles against her creamy skin.

"Let's go home and take care of you, baby."

When we got home, I carried Sage. She insisted on walking, but I wouldn't let her. The way she had to practically hobble her ass to the car tells me I was way too fucking rough with her, and though it felt like what I needed in the moment, now I have this overwhelming feeling of regret, and I need to make it better.

"Trev, seriously, I'm fine. You can put me down," she laughs.

I ignore her though as I carry her through the doors of my bathroom and set her on the bathroom counter before starting up the Jacuzzi tub. I pour in some bubble bath I had my housekeeper pick up for her when I noticed she likes taking baths.

Turning on the water, I adjust the temp until it's searing hot because for some reason all women prefer burning off several layers of their skin in the shower or bath. I look over my shoulder to see Sage watching me with the smallest hint of a smile.

"What?"

She shakes her head. "Nothing. I just can't actually believe Trevor Michaels is drawing me a bath. Never thought I'd see the day."

I roll my eyes as I come to stand next to her, resting my hands on her legs.

"What's that supposed to mean?" I say as I lean in and begin softly kissing her neck.

"Uhm, that you're an asshole?" She laughs.

I pause, genuinely curious if that's the only way she sees me. Have I fucked us over before we even got to begin by being a prick? Will she only ever expect the worst out of me? Maybe some guys would be okay with that, but I'm not one of them. She's a queen, my queen now, and I want her to feel like such.

"But you're my asshole," she finishes with a smirk before pulling my face toward hers and pressing her lips against mine.

My heart immediately begins jackhammering in my chest. Fuck. There is something about her, something special that sends me into a spiral anytime she just touches me. It's like my body can't help itself. She's like my own personal cure and drug. She soothes the hurt while giving me a rush like nothing else this planet has to offer.

I feel her hands start to wander down my body, and I know what she has in mind, but I pull away, attempting to be the nice guy she deserves to see more than every once in a while.

"No, baby. This is about you. I need to make my girl feel good," I say as I grip her hands hovering right over my cock.

"Well, you can make your girl feel good by giving me an orgasm or two," she says as she reaches for my pants again.

I tighten my grip on her before moving to the oversized bathroom sink, turning her with me before pushing her to lay on her back. I press her bound hands against her chest with one hand while I pull down her leggings with the other.

I yank at the thin material of her panties, pushing the useless scraps away as she arches her pussy for me. I don't waste a second, burying my face between her thighs while still keeping her hands trapped. She jolts at the first swipe of my tongue before she lets out a breathy moan.

"Careful," she pants. "I feel like I'm still full of your cum."

My eyes come to her for a moment before I flatten out my tongue, slowly dragging it through her, our eye contact never breaking as I do.

"Does it look like I give a fuck? Come for me, baby. Let me see how good we taste together."

She lets out a needy cry when I do it again and again, licking, sucking, and tongue fucking her until she is a writhing mess. I'm sure a lot of men would be more than a little grossed out to eat a girl out after they came in her. I'd also say those men were little bitches. If I want her to suck her taste off my cock after I fuck her, then I can eat her pussy when she's full of my own cum.

It honestly shouldn't make me as hard as it does, the thought of her full to the brim. The thought that while I'm licking and sucking her, I'm also pushing it in deeper and deeper. I love that I know I'll never have to share Sage. That from now on it will only be my cum filling her to the brim. Fuck, something about that does something to me, causing my pulse to speed up and the tip of my head to leak a bead of pre-cum.

I slip a finger inside her and begin massaging her G-spot before I scrape my teeth against her clit, causing her to buck against me and come all over my face. When I apply the pressure just right, something happens for the first time between us. She isn't just coming, she's soaking me. I greedily take in every drop, relishing the taste of her as she squirts all over my face.

Pride and an ego trip like nothing ever before swells over me as I raise my head up to look at her, her cum quite literally dripping from my chin as I pounce on her, quickly getting her out of her dress and yanking off my pants before submerging us in the bath and fucking her until we can't see straight.

Chapter 28
Trevor

The next few weeks are a blur between games, practices, sponsorship commercials, and burying any of my body parts Sage will let inside her. We are gearing up for the postseason, and it seems like we are going to be ending the regular season at the top of our division.

After the gala, both my parents blew up my phone incessantly, demanding to know where I was and a bunch of other bullshit. I finally answered and told my dad that I wasn't interested in being a part of the business and that I was going to be selling my shares. He was obviously super fucking pissed, but I honestly don't care anymore. I'm tired of trying to please everyone, or at least them. I'm gonna live my life the way I want to, and if they don't like it, well, too fucking bad.

Sage and I have been spending every minute possible together, and honestly, it's not enough for me. I can tell that she still has some hesitancy about us, and I don't blame her. From what I can tell, she has had a shitty dating history, and our relationship didn't start off as the most solid or romantic.

I know the reason she comes across as closed off and unapproachable is because she's scared. She tries to hide behind her bad bitch exterior, but she doesn't fool me. My girl is sensitive and terrified to be vulnerable with anyone, even me. Can't say I blame her— buried deep down, I have similar fears, but I'm trying, for her and for us.

I don't really know when things shifted between us. All I know is one moment, I was bitter and lonely over the woman I thought would be my whole world for my whole life. The next thing I know, I'm thinking about a pair of purple eyes day in and day out. I was looking forward to our banter. I started spouting out bullshit just so she would call me out on it.

There is something about her that is so fucking addictive. I wonder what life could have been like if I had met her sooner. Well, fuck. I guess not too much sooner since she is barely out of high school. Christ. That sounds fucking bad when I say it like that. I've dated plenty of young women, and by date, I mean fucked until our bodies went limp. But not with the same age difference as me and Sage.

Honestly, I constantly forget how many years separate us. I say it's because she's mature for her age. She says it's because I'm a "man-child."

Little shit.

We are hanging out at a tucked-away pub with everyone when Erica speaks.

"Sooo, Sage. What do you want to do tomorrow?"

I lift an eyebrow as I look at the beauty underneath my arm.

"What's tomorrow?"

Sage shrugs. "It's nothing."

Vi scoffs. "Yeah, your twenty-first birthday is definitely not nothing. We have to celebrate! You're finally gonna be all grown up," she coos.

"Slater knows all the great spots in town. Can you get us some VIP stuff, baby?" Scarlett asks her husband.

He nods with a mischievous wink as he kisses the side of her head.

"Hell yes. We gotta do the birthday girl right. No pun intended, Trev," he smirks.

I narrow my eyes at him before looking back to the quiet raven-haired girl beside me.

"Tomorrow is your birthday? Why didn't you tell me?"

Can't lie, it kinda sucks that everyone seemed to know but me. She's my girl. I should know this stuff. I knew her birthday was coming up, but she never gave me a date, and I guess I never thought to ask for the exact date.

Sage shakes her head and laughs.

"Because it isn't a big deal. It's not like I haven't been sneaking into bars for years with my fakes."

"Yeah, but this time you can get one legally, troublemaker," Erica chimes in.

"I'm good. Birthdays are not a big thing for me," Sage practically bites out, effectively ending the conversation. An awkward silence settles over the table before Vi nods sweetly and touches Sage's hand.

"Okay. No problem. Maybe we can all do dinner again soon. Not for your birthday, just because."

Sage seems to relax at that and even gives Vi a smile.

The rest of the night goes fine. Slater talks shit about the team we are playing this weekend, Declan smacks him and tells him not to fuck with our lucky streak we've been on, and Seb actually answered my question when I asked how the treehouse he's been building the girls has been coming.

He wasn't exactly talkative or anything, but the fact he responded to me at all, with no hostility, was huge. When Erica was talking with me, the swarm of butterflies that usually hit didn't. It caught me off guard for a second. I'm sure I'll always love her. I don't think I could ever not. But I also don't think I'm really in love with her anymore. Which is as much of a relief as it is kinda sad. Like I'm losing her in a way but hopefully gaining her in a different way. One thing is obvious, though. The air needs to be cleared. With her. With Seb. If I'm ever truly going to move on, give Sage and me the start we deserve, we all need it.

When Sage and I get home, I go for the protein cookies Sage made the other day in the cookie jar that appeared on my counter one day. They immediately became my latest obsession, and I told her I would do whatever she wanted if she kept them stocked in the house at all times.

"So, are you gonna make your own birthday cake, or do you need me to buy one?" I ask.

"Neither," she laughs.

"What's the deal with that anyway?" I ask, doing my best to keep my tone even so as not to spook her. Getting her to open up is like bathing a cat. You have to be calm and approach her just right.

"With what?" She asks.

"Why didn't you tell me your birthday was coming up? I could have planned something. Taken you somewhere."

"When we are literally going into postseason?"

I shrug. I don't give a fuck. We could have snuck away for a day or two. Aberton would be a little mad, but he'd get over it. Until he found out that the reason I'd be missing practice was because I'd be fucking his daughter.

"Birthdays are dumb. Why celebrate me? All I did was exit my mom's vagina. If anything, she should get the party."

"We could go to the cemetery, and—"

"I was kidding, Trev," she says, cutting me off with a laugh as she shakes her head. "After Mom passed, there wasn't a lot of time for celebrations outside the Crusaders. Birthdays just don't do much for me."

I frown at that, her words kind of breaking my heart. We haven't dug deep into her and her dad's relationship. We don't need to though, for me to know he's been a shit father to her. She deserved better. She *deserves* better. An idea comes to mind as I look around the kitchen before my eyes come to hers.

"Can I take you out tomorrow? No birthday stuff, I promise. Just you and me."

She looks at me hesitantly before slowly nodding.

"What are you up to?" she asks.

I give her a wink as I pull out my phone and start laying out my plan.

"You'll see."

Chapter 29
Sage

The next day, I woke up to an empty bed. I lean up on my elbows and look around to find the bedroom totally vacant. I frown at that, tossing the blankets off me before I open the bedroom door and begin walking downstairs. The smell of something cooking instantly hits my nose, and when I crest the bottom of the stairs and step into the kitchen, I'm surprised by what I see.

A shirtless Trevor Michaels is at the stovetop, folding over what looks like a perfectly cooked omelet.

"What are you doing?" I ask.

He turns to face me, his shoulders slumping as he slides the omelet onto a prepared plate already lined with fresh berries and two pieces of bacon.

"Dammit, I was trying to get this done before you got up."

"Since when do you cook?" I ask as he pushes the plate in front of my usual seat at the kitchen island.

Trev rolls his eyes at me as he walks around the island and wraps his arms around my waist, pulling me into him as he speaks.

"I've lived on my own for over twelve years. I've picked up a thing or two."

"Then why the hell am I the one always cooking?" I grumble.

He smirks at me as he leans down and nips at my earlobe.

"Because you're so fucking good at it."

I scoff and push him away, but he doesn't budge, pressing his lips against the sensitive spot behind my ear as his hold on me tightens. He runs his lips up and down the column of my neck before stopping just above my lips.

Looking up, I see his bright blue eyes stall on me as he smiles gently.

"Happy birthday, baby."

I want to shrug him away, tell him to knock it off, and to please drop the whole birthday thing. But at the same time, a warm feeling spreads across my chest as I feel my throat begin to tighten with emotion. Fuck him. I hate it when he does shit like this to me.

"Thank you," I rasp. Pushing away the building emotion, I blink hard a few times before I speak again.

"And thank you for the breakfast, though if I'm honest, a perfect birthday would have been me waking up to be eaten, not eating an omelet. But I guess beggars can't be choosers," I sigh as I pull away from him and move toward the chair.

Fortunately, I don't make it far before Trevor is on me, literally. He must have forgotten we aren't on the field, and he's not on defense because he tackles me in the middle of the kitchen, spinning us at the last minute so his back is the one that lands against the hard stone floor.

He doesn't even give me time to give him shit, though, before he is yanking down my boy short panties and ripping off his T-shirt that I slept in.

"Come ride my face, babygirl."

Some women are shy about sitting on a man's face, but the way I see it, it gives him the best and easiest access, and if he dies, everyone will high-five at his funeral, so it's fine. I don't hesitate to climb over his body before settling myself right on top of him. His hands grip the flesh of my inner thighs as he squeezes tight and moans.

"Fuck, you taste so goddamn good, baby."

I grind myself against him, letting out a moan as his tongue comes to my clit.

"Trev," I gasp.

"Yes, birthday girl?" he mutters against my skin.

"More," I say as I reach down and wind my fingers through his thick blond hair, forcing his mouth back on me.

I love that he lets me use him as much as he uses me. We know exactly what the other needs before they can even express what they want. I've had some great orgasms in my life, self-produced and from others, but nothing like the ones Trevor gives me. Every. Fucking. Time.

I feel his hands slide between my thighs as one finger slips inside my pussy, moving in the perfect rhythm to have me trembling right on the edge.

"Such a perfect girl," Trevor praises. "Are you going to let me make you feel good everywhere tonight, baby?" he asks as his other hand massages the back of my thigh before one of his fingers applies slight pressure against my asshole.

"Not sure I can handle all you have to offer back there just yet," I admit honestly with a laugh.

Trevor's laugh rumbles against my clit, causing a shudder of pleasure to run through me as he does.

"Don't worry, Raven. We will work up to it. I have a feeling it'll be your new favorite thing before you know it," he says as he presses a little bit more, practically penetrating me as he wraps his mouth around my clit and sucks.

My vision spots as my body practically jerks in response. I feel my pussy pulse around Trevor's finger as I moan and shake against him until my orgasm comes to an end. Blowing out a labored breath, I crawl off him before laying down butt-ass naked against his cool floors.

"Happy fucking birthday to me."

I tried to get a birthday fuck in before Trevor and I had to go to work, but he told me I had to eat the food he made because it took him too long to make it. To which I obviously pouted because what kind of bullshit birthday girl gets denied dick? He promised he'd make it up to me tonight, and he better.

When we get to the training facility, we go our separate ways when he goes to the locker room, and I step onto the field to set up my equipment for the day. I'm honestly getting sick of this shit. I didn't mind it at first, but the marketing department has been up my ass for better quality Q&A content from some of the players who just don't want to participate. I don't know what they expect me to do about it, it's not these guys' job to be a media lightning rod, and it's not mine to make them into one. I mean, maybe it is, but I don't want the job if that's the case because it's not my specialty.

I want to bake, even though I know I'd make virtually no money doing so. I mean, I think we all know at least one if not five people who have opened bakeries, and how many truly last? In a world where money really didn't matter, and I could just do whatever I wanted all day long, that's what I would do. I'd bake and decorate until my hands were sore, and then I'd go home and make Trevor fuck me all better for the next day.

I pause in my steps, that first instinctual thought catching me off guard for a moment. Trevor and I are together, obviously, we have been in one way or another for months now, but I've never imagined us having a genuine long drawn out future until right now. Until it seemed so natural, so easy, so destined. I don't want to invest too much into all of this in case it blows up in my face, but we get along too well. He's too great in his own pain-in-the-ass way, and I feel myself falling harder and faster than I should.

"Sage!" my dad calls out, causing my stomach to twist with displeasure.

I abandon my equipment and walk over to see him texting on his phone in the doorway.

"What's up, Coach?"

He glances up at me before he continues texting while he speaks.

"Your landlord says he hasn't seen you around. Are you not staying there or what? You just wasting my money for the fun of it?"

I do my best to suppress my eye roll at his attitude as I speak.

"No, I haven't been staying there, but honestly, I'm tired of you being in my business. Let the landlord know that I'll take over the rent. Or terminate it, and I'll get my own place, whatever."

"Like you can afford that on the chump change you're making here," he scoffs.

"I'll figure it out, Dad. I know you've got far more important things on your plate than me."

"Oh quit being so fucking dramatic," he says as he pockets his phone.

A few players sneak by us as they step onto the field, and a pair of concerned blue eyes capture my attention in the hallway for a moment before I'm back to looking at the hardened ones of my father.

"I'm just saying, if I'm gonna pay for the place, I expect you to use it."

I don't say anything, mainly because I don't know what to say to him anymore. Trevor seems to think now is the best time to butt in, slipping by us as his eyes come to me.

"Happy birthday, Sage."

He doesn't say more, but his eyes do come to Dad's in a harsh judging glare before he's jogging over for warm-ups. The air around us thickens at his words, and I hear my dad take a deep breath before he speaks quietly.

"Didn't know it was already your birthday."

I shrug, doing my best to keep my tone even as my throat becomes hot.

"Why would you? You stopped keeping track a long time ago."

Without another word, I turn on my heel and head back to my camera to get ready for practice. Dad doesn't try to follow after me, and I'm thankful for it. Being in a room with him is taxing enough.

Chapter 30
Trevor

I do my best to focus during practice, but it's easier said than done when the man that I'm supposed to be listening to is currently the target of my building irritation. I knew he was a shit dad, but how could he forget his only daughter's birthday? The fuck kind of man is he? Sage tries to act like it doesn't bother her, but it's written all over her pretty face. And the fact that the little shit of a man in front of me is a source of even an ounce of pain for her has me ready to bash his face in.

Sage is being the bad bitch she is, not letting anyone see the hurt inside her. She's interviewing the special teams for some bit while the offense and defense are running drills. When we break for water, I jog to the side, cutting toward her first. As smoothly as I'm able, I brush behind her, letting my hand linger on her lower back before I turn to the side and make my way to my bag with my water bottle.

I don't look over my shoulder at her until I'm lifting the bottle to my mouth. Her face is blank, but her eyes are grateful for the small touch. We both agreed to keep things on the down low, first for the sake of both of our jobs considering we were just fooling around. But now that things have evolved into so much more, it's only a matter of time until people figure it out. People like her dad.

Honestly, Coach is about to find out one way or another soon. It's either gonna be he's gonna catch me holding her like she's my whole goddamn world, or he's gonna find my fist buried in his solar plexus if he raises his voice to her one more time.

Tossing my bottle back into my bag, I feel a pair of eyes on me before someone comes up next to me. I raise an unimpressed eyebrow to Jackson Donatello as he lifts a hand up to grip the top of his chest pads.

"See you been hanging with Sage quite a bit," he says coolly, but there is nothing cool about his body language.

"Oh yeah? Where have you seen that?" I challenge.

"Around," he says cryptically. "What's up with that? You bagging her?"

I turn to face him, taking several steps until we are chest to chest, practically nose to nose as I lower my voice to an eerie calm.

"I'm not sure how that's any of your business. Regardless, you can take whatever bullshit you're thinking and shove it right up your ass. I'm not your concern, and she better not be a single fucking thought in your mind."

He scoffs. "Oh yeah? Getting territorial, pretty boy?"

Hearing the nickname only Sage has called me coming from him sends a rush of anger down my spine, and I do my best to breathe through it.

"Fuck. Yes. That girl is mine, and if I see you look at her the way you do one more time, I'll let Coach know where he can find your stash of steroids."

His hardened exterior pales slightly for a moment before he builds his stature up a bit higher.

"Fuck you. You don't know where shit is."

"I was bluffing but looks like you confirmed my suspicions. Stay the fuck away from me and my girl, and you can keep shooting up until you get UA'd."

His eyes harden as he looks from me to her before shaking his head and walking away. I hear him mutter something under his breath, but it's not even worth my time to figure out what it is. I don't think that doper will be a problem for us anymore, especially when I strongly suggest some more rounds of testing should happen before the playoffs. I don't fuck with cheaters.

Thankfully, the rest of practice goes by smoothly, everything is really coming together, and the team is honestly stronger than ever. Since Sage and I have become a real thing, you can feel the tension between Sebastian and I on the field practically disintegrate. I'm probably on the bottom of his favorite people list still, but at least things are finally starting to click with us in the game.

We are in the locker room getting ready to head home for the day when, shocking the hell out of me, Sebastian calls out to me.

"Trevor," he says simply.

I turn to look over my shoulder before giving him my full attention.

"Erica wants you and Sage to come over Friday, have dinner, hang out."

His words are clipped, his body language closed off, but it's probably the most he's spoken to me without threatening me in years.

I nod as I slide on my T-shirt.

"We can probably make that happen."

Seb nods once, and I expect that to be the end of it, until he speaks again.

"You guys are for real?"

"Me and Sage?" I ask.

Seb nods.

I pause for a moment, mainly because I know what he's really asking. He wants to know if this thing with her is just a distraction to get his wife out of my head, or if I'm actually all in with her. If he can finally relax knowing there isn't some pathetic guy waiting for him to fuck up so he can steal his girl. Yep, I used to fucking hope and pray for Seb to do something stupid and drive Erica straight into my arms. Not proud to admit it, but it's not like it was a secret anyway.

I give him a soft nod as I look around us before speaking.

"Yeah, man. She's...special."

Sebastian's eyes narrow on me curiously for a few beats before he nods to himself.

"Good."

With that, he turns, gathers up his stuff and strides out of the locker room. Slater pokes his head from the other side of the lockers and grins.

"Was it just me, or did that sound like progress?"

I let out a short laugh as I shake my head.

"You're way too invested in other people's lives."

"Only because your drama is better than anything on TV. Trust me, Scar and I have tried to find something, to no avail."

I shake my head but can't help but laugh as I zip up my bag.

"Y'all wanna grab lunch or something?" Declan drawls out as he towels his hair dry.

"Sure," Slater says. "You in, Trev?"

"Nah, I have to work on Sage's birthday plans tonight."

"Oh shit. Look at Mr. Playboy getting all romantic." Slater smirks.

I scoff and roll my eyes but don't try to hide my smile as I walk out of the locker room to a waiting Sage in the hallway.

Tonight is gonna be good.

"Is the tie around my eyes really necessary?" Sage grumbles as I guide her through the doors.

"Yes, and if you don't stop whining, I'll turn it into a gag," I say as I pull her to a stop in the middle of the room.

Her mouth spreads into a wicked grin as she blindly looks toward me.

"Now that's more like it."

I bark out a laugh and smack the side of her ass.

"Behave. I'm trying to be romantic and shit."

"Catch me if I swoon," she sighs sarcastically.

Fucking smart-ass.

"Alright, you pain in the ass, take off the tie."

She yanks it down to fall around her neck, her mischievous smile falling away as her eyes widen, and her mouth parts slightly.

I watch as her eyes scan the kitchen around us, nearly every inch covered in some type of shiny object to bake with.

"What are we doing here? Where are we?" Sage asks.

"Sally's Sweet Treats. I rented the place out for the night."

"Why?" she asks, still obviously confused.

I roll up my sleeves as I make my way over to one of the two stations I requested to be stocked and ready to go.

"Well, you know those super boring baking competition shows you've been making me watch lately?"

"You mean the ones that you secretly love and stay up watching even when I fall asleep?" she counters.

"Yep, those. Well, since I couldn't get you onto a show in time because someone forgot to mention her birthday," I say with a faux irritated look.

"Definitely didn't mention it on purpose," she supplies.

"I thought we could have our own little competition."

She raises an eyebrow as she looks around the kitchen.

"You have my attention."

I smirk at her coyness. I can practically see her vibrating with excitement. I'm almost getting a contact high from it alone.

"I had Sally choose three ingredients that we each have to incorporate into a baked good. We have ninety minutes to make our dessert, and the winner gets to choose a present," I say as I lift the two purple gift bags.

"Why do you get a present if it's my birthday?" she sasses.

I give her a wicked smirk as I shake the bag in my left hand.

"Both presents are for you, but one I think I may be more eager to use at first."

"Well, that's chillingly cryptic. Where's the challenge though?" she asks as she begins tying her hair up with the hairband around her wrist.

"Underestimate me all you want, Raven."

She waves me off as she walks over to her station and lifts out the ingredients.

"Sour cream, pecans and...bourbon?" she laughs.

I smirk as I grab two cups from the shelf. I'm not sure if they are measuring cups or actual drinking cups but either way they will work.

"It's your twenty-first birthday, baby. We couldn't go without at least one drink, and it's your favoriteeee," I sing as I pour us each a glass of Pappy.

"It's your favorite. I don't need a thousand-dollar bottle of bourbon to be happy," she says with a haughty look before she takes the glass, clinking it against mine before taking a sip.

I toss mine back before bringing her to me, pressing her lips against mine as I wrap my arms around her. The sharp taste of the bourbon is still fresh on her lips, I can't help but let my tongue chase down the flavor. Then again, I think I much prefer the flavor of Sage over bourbon, and if that's not saying something...

When I pull back, she smiles up at me softly before whispering against my lips.

"Time starts...now."

With that, she's shoving me to the side and racing over to the pantry.

"Cheater!" I call out, causing her to let out a maniacal laugh full of glee.

It's not like I think I actually have a chance of out baking her. She's incredibly talented. But when I was trying to come up with something to do for her birthday that was so last minute, I knew I could combine her two favorite things. Baking and winning.

Knowing that I am definitely going to lose my ass, I may have had Sally tell me the ingredients and already memorized a recipe. Just because I know hers will no doubt look a hell of a lot better than mine doesn't mean I don't want to shock her a bit when it comes to flavor. I'm hoping to impress her with my pecan brown butter sour cream crumb cake, with a bourbon sweet glaze of course.

Because I already have the recipe portions memorized, I take my time as I watch Sage race around the new-to-her kitchen. It only takes her ten minutes before she settles in. From there it's like watching magic. Her body moves so fluidly, from pouring and stirring to baking whatever she's up to. She makes it look effortless. It's never been more clear to me than right in this moment that some people were put on this earth with a purpose, and Sage Aberton has way too much talent to be wasting her days in a sweaty practice facility taking pictures for social media. She's an artist, a master baker, and if she will let me, I'll do everything I can to make all of her dreams come true.

Several times throughout the last hour she has tossed me furrowed looks as I finalize my crumb cake. If I didn't know better, I'd say she was actually worried about losing.

"How'd you come up with your recipe so fast?" Sage calls out as she whisks something in her bowl.

"I'm just naturally gifted, I guess." I shrug.

She narrows her eyes at me. "Where's your phone?"

"In the car. Are you challenging my character?" I ask in mock offense.

"Abso-fucking-lutly."

"Tick-tock, Raven. Time is almost up."

She scoffs before turning her back toward me, causing me to grin. I don't think I'll ever get sick of getting under her skin.

When the timer finally goes off, Sage steps back with a triumphant smile. I don't even have to look at her dessert to know it's incredible. The pride and joy radiating from her face is confirmation enough. When my eyes do drop to her plate though, I'm even more impressed than I expected. It looks like she made some type of cake or bread but it's so artfully plated, it looks like something right from one of her baking shows.

"What is that?" She laughs as she points to my crumb cake that unfortunately turned out heavy on the crumb.

"It's a crumb cake, what do you expect?" I shrug.

"More cake than crumb, I suppose?" She laughs.

"Yeah? What did you make?"

She smiles as she grabs a fork and scoops a bite onto it, holding it out for me.

"Peaches and cream bourbon loaf with chopped pecans."

I wrap my mouth around the end of the fork, the cream glaze hitting my tongue instantly before practically melting in my mouth. Holy fucking shit. As I chew the bite, the balanced sweetness of the peaches to the richness of the bourbon are so perfectly executed, I instantly crave another bite.

Once I swallow, I open my mouth, waiting for my next bite. Sage laughs lightly, a soft airy sound I don't think I've ever really heard from her as she gets another fork full and shoves it in my mouth. I chomp at it, causing her to giggle as I chew the bite quickly and wind my hand around the back of her neck.

"Alright, you win, Raven. Go pick your prize."

"Well, hold on. I haven't tried yours yet, despite the...unique look, maybe it's really good."

I chuckle as I place a kiss on her exposed shoulder.

"It's not. I turned the browned butter into scorched butter, and I'm pretty sure I used salt instead of sugar. I even cheated too and planned out my recipe ahead of time."

Her mouth drops open, and she punches me in the arm.

"Fucking asshole!"

Sage walks over to the two displayed bags as she begins tearing into them.

"Just for that, I'm opening both."

I laugh and nod as I lean against the table and watch her. The first bag she opens is a bottle of her favorite perfume, a few scented candles, and a pair of car keys.

She holds up the keys with a stunned look.

"What are these for?"

"The shiny black Mercedes GT-S sitting in our driveway at home."

Sage stares at me for a moment, seemingly speechless.

"I'm not sure which part has me more thrown, the fact that you casually bought me a luxury car for my birthday or the fact that you called it 'our' driveway."

I push away from the table, closing the distance between us before reaching my hand up to cup her jaw.

"It is our driveway. Let's be real, even if you wanted to leave, I'm not letting you go. You're stuck with me, so that should come with some perks."

She licks her lips softly as she exhales.

"Like pain and suffering compensation?"

I chuckle lightly as I nod and brush my lips against hers.

"Exactly."

"I don't know what to say."

"Hmm, thank you usually works," I say as I run my mouth over her jawline.

"Seriously, Trevor," she says, something in her tone causing me to pull back.

I look down at her to see her gem-colored eyes full of emotion as she looks up at me.

"Thank you, I love all of it. It's so sweet."

The sincerity in her words has my chest thumping rapidly as I wrap my arms around her.

"Anything for you, baby. Now, be a good girl, and open the other bag."

"I take it this is the one you're excited about?" she asks as she grabs the bag.

I allow her to step out of my reach just a hair as I nod and watch her closely.

When she peels back the tissue paper, her eyes widen before a tint of red stains her cheeks.

"Are you fucking serious?"

Grinning at her, I pinch her side.

"You ever used these before, baby?"

"No, never," she huffs, seemingly trying to compose herself.

I waggle my eyebrows at her as I take her hand in mine.

"You won't be able to say that after tonight."

Chapter 31
Sage

A s Trevor races through the night-drenched streets of Seattle, my mind is whirling. I can't believe all the effort he went through for my birthday. I don't think anyone has tried so hard since my mom built that balloon arch that ended up falling over in the middle of my eighth birthday party.

I glance down to see his right hand resting on my knee absentmindedly as he continues driving. It's always there. Even if it's a five-minute trip to the grocery store, we get in the car, and his hand goes right to my knee. I'm not sure if it's done for his comfort or mine, maybe both.

Trevor pulls up to the house, parking in his usual spot when I notice the brand-new Mercedes he was talking about right beside us.

"If you're fucking with me about the car, I'm gonna kill you," I say.

He glances out the window and back to me before smirking.

"I gotta say, I was anticipating a fight on that. Thought you were gonna be too strong and independent to accept a gift like that."

I scoff as I grab my door handle.

"I'm strong and independent, not stupid. If you want to drop well over one hundred k on a birthday present for a woman you just started dating, I'm sure as hell not gonna turn it down."

Trevor barks out a laugh as he steps out of the car, meeting me on my side before wrapping an arm around my lower back.

"You never cease to surprise me."

"Someone's gotta keep you on your toes. You get way too self-righteous and douchey otherwise."

I feel Trevor's palm come down to my ass, clapping down over it before smirking against my lips.

"Get your fine ass upstairs and into our bed, take your clothes off and wait for me. We aren't done celebrating you just yet."

Anticipation flutters low in my belly at the reminder of his other present. Trevor takes a step away from me, to allow me to go before giving me a wicked smile that promises all sorts of naughty good fun tonight.

Perfect.

The silk of Trevor's sheets brushes against my skin in a soothing way. If my heart wasn't hammering inside my chest for what comes next, I have no doubt I would already be asleep due to the buttery goodness of his bed. However, with every heavy footstep of his up the stairs, my adrenaline spikes, until he is standing in the doorway.

He pauses for a moment, leaning against the wooden door with a predatory smile as he eyes me.

"Such a pretty birthday girl. You ready to play?"

I sink my teeth into my lower lip as I nod softly. He grins wider this time as he takes the gift bag in his hand and sets it down on the bedside table. I watch as he shucks off his shirt and pants until he is left just in his boxers before he crawls onto the bed between my legs. His arms come beneath both my knees before forcing me to spread open for him.

"But first, a snack," he rumbles as he buries his face in my cunt.

The initial feel of his tongue causes me to leap before I intertwine my fingers in his golden hair and pull him closer. You can say a lot of things about Trevor Michaels, but one thing you can never say is that the man doesn't eat pussy well because shit, I've never had better.

He slips a finger inside me and begins slowly working me over as his mouth practically sucks my clit off.

"Fuck!" I moan as his eyes come up to me, not moving his mouth for one second.

He gives me a quick wink before he pushes a little deeper toward that magic button that sends me shattering apart. I feel him lick my orgasm clean before he moves to sit on his knees, his mouth glistening as he grins.

"Fucking delicious."

He leans over me to reach the bedside table to grab the bag before coming back between my legs.

"Close your eyes, Raven."

"No way! I want to know exactly what you're doing with that thing."

"Trust me?" he asks.

"Barely."

What almost looks like hurt flashes across his face, causing me to eat my words really quick.

"Sorry, I was kidding. I trust you," I say as I begrudgingly close my eyes.

I feel the warm tips of his fingers run up and down my bare thighs, leaving a wake of goose bumps in their path. Slowly, he begins massaging me. My thighs, my calves, even my ass cheeks. The tension I previously felt slowly begins to dissipate as I sink into his touch.

Suddenly, I feel a cool liquid hit my asshole, causing me to jerk before Trevor's hands push me back against the bed.

"Relax, babygirl. Deep breaths."

I do as he says, keeping my eyes closed as his fingers gently massage the liquid against and into me. I feel him slowly work the tip of his finger in and out of me as he speaks.

"Good girl, such a good girl. Nice deep breaths just like that."

I exhale a long breath when I feel him pull away from me. On the next exhale, I feel a cool object pressed against my hole before it slips in with a pop. My eyes fly open as I look down to see Trevor's eyes greedily taking up the sight before him. He looks up at me and nods, giving me a reassuring look as he pushes the beads in a little more, then pushing the next bead in.

Each new bead has my toes curling, and my pulse thundering. I saw how long that strand was. There is absolutely no way it's all going to fit. But one by one, Trevor continues filling me up.

"Touch yourself, baby. Play with that pretty little clit."

I don't hesitate, rubbing my fingers against my clit, relieved to feel that familiar tingle of pleasure to distract me from the building discomfort of each larger-sized bead.

"Trevor, I don't think I can take much more," I say softly as I continue rubbing my fingers in tight circles.

"You can take it all. Deep breaths and focus on playing with that pretty little pussy."

I let out a shaky nod as he pauses, allowing me to relax a little more. A soft moan falls from my lips, causing Trevor to groan.

"I love your little noises. So fucking sexy."

I let out another one just as Trevor pushes the largest bead so far in. It makes my toes curl at first, and it takes several seconds to adjust before I blow out a shaky breath and allow my body to relax around the beads.

"That's all of them. You did so good, babygirl. I'm so proud of you," he says as he presses a kiss against my inner thigh.

His praise causes a fluttering in my lower belly as I look at him and smile.

"What does my girl want now?"

"You. Come fuck me, Trev."

He pulls down his boxers and tosses them to the side before lining himself up to me.

"Don't move too much. I want those beads to stay there until you come, understand?"

I nod quickly as I feel the warm head of his tip press against my slick hole. He presses inside in the next moment, causing a louder more satisfied moan to slip out of me. Trevor keeps pushing until he bottoms out and grumbles out a pleased sound.

Slower than normal, he begins fucking me, his thrusts extremely purposeful as he pulls in and out of me. If I wasn't already a writhing mess, I'd already be close, but from every kiss and touch he's given me thus far, I'm ready to fucking lose it.

"Fuck, your cunt is pulsing. You're gonna come, aren't you, Raven?"

"Uh-huh," I whimper.

"One sec, baby," he says as he adjusts our position slightly until his hand is behind my lower back.

Just him moving has my pussy squeezing once, my orgasm literally a breath away.

"Shit, shit, shit. I'm trying to keep it together, but you've got my cock in a goddamn chokehold, baby."

He blows out what sounds like a settling breath before his eyes come to my own. His chest rising and falling as rapidly as my own. I get lost in those blue eyes for a moment, so many things lying just below the surface, like two infinitely deep pools I could dive right into. I'm so lost in him right now I almost don't hear the low rumble of his voice.

"Come."

That single command sends me splintering apart. I feel my pussy clamp down on him one final time before it triggers my orgasm. In that same minute, Trevor pulls the beads out of me in one swoop, ratcheting my already powerful orgasm into a blinding combination of excitement and ecstasy. I scream out my release as my body spasms and flutters, a feeling like I've never experienced racing through me.

This isn't my first time with butt play, but this is definitely my first time with anal toys, and holy shit, I hope it's not the last. I feel Trevor's cock pulse before emptying his hot cum inside me, coating my walls as he moans out his own orgasm.

"Fuck!" he barks out before his thrusts in me slowly.

He slumps against me before nuzzling his face into my neck. I almost tell him to get the fuck off of me, but the way his arms wrap me so tightly next to him has a safe, protected feeling practically blanketing me, so I settle for only being able to breathe out of one lung for now.

Chapter 32
Trevor

After practice the next day, I came home to find Sage working on her laptop. We decided to order in. We are currently lying in bed eating takeout and watching one of Sage's baking shows when she speaks.

"What's the story between you and Erica?"

The question catches me off guard and has me turning to face her.

"What do you mean?"

She sets her food to the side as she turns her head to face me.

"What's the story? The full one. I know you said you used to date, and then she started dating Sebastian, but it feels like there is more to it. Caldwell wouldn't hate you so viscerally if he stole *your* girl, you know?"

"What does it matter?" I say with a half shrug, hoping she will let it go. It's not my proudest moment, and it's something I try to forget about constantly.

"It matters to me," she says seriously, causing me to exhale a heavy breath and run a hand through my hair as I nod.

"We broke up when I went to Brighton U, right? Well, we were good after that, better than ever really. It wasn't until the summer before she started at Brighton that I realized how bad I fucked up. We had been split up for two years then, and at the time I was convinced we were meant to find our way back to each other.

"So, when she came to school, I tried to repair what I had broken. Tried to take my time but make my intentions clear. Little did I know she and Sebastian had met at a party her first night on campus and hooked up, in the laundry room of all places," I laugh dryly as I shake my head.

"Seb knew all about Erica, but he didn't know what she looked like until I brought her to the house the next day. I guess from there they decided to stay away from each other. Seb knew I was in love with her, and he was my best friend, and Erica thought he was an asshole for how he treated her after."

"Sebastian? The man that practically worships the ground she walks on?" Sage asks with a dubious look.

I nod. "He was trying to be a good friend, push her away so I could have my chance with her. It was already too late, though.

"Somewhere along the way, they decided to stop fighting it, and they started seeing each other, on the down low."

Sage winces. "And I'm guessing you found out."

"In a shit way," I fill in.

"I was mad, so fucking mad," I say as I shake my head, the memories of the past practically dragging me under as I recall that night with perfect clarity.

"I couldn't believe what I was seeing. My closest friend and the girl I was in love with since I was a kid kissing, touching...I saw red. Seb and I got into it, I stormed off, got into my car and lost control."

"Trev," Sage says softly as she reaches out to me. Her soft hand covering my own as sympathy covers her face.

"I wrapped my car around a telephone pole, broke my arm, and was taken to the hospital. It took me a bit to wake up, and when I did, I heard them talking in my room. I heard them telling each other how much they loved each other and would be by each other's side through anything. I-I don't know what I was thinking, in the moment I was still so fucking hurt. I felt so betrayed and like he had fucked me over. I didn't feel like I even had a proper chance with Erica before he tried to steal her. In my mind he played dirty, so I guess I figured it was my turn to do the same."

Tilting my head up to the ceiling I shake my head as I continue speaking.

"I just wanted some time with her, to get her away from him, to show her how good we were together. I'm not proud of it, but at the moment, I felt desperate, like it was my last chance."

The air is heavy between us as we sit in silence. Sage waits patiently for several seconds before she finally asks.

"What did you do?"

Slowly, I turn to face her, hoping to God she won't judge me too harshly for what I say next.

"I lied. I faked amnesia, acted like I thought it was two years prior, right before we had broken up. I acted like I thought Erica and I were still together to push them apart, to bring her to me."

I pause, watching for her reaction. Sage's eyes are wide, her brows knitted, and her mouth slightly parted.

"That's...really fucked up," she says bluntly.

"I know," I wince. "I was young and dumb and fucking desperate. Seb and Erica ended up breaking up for a bit, I felt guilty as shit for lying to everyone, but it was working. Erica and I were practically inseparable, we even had a few moments. I thought she was going to be mine...until the truth came out."

"What happened after that?" she asks.

I shrug. "What do you think? They both basically told me to go fuck myself. Seb was too stubborn to go after Erica, though. He thought he wasn't good enough for her, but I knew the truth then. I was the one who wasn't good enough. I told him I'd give him this chance to go get her, but he'd only get one. He hasn't fucked up to this day. They got married, had the twins, and have been living happily ever after since."

A heaviness settles on my tongue at those words, but ironically, a lightness lifts off my shoulders at having the whole truth out there. Sage deserved to know. It was long overdue.

"And you've just been not so secretly in love with her ever since? Doomed to watch them fall deeper in love while you're ostracized for what you did?" Sage asks, the raw truth to her words scraping against me.

I nod and shrug.

"Pretty much, I guess."

"Wow."

She doesn't say anything else for a minute or so before she continues.

"Well fuck, let it be known, when Trevor Michaels wants something he goes after it at all costs." She laughs hollowly.

I don't laugh, though. I know she's trying to mask her disappointment in me with humor. There is no point in masking it, though. She could never look down on me as much as I look down on myself. It was easily the lowest point in my life, that one thing I did and wish more than anything I could take back. But I can't. Sometimes we have to live with our decisions, and we don't get a do-over. You just have to keep moving.

"And now?" Sage asks, shaking me out of my thoughts.

"Now what?"

"How do you feel about her now? Do you still want her back? If she came to you tomorrow and told you she was leaving Sebastian, what would you do?"

I hear the hesitation in her voice, like she's terrified to hear the answer. I hate that it's there. I hate that there is even an ounce of doubt in her about us, but I don't blame her for having it. I've been a fucking wild card for years when it comes to Erica, but things have changed.

I settle back into the bed, reaching over to her before dragging her into me. She comes easily, but I can practically feel the wall she's trying to build. I can see the vaults she's locking her heart away in as she looks up at me.

Cupping the side of her face I shake my head.

"I honestly don't know what I'd do, probably try to talk her out of it because I've never seen anyone love someone as wholly as Sebastian does to Erica. If the question you're really asking is if I'd leave this for another chance with her?" I say as I gesture between us.

"No," I say simply with a shake of my head.

She watches me with trepidation, but slowly she nods, accepting my answer before sinking into my touch. Less than two minutes later I hear the soft sounds of her sleeping. I'm wide awake, though. I hate that I didn't say more, reassure her more. She deserves more, and I want to give it all to her. She doesn't deserve to be in a relationship where she's waiting for the other shoe to drop. Words are meaningless, though. I have to prove how committed I am to her, to us.

The next morning, things are a little tense, but as our morning routine goes on, things fall back into ease. She wasn't supposed to come to practice today, but she made up some bullshit excuse of why she was riding with me. I knew it was because she was trying to feel closer to me after last night, and I sure as hell was not about to turn down an opportunity for more time with her.

Instead of holding her knee in the car, I wrapped my arm around the back of her shoulders, pulling her as close to me as the center console would allow. I kissed her like I was about to lose her before we walked into practice and did the same when we got back to my car after.

This shit has to end—today. It's time, long overdue. And I won't let my past ruin the bright future I have just within reach. I need to let go, fully, so I can hold on to Sage with both fucking hands.

Sage and I are walking up to Erica and Seb's house hand in hand when I knock on the door. Little Rosie answers the door almost immediately, bouncing up and down before jumping into my arms.

"Uncle Trev! Uncle Trev!" she exclaims.

I can't help but smile as I hold her.

"Hey, sweet girl. Where is your sissy?"

Daphne comes out of nowhere, practically tackling me to the ground and giggling in the process. I let out a laugh as I scoop her into my arms too, hiking them both up over my shoulders as I step inside. They are both giggling and squealing as I haul them through the house, and I turn to see Sage following us with a soft smile. I shoot her a wink before dumping the kids onto the couch. They quickly scramble to their feet before taking off down the hallway.

Erica comes out of the kitchen with a smile on her face as she greets us. She pulls me into a quick hug before doing the same to Sage.

"Hey, guys! Dinner is almost done."

"We brought booze," Sage says as she lifts up the two wine bottles in her hands.

"Ah, I knew you were my favorite for a reason," Erica says as she takes one of the bottles from Sage before placing her hand into Sage's and leading her into the kitchen.

I smile at them as I turn to see Seb standing in the doorway with his arms folded watching me. A small bit of the lightness I was feeling dims as I look at him.

"Hey, man," I say.

He dips his head in acknowledgment, and surprising the hell out of me, he crosses the hallway to me before clapping his hand against mine.

"Hey," he says simply.

I'll take it.

Seb and I talk about work a bit while Erica and Sage talk during dinner. Things are actually comfortable for the first time in literally a decade. I look around to see the twins playing with their chicken more than eating it while Seb attempts to gently parent them. Sage and Erica are just finishing the first bottle of wine and laughing to each other as they whisper about god knows what. Sage looks up to see me watching her and gives me a saucy wink that has my heart tripping up in my chest.

God, what is it about her that sends me racing? Things with her are just so natural, so perfect, and at this moment I'm more sure than ever that Sage is something special, someone that I need to protect at all costs.

Once dinner is over I volunteer to do dishes while Seb and Sage get drug into a game of Candy Land with the girls. I'm just finishing up the last dish when Erica comes into the kitchen, hip checking me a little harder than I'm sure she meant to as her wine glass almost sloshes onto the floor.

"Oh shit!" She giggles.

"Easy there, you lush," I tease as I take the glass out of her hand and rinse it out.

"Your girlfriend is the instigator. These young 'uns can drink better than me. I had to at least attempt to hold my own."

"Yeah, she's trouble," I smile as I set the glass down to dry.

Erica is watching me with a dopey grin that causes me to laugh.

"What?"

"So it's true?"

I raise an eyebrow for her to elaborate, causing her to shove my shoulder.

"You and her. You're together. You're in a relationship, Trevvvv. After how many years? I can hardly believe it."

I smile and nod as I look out into the living room where Sage is whooping in celebration as she begins moving her yellow character across the board.

"I'm happy."

"I can tell. I'm so happy for both of you." Erica smiles up to me.

Looking down into her turquoise eyes, I can't help but feel the gentle stir of past feelings. They aren't necessarily coming to the surface but more like stirring in a reminder of what once was, what will possibly always be there, but not in the same capacity.

"Can we talk...in private?" I ask seriously.

Her smile falls as she nods and loops her arm through mine, leading us out of the kitchen and through the back doors to the pool.

Chapter 33
Sage

I just arrived at Candy Land. I know I'm impressive as fuck. Did I make a couple of little girls cry in the process? Yes, yes I did. But that's life.

No, seriously. Sebastian and I tried to cheat so one of the girls could win, but every card I drew was a dessert, and I guess fate just had other plans. After Daphne threw her cards and ran upstairs, and Rosalie pouted until tears built up in her little round eyes, Sebastian decided it was time to call it a night. He took them upstairs to start their bedtime routine while I started cleaning up.

As Sebastian was carrying Rosalie upstairs, I noticed out of the corner of my eye Erica and Trevor walking arm and arm out of the kitchen to the backyard. I tried not to let the jealous pang run through my chest at the sight, but it was no use. I'm an extremely jealous person, and when it comes to Trevor and Erica, I'm practically on edge with every word exchanged.

I'd be lying if I said that it wasn't my main concern when Trevor and I were contemplating starting this thing, but I've tried to push it to the side, focusing on the time we spend together. What it feels like when he holds me, when he whispers to me all the assurances and praise in the world. Well, apart from last night. I can't lie that I was more than a little disappointed at his lack of words when I asked him what would happen if Erica and Seb split. Maybe it was stupid to ask. It's not like in my gut I don't know the answer.

I don't know how Sebastian has dealt with this turmoil for almost ten years. I'm a few months in and feel like I'm ready to go crazy. I grab the board game, taking it to the kitchen instead of the closet I saw it grabbed from because I can't resist looking out the glass back doors.

A sinking feeling suddenly fills me as I stand, my intuition is screaming not to go over there, that I don't want to see whatever is going on. But I can't help it. I have to know, once and for all. Taking slow breaths, I take my time setting the board game on the kitchen island before I slowly turn to face the backyard, my heart stalling out at what I see.

Erica is leaning against Trevor's shoulder, her head resting on him as she looks up at him. They are sitting at the edge of the pool, their feet just barely touching the water as he smiles down at her like she hung the moon. I knew it was going to hurt, but fuck, I didn't know it was going to hurt this bad. Trevor lifts a hand to brush a piece of Erica's curly hair out of her face as he speaks, and she blinks up at him like she's never loved another.

Like a knife has been sunk into my chest, I can't breathe. I knew better. I knew from the first time I saw them together that there was something there. I had the facts, maybe not the full ones until last night, but I knew there was history there, chemistry. No matter how badly he fucked up and how much she loves Sebastian, they will always love each other. I'll always be the second choice, and I hate to admit I'm insecure enough to say I can't handle that.

I stumble backward several steps, not having it in me to watch them love each other from afar anymore. I grab my jacket and phone, and I run. I throw the door open, slamming it shut before running down their long driveway. More tears fall down my face as I shakily pull my phone out and order a ride to pick me up down the road.

I'm being dramatic, I know that. It's not like he cheated on me, at least not that I saw. But how long will we be together before he does? He can only subdue his feelings for so long before he breaks, before she breaks. Before they fuck right there on the kitchen island, kids and Sebastian upstairs be damned. I can't stick around for that. I can't settle to be someone's backup plan. I won't.

My ride arrives in record time, and I hop in quickly, avoiding the awkward small talk he attempts to make before he drops me off at Trevor's house. I quickly enter the gate code before running up to the front door. I scan my finger and step inside before slamming the door shut behind me. Who knows how long they will be out there making eyes at each other? If Trevor doesn't want to end up drowning in the shallow end of a pool, he should probably stop before Sebastian gets done putting the girls down. Regardless, it won't be long before he figures out I'm gone and even less time before he comes looking for me here first.

I grab the duffle bag that I brought here and quickly begin packing it with my things, leaving behind anything Trevor has bought me in the last few months. I don't give a shit what I leave honestly. I just need to get the fuck out of here.

I can feel myself slowly shutting down, compartmentalizing the weaker broken pieces of me and shielding them with the bad bitch exterior I've wielded so well over the last few years. You will not cry. You will not break over a womanizing pro baller. How cliché could you possibly get? You're better than that, better than this.

At least I still have my apartment to fall back on. Who knows if Dad has called to cancel the lease early or not, but it's a good place to start for the night. I'm just finishing zipping my bag, slinging it over my shoulder when the front door bursts open.

"Sage! Sage, are you here?!" Trevor's panicked voice calls out.

A lead ball sinks in my stomach at the sound of his voice before I let out a heavy exhale.

Don't feel. Don't feel. Don't feel.

His footsteps thunder up the stairs, panic splashed across his face before relief washes it away when he sees me.

"Jesus, you scared the hell out of me. What happened? Are you okay? Why didn't you come get me?" he asks, pausing when his eyes zero in on my bag.

His entire body language changes from one of panicked relief to caution, like I'm an animal he's trying not to spook.

"What's going on?"

"Nothing," I say with a shake of my head remarkably smoothly if I do say so myself. "Thanks for letting me stay here. You didn't have to, but it was really nice. It's more than time to get back to my real life, though."

"Your real life?" he reiterates stoically.

"Yeah, I mean, I can't crash with you forever. Cramping that bachelor lifestyle, you know?" I attempt to joke, though it falls flat.

I try to move past him, but he stops in front of me, tilting his head to the side slightly as he leans in.

"What are you talking about, Sage? Where are you going?"

"My home, you know, the one you spent gobs of money redecorating for me. I'll pay you back for all that as soon as I can. I just need to—"

"I don't give a fuck. I don't want a single dime from you. Where the fuck are you going when your home is here?" he asks, emotion cracking through when he says here.

I watch as a million emotions flash through his blue eyes as he shakes his head at me. I try to keep my emotions buried as I shrug my shoulders.

"C'mon, Trevor. We had a good run, and it was a great way to kill some time, but let's be real. You and me? We could never be more than just fuck buddies."

"Fuck buddies," he deadpans.

"Yeah, no hard feelings or anything. Trust me, I won't be one of those girls who calls you day and night," I laugh, though it sounds hollow even to my own ears.

My words must have shocked him because when I go to move around him, he doesn't stop me this time. I take each step carefully while also trying to hurry as fast as I can. The farther I get away from him, the better.

I almost make it to the front door before I'm being spun around, my duffel bag dropping to the ground, and my back bumping against the wall. Trevor is caging me against the wall, his hands on either side of my head and his leg wedged between my thighs to pin me in place.

"Okay, we need to start from the beginning because I don't know what the fuck is going on right now. You act like we've been messing around and barely tolerating each other when we've been in a full-blown relationship for weeks now."

"Trevor. We were just—"

"No, cut the shit. What the fuck happened between me and my girlfriend having a nice dinner at our friends' house, to you acting like you can hardly look at me?"

Hearing the word girlfriend on his lips chips at my armor and has my face wincing as I look away. He doesn't allow it though, his hand gripping my face and forcing me to look at him as his eyes drill into me in search of the truth.

"What happened, Sage?"

This time I'm not able to keep my tone even or cool. It's wobbly and weak as my throat tightens with each word.

"I saw you, out back, with h-her."

His hardened look softens, and he drops his hold on my face before lowering his forehead to mine. He blows out a heavy breath before his eyes come to me, not moving his head as he speaks.

"That's what this is about?"

"No, it's just time for us to go separate ways. I can't get any more involved with someone who is still clearly in love with another woman. It just spells disaster for all parties, so I'm taking myself out of the game. You and Erica and Sebastian can figure your own shit out. Maybe even have a little throuple. You all deserve to be happy, and so do I."

He shakes his head vehemently as he speaks.

"No, that's not what I want. Not even fucking close. We were talking tonight because we needed to. I—"

"I'm not her. I'm never gonna be her, Trevor. There is only one Erica."

I feel another tear slide down my cheek, and I fucking hate myself for allowing it to slip by. Trevor's thumb reaches out and catches it instantly, brushing it away like he could brush away my pain if he tried hard enough.

"Baby girl, it's not about you not being her. It's that she's not you."

His words suck all the air from my lungs as his face crumples with sadness.

"I'm so fucking sorry. I'm trying to do the right thing, and I fucked things up even more," he says with a shake of his head as he pulls back slightly.

"Erica and I were talking tonight, about heavy shit."

"Everything with you two is heavy," I attempt to tease, but it just breaks off into a half sob.

Trevor nods as he continues.

"I was telling her how I love her, I've loved her my whole life, and that will never stop."

If you could feel the way my heart shatters in this moment, I doubt a weaker woman would be able to stand. Miraculously, I do, though. I brace for impact as everything I thought I was building with Trevor comes to a fiery death.

"I was also telling her," he continues, "how I'm not in love with her anymore."

My brows furrow at that.

"I was telling her how every time I saw her for the last ten years, I got butterflies. How any time she'd hug me, I'd hold on a little bit longer than I knew I should because I was desperate for every second with her. I told her that I never imagined caring for anyone half as much as I did about her. Until I met you."

I swallow heavily, doing my best to stay silent as he continues.

"I knew from the moment that I met you, there was something strong between us. At first, I thought it was lust because you were so goddamn beautiful. Then you opened your mouth, and I thought for sure it was hate, and god did I hate you so much. But then things shifted, and I realized that I loved you so much better."

Another tear drips down my face from his words because I want to believe him so badly. All I want to do is fall into his arms and beg him to never hurt me, but I know I can't. Loving him is too reckless, too risky.

"This isn't a romance novel, baby. There is no third-act breakup for us. You are mine, and I am yours. Period."

He blows out a breath as he closes his eyes before opening them again, a newfound flare in them as he speaks.

"I love you, Sage. More than I know what to do with, more than I know how to express. I'm a fuck-up by nature. I'm gonna continue to fuck up, and I'm sorry for that. I'm about the least perfect man in the world, but I can promise

I'll do everything in my power to make up for every single fuck up. I can promise that I'll do anything and everything to always make you feel like the queen you are. You are the only woman I want to wake up to every morning and the only one I want in my arms at night. Words aren't shit when it comes to things like this, so I'm going to prove it. Just give me the chance, babygirl. Give us the chance. I fuck up a lot of things, but I won't fuck this up—not when it's this important."

I feel each layer I've attempted to shield myself with, every ounce of armor and bravery fall apart at that. Not because of his words, but because of the earnest desperation on his face. The sincerity pouring out of him. Call me stupid, call me easily manipulated, but I've never felt more safe, more cared for, or protected than I do in this man's arms. Sometimes, you have to go out on a limb and take a risk. I know I'm risking everything for Trevor Michaels, but at the same time, I'm not sure it's even my choice at this point.

Because I love him too.

Slowly I nod my head, not having it in me to speak. Trevor doesn't seem to need my words either. He cups my face with his, gripping me in a firm hold as he presses his lips against mine.

"I love you, Raven. So fucking much," he says in between kisses.

I nod again in response, causing him to let out a relieved laugh as his hands wander down my body, lifting me up by my thighs. I wrap my legs around his torso as he begins carrying me up the stairs and straight to his bedroom, our bedroom.

He lays me down on the bed before pulling off his clothes.

"I need to feel you, baby. Can I get close to you?" he asks softly.

I nod again, spurring him on to pull my pants down before laying on top of me. He slips into me instantly, letting out a shuddered breath when he is fully seated inside me.

"Trev," I gasp softly, causing his eyes to come to me.

"Shit, I almost lost you, didn't I, baby?"

I swallow but don't respond before he shakes his head and curses as he begins thrusting.

"I know I did, and I'm so sorry. I knew I needed to close that chapter of my life for good before we could start our own. But I'm sorry, I should have talked to you first," he says as he rubs his head against my G-spot. "Reassured you…" He thrusts again. "Told you how I can't fucking breathe when you're not near me."

"Trevor," I moan as my eyes water.

"No more tears, baby. Just let me love you."

"Please," I say softly.

"Always," he promises.

Chapter 34
Trevor

I t's official. Sage Aberton has broken every single rule of mine, and I don't even care anymore. I'm in love with her, and I know she's in love with me too. She wouldn't have tried to leave last night if she didn't love me. Fuck. I can't believe I almost lost her. I can only imagine what she was thinking when she was an outsider looking in. If only she would have been there to hear our conversation.

"You're not just dating. You're in love," Erica smiles at me.

I practically blanch at her words. I really care about Sage, and I fucking hate being away from her these days. But I don't know if I'd call it love. I've only loved one person, and that didn't turn out great the last time.

"I don't think I ever want to fall in love again. It gets a little too complicated," I say as I give her a look as I gesture between the two of us.

Erica shrugs her shoulders.

"Whether you want to or not is irrelevant, you're in love with her, and she's in love with you."

"Really? She said that? What did she tell you?" I say as I turn to face her, holding my breath with anticipation.

"No, she didn't tell me anything. I can just see it on her face, on both of your faces. Really think about it, though, Trev. If you didn't love her, would you have gotten as excited as you just did at the idea of her loving you?"

I turn to stare off into the still water of the pool as I mull over her words. Love. Is this what love is when it's not the person you've always known? Is this what falling in love is like? One minute you hate them, the next you want to protect them from every bad thing in the world? You crave their touch like you can't take your next breath without them?

"I'm in love," I say, more to myself than Erica.

"Wow, I think I just literally heard your little rule break inside your head," Erica says with a know-it-all smile.

Turning my head to face her, I can't help but smile as she leans on my shoulder and hugs my arm.

"I'm so happy for you, Trev. You deserve to have it all."

I couldn't even speak before Sebastian was opening the back door, asking what I had done to Sage. He watched her take off down the street to god knows where, and I was up, on my feet and running after her in the next moment.

Sage and I just pulled up to the practice facility. We only have a team meeting today since tomorrow is a home game. She said she could use some film of just the facility so she decided to come with.

I get out of my side before jogging around to grab her door. She smiles in thanks and goes to step around me when I grab her hand, lacing our fingers together.

Sage frowns at me as she raises an eyebrow.

"What are you doing?"

"Walking with my girl," I say simply as I lock the car.

"Okay, but don't you think someone is going to see? You need to let go of my hand," she says as she tries to wiggle out of my grip, but I only tighten my hold.

"Babygirl, you're not nearly as smart as I thought you were if you think there is a chance in hell, after last night, that I'm not shouting how in love with you I am from the motherfucking rooftops."

"Please don't, that sounds like something Santos would do," she says with a curled lip.

I bark out a laugh as I let go of her hand before wrapping my arm around her shoulder and pulling her into me. Bending down, I press a kiss to the side of her head as we step into the hallway.

"What? You embarrassed to be seen with me? Any woman would kill to be in your position."

She cuts me a narrowed glance as she speaks.

"And if any woman finds herself in my position, I'll kill them."

I can't help but grin as I hold her to me tighter this time.

"It's fucking hot when you get all jealous."

Sage rolls her eyes but doesn't pull away from me. We almost make it to where we will split off when Coach appears practically out of thin air, steam rolling out of his ears as he barrels down the hallway.

"What the fuck is this?!" he shouts.

I give him a laid-back look before glancing to Sage and back to him.

"What's what, Coach?"

"Don't be a fucking smart-ass with me, Michaels. Do I have to spell it out for you? My daughter is off fucking limits. If you want to see a second of time on the field for the rest of the year, I suggest you back away and lose her information."

I can't help but scoff.

"No can do, Coach. If you have to bench me because your adult daughter and I are in a relationship, I guess do what you gotta do. Going into the postseason and losing your starting quarterback doesn't sound like a great way to maintain your position if I can be so bold."

His chest heaves, his nostrils flaring as he storms up to us. I'm ready for it, but at the last moment, he switches directions and comes face to face with Sage.

"You're such a fucking attention whore! Always trying to get a reaction. Well, here is your fucking reaction! Now get the fuck away from my player."

"Or what? I'm not gonna break him, Dad," Sage says, her tone hard, but I notice a slight tremble to her vibrato.

"You little fucking shit!" Coach shouts before raising his hand.

Sage flinches slightly in preparation, and it's all the warning I need to move. I push Sage behind me quickly and catch Aberton's hand midair, not releasing him as I lower my voice to a deathly sound.

"If you touch her, I'll fucking bury you."

Aberton's anger is wild and strong, but he must see the promise in my eyes because I watch that fire in his quickly dampen. I toss his hand away from me, back at his fat piece of shit side as I continue.

"Lay a finger on her. I fucking dare you."

The death glare he is giving me is one where I know he is wishing I just burst into flames right here and now. Unfortunately for him, I'm still standing, and I'll be damned if he gets anywhere near my girl.

"This isn't going to end well," he says, his eyes attempting to go over my shoulder to Sage. "Just like the last one. You always pick the worst kind, and this time you'll be far worse off than a couple bumps and bruises."

With that, he turns and storms back to the film room where our meeting is being held. I don't turn my back until he is gone, but as soon as I hear that door shut, I spin on my heel. Sage is breathing heavily, staring at the floor like she's in another place, another time. The look on her face honestly scares the living shit out of me.

"Baby? Baby?" I ask, causing her to startle as she looks up at me.

Her bright eyes snap to my own, a thin, watery layer covering them as she quickly swipes at her face.

"Thanks."

I frown at that. "Thanks for what? I would never let anyone even think about hurting you. Has he ever hurt you before?"

She shakes her head. "No, never. I-I've never seen him like that. The most I've ever gotten from him was indifference."

"And what about that thing he said about a couple of bumps and bruises? He talking about your ex?"

She doesn't speak, and the look she gives me begs me not to pry. I want to say to hell with that, strap her to a chair and force her to give me names and addresses of every man who has ever hurt her. That won't work, though. I need her to come to me when she's ready, to trust me. So I'll give her that, but if she doesn't give me details soon, I'll take matters into my own hands. If my girl is in danger, I need to know about it so I can protect her with everything I have.

"C'mon, let's go home," I say.

"You need to go have your meeting," she argues.

"Fuck him. What's he gonna do? Bench me? Let him."

I reach down and wrap my hand around hers as she looks up at me with a look that is drenched in vulnerability. It pains my heart and causes me to abandon her hand and wrap her whole damn body around my own. I can never be close enough to her, ever. Especially when she's hurting. The only thing I know how to do in situations like this is hold her close and make sure nothing else can hurt her, not when I'm around.

Chapter 35
Sage

To no one's surprise, Dad didn't bench Trevor at the game. I was on the sidelines for the first quarter, and obviously we arrived together, so I heard him tear into Trev when we first got there, but he was out on that field when the game kicked off. The cocky asshole was right, doesn't matter how much my dad may hate him, Trevor is invaluable to the team and really their only solid chance of making it to the Super Bowl.

The Crusaders won, again, a huge thanks to Caldwell who really shined this last game. Trevor scored three touchdowns and had one interception, all in the first half of the game. The crowd was going absolutely apeshit. He's always been a star player, and after this game, there is buzz about him being considered for the Offensive Player of the Year award this year if his performance continues.

Trevor has been giving me space emotionally. There is no physical space between us ever. When he is in the room, I'm basically on top of him, due to no desire of my own. Okay, maybe I like it a little bit, but I never imagined a big, womanizing playboy would be so cuddly all the time. Maybe it's his own insecurities coming to light. Or maybe I'm just so hot he can't keep his hands off me.

Duh, that's obviously it.

I'm thankful for the space, though. Obviously Dad said shit that raised red flags in Trevor's mind, and I know him. He's desperate to hear it all. He wants to know about my past, if I'm in danger, how he can protect me. If I'm being honest, though. I don't know how to tell for sure.

Calista and I have all but lost contact, and it's taken everything in me not to jump to the worst conclusions. I know it'll do no good, though. Hammer would never let anything bad happen to her, so I know she's at least safe. But if she hasn't been able to reach out to me in months....something bad is going on at the clubhouse, and that sends a fear like no other racing down my spine.

I'm unpacking my duffel bag in Trevor's room, sorry, *our* room, because every time he saw it in the corner of the room, he practically sneered at it like it offended him. Maybe he didn't like the reminder that I tried to walk out on him, or maybe it's his OCD coming to light. I joked about unpacking it into the spare bedroom again when he leveled me with a look that could kill.

"If you know what's good for you, you'll put your things away permanently in our bedroom. Don't act like there isn't more space than you know what to do with in here."

"Hey, want to grab some dinner?" Trev asks as he slips his arms around me from behind and places a soft kiss on the base of my neck.

I smile at the touch before I turn to face him.

"Yeah, give me a sec. Almost done," I say as I grab a stack of shirts and turn to place them in the drawer.

Trev nods as he bends down to my bag and reaches in, his eyes going wide when he pulls something out.

"What the fuck is this?"

When I spin to see what he's talking about, I laugh. What else am I supposed to do when I turn around to see my boyfriend holding a thick eight-inch dildo in his hand? The look on his face is a mixture of horror and maybe a glimmer of intrigue.

"Why the hell do you have this?" Trevor asks as he shakes his head and looks at me.

"Uhm, to fuck? Or I guess for it to fuck me."

His eyes widen. "That's what I'm here for, though."

"Not always. A girl has needs, and sometimes she doesn't want to deal with the bullshit that comes with the other ninety-five percent of a man."

He stares at me for several more seconds before his head tilts to the side, and he slowly stalks toward me. I don't bother to evade him, he always catches me, and I like the feeling of adrenaline coursing in my veins as he eats up the distance between us.

When his chest brushes against mine, he bends down until his lips are against my ear.

"Show me."

I lean away to look up at him with furrowed brows.

"Show me how you fuck yourself, babygirl," he says as he hands the silicone cock to me.

A thrill runs through me, and I don't hesitate to take it from him and move to the bed. An approving sound vibrates through Trevor as he follows after me, tracking my every move as I climb on top of the bed and lay on my back. Honestly, I'm even impressed with our comfort level with each other. I feel like most couples would fumble through this, maybe get a little awkward, but I honestly see this only working out in my favor, and it's not like I haven't used this thing dozens of times so what's the downside? It's all the fun with the thrill of an audience.

Trevor reaches out for the waistband of my leggings before I can, slowly pulling them and my panties down before peeling them off my legs.

"Hand me the lube," I say as I grip the dildo in front of me.

Trevor does as I ask, even squirting a bit on the tip of the dildo for me before he undoes his pants and applies some to himself as well. I raise an eyebrow but can't deny the fluttering of butterflies in my lower belly at the idea of him touching himself while I'm touching myself.

Keeping my eyes on him, I take the head of my dildo, feeling the cool tip of the lube rest against my pussy before I slowly start pushing it in. The combined intrusion and chill of the lube has my body shuddering as Trevor begins slowly stroking his cock.

"You like that, baby?" he asks in the raspy voice he only reserves for the bedroom.

It's probably for the best that he does. He's already a national sex symbol. If these women heard the voice he uses and the things he says in the bedroom, all hope would be lost for panties everywhere.

I bite my lower lip and nod as I continue pushing the dildo inside me inch by inch until it is fully inside me. I let out a shuddering breath as Trevor's pace slowly increases.

"Ride that cock, babygirl. Show me how well you take it."

My pussy pulses at his words as I begin slowly moving it in and out of me, pleasure racing through me with every motion. I let out a breathy moan as Trevor swears.

"Goddamn, this is so fucking hot."

His strokes become a little more choppy as his eyes stay fixated on my pussy.

"You like watching me get fucked by another cock?" I ask with a small smile.

Trevor's eyes darken as he looks up to my own.

"No. The only cock that belongs inside you, is my own, this is as close to another cock as you are going to get, and I can think of dozens of ways to make you come between the two of us."

"Well, don't be all talk," I tease as another soft moan escapes me.

Trevor lets go of his cock before he crawls onto the bed, pushing my legs up until my feet are planted on the bed. He slips between my thighs, and I think he's about to take the dildo out of me so I stop pushing it in and out. But then I feel him grab my hand, setting it back on the base and forcing it back inside me.

"Fuck," I whimper as his hand guides my own.

"Just like this. You have to get that slight rotation if you want to rub your G-spot, sweetheart."

True to his words, sparks flash behind my eyes when he makes my hand angle up just a bit.

"Thanks for the tip," I breathe. "You can go now."

He barks out a short laugh as he grumbles against my inner thigh.

"Not on your fucking life."

Before I can give him another sassy remark, his tongue sticks out, slowly tracing a line from my inner thigh down. He keeps going until he rests on my asshole.

"What are you doing?" I ask.

"About to eat this delectable ass," he says before his tongue traces over me, causing me to buck against him.

He wraps an arm around my stomach to hold me down but doesn't relent as his tongue flicks against me. It's not as good as getting your pussy eaten, but fuck if it isn't second place. I can't even focus enough to keep my rhythm up when he pulls away, reaching out for the lube before spreading a few cool drops against me.

"You ever been double stuffed before, Raven?"

"No."

"Better get ready, baby."

Trevor lines up his cock to my ass before he slowly starts pushing in. Trevor and I have been doing a lot of experimenting lately, and it's blatantly obvious that we both love anal and normally I'm able to take him with minimal pain. But right now when my pussy is already full and now he's trying to fill my ass too. It's too much.

"Trev," I gasp. "I can't. Too much."

"You can take it. Be a good girl and keep that cock in your pussy. I'll go slow."

I feel my pussy clench around the dildo, and inadvertently, my ass around Trevor.

"Christ, we starting this already. You have to at least let me get all the way in before you make me come," Trevor says with a gentle swat to the side of my ass.

I blow out a breath as I nod, doing my best to relax as Trevor slowly pushes inside more and more. There are a couple of points where I don't think I'll be able to do it, but Trevor continues praising me through it.

"You're doing so well. Almost there, baby. Fuck you're so perfect."

As soon as he is fully seated in me, something like relief takes over as Trevor smiles down at me.

"I'm so proud of you."

I pulse at his words, causing his eyes to roll into the back of his head for a moment before he grins again.

"When you're ready," he says.

I nod and begin moving the dildo inside me once again. It's not too much until Trevor starts moving. His movements are slow and gentle, and soon the discomfort falls away because this has got to be the hottest thing I've ever done in my life.

"Fuck yes, look at you getting all relaxed. Your tight ass is squeezing the fucking life out of me, but you're fucking that dildo like you want more."

"No more!" I practically shout before chuckling softly.

"Why's that?" Trevor rumbles in a low voice.

"Too much. T-too full," I ramble as my eyes attempt to stay open when waves of pleasure continue to crash into me over and over again.

"Never enough, baby. You could take more if you wanted to but we will save that for another day."

I'm not sure if it's excitement or fear that makes my stomach flip in anticipation. Probably a healthy dose of both.

I angle the dildo a little more, trying to rub against my G-spot as Trevor curses.

"Are you okay?" I ask with a slight dip of my eyebrows.

"Fine," he grits through clenched teeth.

I continue my rhythm, enjoying the sensation the head of the dildo is giving me combined with Trevor when he curses again.

"Are you hurting?" I ask again.

He chokes out a laugh as he shakes his head and looks at me.

"No, baby. I can just feel *everything*."

"Everything? What do you mean?"

He presses into me a little deeper as he speaks.

"Every time you angle your dildo like that, I can feel it rub against my cock through you."

Understanding dawns on me before I give him a wicked smile. I adjust the angle even more, to the point it's not overly satisfying for me but the look of uncontrolled pleasure that splashes across Trevor's face makes it worth it.

"Like this?" I ask innocently.

"Yes," he groans as his eyes close, and his thrusts become jerkier.

"Do you like it?" I ask.

He doesn't respond as his grip on my hips tightens, so I get his attention by wiggling the dildo side to side, purposefully rubbing against where Trevor's tip is. His eyes fly open as his mouth parts, and he lets out a breathy gasp.

"Do you like it?" I repeat, kind of loving the power I'm getting from this.

"Yeah," he strains out.

I smirk at that as I speak.

"Bet you'd love it even more if it was a real cock inside me, rubbing against you."

Trevor frowns at that.

"Fuck that. No man will ever be graced with the sight of you again, let alone touch you."

I shrug. "Fine, but I wouldn't mind sharing you with another man."

Now Trevor laughs.

"Keep letting that fantasy live in your head, baby, because it's gonna stay there. Just because I like the feeling of something rubbing my cock while I'm balls deep in my girl's ass doesn't mean I want to get fucked in the ass myself."

I pout at that, the idea of having a threesome with Trevor was actually turning me on. The guy wouldn't even have to touch me. I'd be happy just to watch. But then he had to go and ruin my fantasy.

He lowers himself down, hovering over me as he continues thrusting in and out of me.

"Aw come on, baby. Don't pout. I'm sorry I don't want to fuck other people."

"Let's be clear, guys, not girls. If you said you wanted to fuck other girls, you'd wake up to a missing penis, but if you told me you wanted to explore your sexuality, I'm all for it."

Trevor rumbles out a soft laugh as he runs his nose along the side of my neck.

"You'll be the first person I come to."

Excitement runs through me. *That wasn't a hard no.*

"Now stop thinking about other cocks and focus on mine and your dildo," Trev says as he pushes deeper into me.

I let out a gasp that turns into a moan as he continues.

"Play with your pussy. I want to feel you come."

I reach my free hand down to my clit as I begin rubbing while continuing my motions with my dildo. The violence of this orgasm is going to be unlike anything I've experienced before, I can tell just by the build up. My pussy is spasming in hard pulses as I feel it building and building.

"You're so close. Are you going to fall apart for me? Stuffed so full and needy for a release?"

I nod shakily as my breath begins coming out in spurts. Trevor reaches out and takes my hand away from my clit, pausing for a moment, and it's as if he has turned all the sound off in the world. Everything freezes at that moment. I don't even breathe before he rests just the pad of his thumb against me.

"Come."

As if a detonation has gone off inside our bedroom, I explode. Sound ignites in my ears like a wild roar as pleasure tears through me, wave upon wave demolishing my being as I scream, moan, and shout his name. It's like nothing I've ever felt before, I practically crawl the wall, either to get away from the sensations or make sure they never leave.

I think I heard and felt Trevor come too, but honestly, I practically blacked out so here's hoping he took care of himself because I honestly don't have it in me to care about anything right now.

Slowly, I feel the dildo slide out of me before Trevor pulls away too. It hurts for a second before satiated relief hums through every nerve ending in my body. I lay on the bed, a sweaty naked mess, for I don't know how long before Trevor picks me up, carries me across the room, and slowly lowers us into a warm waiting bubble bath. I nestle my head against his shoulder and close my eyes.

Well, we should definitely do that more often.

Chapter 36
Trevor

It's officially postseason which means it's fucking go time. We are the number one seed for the NFC, which is a pretty big fucking deal. I guess the Crusaders haven't been the number one seed since '98 and haven't made it to the Super Bowl in the last five years, so everyone is riding a good buzz. Since we are first in our division, we get a bye for wild card weekend. Only a few more games until the Super Bowl.

Honestly, getting another ring isn't the end all be all for me. I have enough, and it's not that I don't take pride in my work or love to win, because it's a yes to both, but I think everyone is really pushing for this because it is definitely going to be at least two of our star players' last season. Declan and Seb deserve to go out with another ring.

Speaking of the devil, we just finished up practice when Sebastian comes off of the practice field and into the locker room. I've been waiting for the right time to talk to him, the right place, but I finally figured I need to just sack up and have it out with him, and if he punches me in the face, let's be real, I probably deserved it.

"Hey," I say as he goes to his locker. "You got a minute?"

He looks at me for a few seconds, long enough to the point that I think he's going to blow me off before he turns away from the locker, giving me his full attention as he nods. I let out a long breath as I look up at my former best friend and try to cram a decade's worth of apologies into a handful of words.

"I'm sorry."

Nailed it.

Sebastian lifts an unimpressed eyebrow but doesn't speak, so I continue.

"I'm sorry for a lot, too much. I'm sorry for the shit that happened back in college. I'm sorry for how I reacted when I found out you and Erica were together. I'm sorry I manipulated everyone with the fake amnesia." I pause for a moment, mustering up the words that are the hardest to say out loud.

"And I'm sorry that I couldn't stop loving your wife. I felt the way I did, and I couldn't change it at the time, but I could have restrained it better, distanced myself more. I was selfish and fucking terrible. Honestly, I don't know why you didn't beat my ass years ago."

"Wanted to. Erica told me I couldn't," Seb says stoically.

I let out a humorless laugh as I nod. Of course she did, always trying to protect me.

"You should have anyway. You had every right. I know I caused you guys problems through the years. Fights you didn't need to have, tension that should have never existed, and for that, I can honestly never be sorry enough. If I knew there was a man out there that was desperate for Sage, that would do anything to have her I'd..." I pause, flexing my hands at my sides and shaking my head. Can't even fucking finish that thought. All I can say is Sebastian is a better man than I.

"You really love her, don't you?" Seb asks, surprise coloring his words.

"Sage?" I ask.

He nods.

I let out a heavy breath as I put my hands on my hips and shake my head. I can't help the smile that spreads across my face before nodding.

"A lot, man. More than I've ever loved anyone."

"Anyone?" Seb asks with a dubious look.

Erica was my first great love, we were best friends. Things were perfect. But we were young, life was easy for us back then, and therefore, the relationship was easy. Despite how deep our friendship runs, I don't think the love for each other ever ran as deep. Not as deep as it runs for her and Seb. Not as deep as I feel it in just a touch from Sage. I loved Erica, but then I think I just loved the idea of her. The idea of a life where my parents were proud of me, we had no responsibilities, and I could just be myself around my best friend.

I was too young to understand that I could still have my best friend. We didn't need to be in love too. And then I just continued fucking things up from there one mistake at a time.

Things with Sage and I are different. I think because we started off so rocky, literally hating each other, it's already made us stronger than Erica and I ever were or ever could have been together. When I wasn't around Erica, I missed her like crazy, wanted to be around her. When I'm not with Sage, I can't fucking breathe. Can hardly think until she's in my sights again. I loved Erica selfishly, but I love Sage wholly.

"Anyone," I confirm with a confident nod that has Seb's dubious look giving way into what looks like awe.

"Fuck, well alright then."

I frown.

"Alright then?"

"Yeah." He shrugs.

"That's it? You don't have anything to say?"

He shrugs again. "All I wanted you to do was fuck off my wife. I knew you were sorry, you looked like a kicked puppy dog anytime you even glanced in my direction. But being sorry didn't make up for the fact that had something bad happened to me or Erica, and I didn't work out, you would have been there in a heartbeat to take my place."

"I know. I was a piece of shit."

"For years," Seb fills in.

I nod and lower my head because what else can I say at this point?

"But Erica really likes Sage, and so do the girls. I don't see them letting her go anytime soon so, maybe we should all go do something this weekend. Go over to the coast or something?"

"Really?" I ask, surprise evident in my words.

Sebastian shrugs. "Erica has been wanting to go."

"Yeah, that sounds good. I'll talk to Sage."

"Cool," Seb says as he turns around to resume taking off his gear, like nothing even happened.

I'm surprised by the guy's nonchalant attitude, but honestly, am I? The man is practically a gargoyle. He doesn't show any emotions unless one of his girls is around, and that's the way he likes it.

I'm not naïve enough to think we could ever be as close as we were in college. That bridge is probably permanently burned and rightfully so. But if we can get along, have a drink or two without getting ready to come to blows, I'd say that's progress.

Chapter 37
Sage

"Erica, it's January in Washington. Why the hell do you want to go to the ocean?" I say as we step outside of the mall downtown and onto the sidewalk.

"I love the water. We can always bundle up, and I just want to get out of the city for the weekend, let the girls run and play, you know?"

"That's fine but if they run and play, they are going to run and get a cold. It's cold and raining practically nonstop on the coast. Especially this time of year," I say, attempting to talk some reason into my naïve friend.

She shrugs. "We will probably spend most of the time in the hotel anyway."

I blink hard, still trying to understand what the fucking point is of us even going then, but I just shake my head. Trevor said we could go if I wanted or stay home and just relax. Erica wasn't as easygoing. She demanded that we come with and promised it would be a lot of fun, though I'm failing to see the fun part.

"Why are you even bothering with getting a new swimsuit? You're not gonna swim," I say.

"Well, not in the ocean, but the hotel has a pool. Why are you being sour? Just say yes already so we can both stop pretending like you may not come."

I can't help but laugh as we cross the street to the parking garage we parked in. Erica hits her trunk button and begins emptying her arms full of bags into the car. I go to poke fun when a loud roar sounds from behind me. I whirl around to see a white van come right up to us, squealing to a stop before the side door is thrown open.

My stomach bottoms out to the floor as two guys tattooed within an inch of their lives hop out.

No. No. No.

"Erica, run!" I scream at the top of my lungs just as one of the guys grabs me.

"Oh my god! Help! HELP!" she squeals, hitting an octave I didn't know humans were capable of.

I fight against the hold of the guy grabbing me as he attempts to drag me into the van while the other guy pins a thrashing Erica against the car.

"What do I do with this one?" he asks.

"Leave her, he only wants this one," the guy holding me says.

Just the mention of him sends a chill running down my spine, and my fight mode kicks in. I stomp on his foot as hard as I can, satisfied when I hear a sickening crunch. He lets me go with one of his arms, and it's just enough to get some space between us. I spin out of his hold before I drive the palm of my hand against his nose, effectively breaking it instantly.

"Fucking bitch!" he roars as blood spews from his face.

I hear the man behind me scream as I turn to see his hand covering Erica's mouth as she sinks her teeth into his finger. She pushes against his back hard enough for him to let her go before she turns around and kicks him in the balls so hard, I wince for him.

Erica shakily grabs her phone quickly calling for help as Mr. Broken Nose comes at me again. Unfortunately I don't miss him in time, and I catch a fist to the side of the face that sends my ears ringing. I lose my balance for a second, and he grabs my arm, dragging me halfway into the van.

"Let her go!" Erica screams as a tennis shoe hits the guy in the back of the head.

Really? A shoe Erica? I guess I appreciate the effort, but the girl is out of her depth. The guy holding me lets me go, turning to face Erica as he reaches for a gun at his side. Fear seizes me as I shove him into the side of the van, scrambling out as I run toward Erica and practically tackle her for coverage. We run behind the car as the guy lets out the first shot, causing her to startle as she lets out a cry.

Fuck, fuck, fuck. We have no weapons, no escape route, and no time. Then, like an angel from above, a couple of security guards for the parking garage crest the corner, instantly taking in the scene in front of them. They both simultaneously pull out the guns at their sides before pointing them at Mr. Broken Nose.

"Put the gun down!" one of them shouts.

He turns to face the guys, calculating his odds before he curses, yanking his stumbling friend who is still recovering from that devastating dick kick before yanking him into the open door of the van. It peels out of there in the next minute as the guys run over to us.

"Are you guys okay?" one of them asks quickly.

Erica nods shakily, but I don't speak because I know what this means. We got lucky today, but next time I might not be able to say the same. And if what they say is true, if he wants me, then I'm as good as gone.

Chapter 38
Trevor

We are taking a break during practice when Sebastian's phone starts ringing. He frowns before digging into his bag and pulling it out. His frown deepens when he looks at the screen before answering.

"Hey, baby, we're still in practice. What's—"

The look on his face shifts in a moment, and it's a look that sends a chill straight down my spine. He goes practically pale white before he's grabbing his keys and running. I don't know what's happened, but Sage and Erica are shopping together, and something heavy settles in my gut, telling me to follow him.

I hear several of the coaches shout out after us, but that doesn't slow us down in the slightest.

"Stay on the phone, baby. I'm coming, I'm coming," he says as we reach his car in record time.

It's a little hard to get in with all of our gear on but we manage, and Sebastian is peeling out of the parking lot in the next second.

"Erica? Erica!" Sebastian barks into the phone.

"What the fuck is going on?" I ask.

Sebastian's hand is shaking as he puts his phone on speaker as he runs a red light, maneuvering around honking cars as he continues.

I don't hear anything at first, then the faint sound of Erica's voice in the background comes through.

"Let her go!"

Panic races through me at her words.

"Her?!" I shout. "Her who?!"

I'm pissed I didn't have the foresight to grab my own phone because I need to hear Sage's voice. Need to know she's okay. In the next second, a gunshot rings out that has both Sebastian and I holding our breath. The air inside the car is so dangerous, so silent, it feels as if time has frozen despite the speed with which we are racing down the busy streets of Seattle.

"Erica?" Sebastian rasps roughly, but no one responds.

Oh my god. Oh my god. Oh my god.

Sebastian is practically drifting his Suburban in the parking garage before racing up floor after floor.

"Are you guys okay?" a man's muffled voice sounds through the phone just as we come around a corner to see two men standing over our girls.

Sebastian doesn't bother finding a spot. He slams the car into park in the middle of the road and races out of the car, but I'm faster. Sage and Erica are both sitting on the ground while the men are standing over them. My eyes instantly go to Sage, scanning over her for injuries and coming up empty, thank God. I set my sights on the man closest to her before full-on tackling him to the ground.

We tussle a bit before I hear Erica's voice.

"Trev! Seb! Stop! They helped us!"

I pause, looking down at the man beneath me, noticing the security-labeled clothing he's wearing before I look up at her.

"You sure?"

She nods quickly, causing me to release him and scramble toward a silent Sage. I grab her face and force her to look at me.

"Baby," I breathe out, my heart beating like a jackhammer. "What the fuck happened? What's going on?"

Her beautiful purple hues are cloudy with pain and fear, a watery layer of tears dimming their shine as she looks at me.

"T-trev?"

"I'm here," I say as Sebastian speaks.

"How did they save you?" he demands, looking like a crazed man, still not releasing the man beneath him.

"They scared the guys off, thankfully," Erica says, her voice breaking off on a sob that has Sebastian abandoning his target and gathering his wife into his arms. She falls apart, sobbing and clinging to him like she might drift away otherwise. My heart hurts for her, but I'm far too concerned with what happened and why my girl has hardly said a word yet.

"Sweetheart," I say gently, brushing away the silent tears that are currently streaming down her cheeks. "Talk to me," I beg.

I watch as her lower lip begins to tremble before she blows out a rough breath and speaks.

"He's coming for me."

"Who?" I push again, but she stays quiet.

"A couple of guys pulled up in a van, they tried to take Sage," Erica says.

"Both of you, you mean," Seb says as he holds her tighter.

Erica shakes her head, though, as she shares a heavy look with me.

"No, just Sage."

The panic I felt in the car is nothing compared to what I feel now. I gather Sage's body into my arms, holding her as tightly as I possibly can as I blow out a staggered breath.

"We got the license plate," the guy who took the punch from Seb says. "Police are on their way."

We both nod as Sebastian holds out his hand.

"Thanks, sorry I punched you."

He shrugs. "Would have done the same thing, and if I had to be punched by anyone, it's cool that it was Sebastian Caldwell."

He tries to laugh, but it doesn't land. The four of us just stare at him, causing him to share an awkward look with his buddy. A police car pulls up at the next moment and begins questioning everyone. Sage doesn't say much, she just tells the exact same story as Erica without sharing any extra details.

"He said, 'Leave her, he only wants this one' when he was holding Sage."

"Who is he?" the cop asks Erica.

She shrugs before looking toward a practically catatonic Sage.

"Ma'am, can you tell us anything? Give us a name? Something?"

"No point, you'll never get him," she says numbly.

"We have a lot of resources at our disposal, and you're clearly in danger. Let us help," the cop tries to reason.

Sage's eyes harden as she looks up at him, a hard clamp to her jaw as she speaks.

"Alec Hale. The Snakebacks president of the Sante Fe chapter."

I watch as the cop visibly swallows, and his eyes widen.

"What the fuck does that mean? Who is that?" I ask the cop before facing Sage.

She looks at me but doesn't speak as she shakes her head. My eyes come to Erica who seems to know exactly what I'm thinking. She comes beside Sage, taking my place as I walk over to the cop and take him to the side.

"What's going on? Do you know this guy?"

"Not personally," he says as he jots something down on his notepad.

"What is he? A gangster or something?" I ask.

"The Snakebacks are a national Motorcycle Club, one percenters. No one you want to mess with."

Motorcycle club? What the fuck? Like Sons of Anarchy shit?

"What about Sage? What does it mean he's coming after her like this? What can we do until you catch him?"

The cop huffs out a laugh as he shakes his head.

"I'm afraid it's a hell of a lot trickier than that. We have the license plate the guys gave us, and we will do our best with that lead, but these guys have a reputation, and it isn't for being good citizens with their properties in their name or paying their taxes. We've been trying to nail the Seattle chapter for years with no luck. In my experience, they only come out of the shadows when they are ready to."

"Okay, well why the fuck is this prick biker targeting my girl?" I say, doing my best to keep my fear for Sage under wraps as I get some answers.

"You tell me, she clearly isn't talking to us."

I shake my head as I look over my shoulder to see her staring off into the space in front of her, Erica holding her comfortingly.

"My guess," the cop continues, "is that you're shacking up with a Snakeback president's old lady. Between you and me, if I were you, I'd be getting the hell away from her as fast as possible before you get a target painted on your back."

I turn to face him, disgust filling my face as I sneer at him.

"Not a chance in fucking hell."

The cop shrugs. "Then I'd suggest some private security until we have an update."

"Done," I say before turning on my heel and getting back to my girl.

I'll call a company in a bit, for now, I need to get my girl home and have a serious fucking talk with her.

It's time.

Chapter 39
Sage

Once the police were through with us, Trevor took Erica's car and drove us home since she was definitely not okay to drive. I feel bad. I feel like I should have protected her more, at least comforted her more. I was in fight or flight mode at the time, and then when that passed, a familiar numbness sank into my bones, and it has yet to fade.

When we get home and settled inside, I expect Trevor to start drilling me with questions. Instead, he sits down on the couch beside me, not too close to where I feel crowded but close enough that I know he's beside me. We sit there in silence for I don't know how long, and honestly, it's exactly what I need. He always seems to know exactly what I need exactly when I need it.

Which is why when I turn to face him, he's sitting there quietly, waiting for me once I'm ready to speak.

"So, I have a pretty psycho ex-boyfriend," I say dryly.

I think I was attempting to be funny, but honestly, I don't even laugh. Trevor just stares at me which tells me I need to just get this shit out of me.

"What do you want to know?" I ask.

"Everything. Anything." He pauses before shaking his head. "Where did you even meet a guy like him?"

"Seattle. I was sixteen the first time I met him. He was thirty-two."

"Jesus," Trevor exhales with a shake of his head.

I nod. "It was at a party in a sketchy part of town. I told Dad I was staying the night with a friend, and we snuck out to go. Some college guy my friend was hooking up with was holding the party. Some bikers were there, one was giving me a hard time before one of the guys jumped in, beat his ass, and watched over me for the rest of the night."

Trevor lets me continue, only reaching out and resting his hand on my leg in support.

"Then the next day he showed up outside my school, took me on a ride on his bike. We hooked up that night and became pretty much inseparable."

"At sixteen?" he cuts in with a disgusted shake of his head. "That guy is a fucking predator. Where the fuck was your dad?"

"Busy. Trying to coach up some of the best players in the NFL and no time for a troublemaker daughter."

Trevor shakes his head but doesn't say more.

"Anyway, when I turned eighteen, he got the opportunity to join the Santa Fe chapter. He was just an enforcer up here, but his best friend ran the chapter down south and wanted him to be his VP. So, he packed a bag for me that night, and I left a note for my dad telling him I'd see him around. Dad didn't try to call, and I didn't look back. I know it sounds dumb, but I was happy. He gave a shit about me, took care of me."

"Until?"

"Until we got down there." I look down at my hands, rubbing my fingertips together, mesmerized by the movement. Or maybe it's just better than looking at the disappointment on Trevor's face.

"Everything was fine for a bit. Everyone welcomed us like an arriving king and queen. I even made some friends. My best friend Calista is still down there. She's married to Hammer, their enforcer. I haven't heard from her in a while which should have tipped me off that something wasn't right," I say, finishing my sentence in a whisper.

"What happened when you were down there?" Trevor says, redirecting my train of thought.

"Nothing until some shit went down. The president ended up dying, and Alec lost it. Started dipping his fingers into the product they were pushing, something he never did before. He got mean, violent. Hammer and Calista got really good about hiding me from him when he was at his worst, but one night they couldn't and…"

Trevor's grip on me tightens as I breathe through the painful memories. I look over at him, doing my best to smile as a tear drops down my face.

"Suffice it to say, I got a little messed up. Couldn't walk for almost a week because of my broken ribs. Took me longer to go out in public because of the black eyes I was sporting. I was scared, and I didn't think I had any options until Calista bought me a bus ticket and put me on it, in the middle of the night, when they were off doing a pickup."

"That was back in April. I've been trying to lay low here ever since. When I was here for several months and didn't hear from him, I thought he moved on. Even heard he was spending time with one girl in particular. I thought I was off the hook. Now I realize I was just being naïve."

"Hey, look at me," Trev says, and I blink a few times before realizing I'm staring at a blank wall as I meet his deep blue eyes.

"I'll never let him touch a hair on your head again, you have my word."

I give him a sad smile as I shake my head.

"You can't keep that promise, Trev. I know you want to, and I know you believe it, but you have no idea the reach these guys have."

"Don't give a fuck. I'll send you away if I have to. To the East Coast, Europe. I'll take you as far away as it takes until you're out of his grasp, you hear me?"

"He always gets what he wants," I say almost to myself as I lick away the fallen tear that's smeared across my lips. "And according to his henchmen, what he wants is me."

Trevor's hand leaves my thigh before cupping my jaw.

"Well, he can't have you. You hear me? You're mine, and I'll kill anyone who touches what's mine. We are going to keep you safe. *I'm* going to keep you safe."

The ferocity he says those words with have me almost believing him.

Almost.

"I'm gonna call a private security company. From now on, your ass is locked down. You won't be out of my sight any more than physically required, and when you are, you'll have two men on you. We're gonna get another gate, more cameras, more—"

"You don't have to do all that," I say with a shake of my head.

He looks as if I've slapped him as he reaches over and pulls me into his lap, clasping his hand behind my neck as he speaks.

"Of course I do. You are the most precious thing in the world to me. And I'm going to do anything and everything to not only keep you safe, but make you feel safe. Money doesn't matter, resources don't matter, you are all that matters to me, Sage."

As if he could ease my anxiety with just his words, my breathing comes and goes a little easier as I nod my head softly.

"Okay."

"I love you, babygirl, so fucking much."

I close my eyes, allowing his words to coat me like a balm, to my previously bruised and cracked heart, before I open them to look at him.

"I love you too, Trevor."

The smile that spreads across his face is like nothing I've ever seen as he brings his lips to my own. I lose track of how long we stay like that, wrapped up in each other, whispering promises and declarations of love and what will come after all of this ends.

I don't have the heart to tell him that the ending will no doubt be much more sorrow filled than he's envisioning.

Chapter 40
Trevor

I'm barely even here. I mean, I'm here physically, but mentally? Not a fucking chance. We are playing the Salt Lake City Tigers today, winner moves on to the NFC championships, and I could honestly give fuck all.

"Hey," Slater says, jarring me out of my head as we line up for the next down. "You good?"

I turn my head to the sidelines, making sure for the twentieth time this quarter that she's still there.

"She's good, man. She's safe. You've got a whole team of brothers looking out for her and your two goons are right there in the tunnel. No one is getting to her."

I blow out a breath as I nod my head. I called Precision Security, one of the most extensive security companies in the country, and had two guys on my property within eight hours. They have practically glued themselves to Sage's side since then, which makes the 2k a day more than worth it.

It's been a little over a week since Sage and Erica were attacked. The police couldn't turn up shit with the license plate. Guess it was a stolen van that was wiped clean of prints and found in a ditch a few days after. They know where the Seattle chapter's clubhouse is, but without more solid evidence, they can't do shit.

Delcan and Slater both tried to come by the house to check on us once they heard but Sage needed the time away from people to just be, so I told them to hold off. She's too strong for their pity. She doesn't need or want it. I can see how on edge she is, though. The way she jumps when I shut the fridge too hard or how she has to turn every light on in the house when she needs a drink of water. She's terrified, and I fucking hate that I can't ease that fear for her. The only thing that will is getting this Alec guy behind bars, and I'm working on that too, but this stuff takes time, unfortunately.

When I asked Sage if she thought Alec was responsible for her break-in months ago, she cringed and shrugged. She said the idea had crossed her mind, but she wanted to believe it wasn't. I still don't have all the facts, so I'm not sure what to connect yet, but it's obvious to me this guy never forgot about Sage. He was just biding his time.

Her dad heard about the altercation somehow, and the bastard actually seemed concerned, asking if there was anything he could do to help. I took way too much joy in telling him I was more than capable of protecting her unlike some. I ran a fuck ton of lines that day, but it was worth it. Fucking prick.

The ball is tossed into my hands, and I have to blink out of the heavy thoughts plaguing my mind as I scan the field. I find Seb trying to break free of his man before I look to the other side and see Slater spin around the guy covering him. I toss the ball to Slater just before I'm taken down.

When I pop back up, I watch as Slater crosses over into the end zone. Fuck yes. I look up at the scoreboard to see that the game only has five seconds left and the clock runs out. The final score is 27-13. Looks like we are going to the NFC championship.

I run over to the sidelines, wrapping Sage into my arms before she presses her lips against mine.

"Nice toss, QB." She smiles.

"Thanks, Raven." I smirk before setting her down.

Everyone around us is going wild, bouncing around excitedly as family and friends filter onto the field. I've got my family right here and my friends I can celebrate with later, so when I set Sage down, I wrap her hand in mine and start walking toward the exit. I'm not even going to attempt to get changed and leave Sage outside all by herself, apart from her two bodyguards I guess, so I figured that can be taken care of when we get back to the house.

"Isn't Dad gonna be pissed if you don't stay for the after-game huddle?"

I roll my eyes at her.

"Your dad can choke on a fucking dick."

"Like father like daughter, I guess," she nods in agreement.

I bark out a laugh as I swat her ass.

"Don't make promises you don't intend on fulfilling."

"Well, it's your job to do the filling."

A muffled snort comes from behind us, and I turn to see one of her body-guards, Jake, covering a laugh.

"It's okay, you can laugh. She's crude but hilarious."

"They know. I have this game to see how red I can make their faces. Jake loses every time. Meanwhile Alberto is like a fucking palace guard," she says, gesturing to her surlier guard.

"They are not here for your enjoyment. Leave them alone," I say with a sigh.

"Well someone has to lighten the mood. It's depressing to think they are only hanging out with me so I don't end up dead or kidnapped."

I frown at her words, tensing at even the thought of it, which causes her teasing smile to fall.

"Hey, I'm kidding. I'm sorry. I'm just trying to cope, and you know the funniest part of me comes from all of my trauma."

Shaking my head, I kiss her temple. "I guess whatever makes you feel better."

"What would make me feel better is your head between my legs and a few dozen orgasms. Think you can make that happen?" she taunts as we walk out to the parking lot where Alberto gets in the driver's seat while Jake holds the door open for us.

"Well, our flight isn't for another eleven hours. I'd say I'm up to the challenge."

Chapter 41
Sage

Once we got home, we're barely inside the house for ten seconds before it hits. That intuition that every woman gets before the actual feeling of what comes next. I change directions, heading straight for the hallway bathroom and curse when I confirm.

Shark week.

Thankfully, I have some tampons stashed in here and am able to take care of that side of things, but I know the cramps, bloating, and overall misery will set in soon enough.

When I make my way out of the bathroom, Trevor is leaning against the kitchen island shooting off a text when he smiles and turns to face me. One look at my pout has his eyebrows dipping.

"What's wrong?"

"My uterus is being a psycho bitch because I didn't give her a baby so she's making herself bleed."

Trevor blinks several times before he nods.

"You're on your period."

"Isn't that what I just said?"

"Not even remotely, but that's okay. I'll get the provisions," he says as he fires up the tea kettle while grabbing most of my go-to snacks.

In less than two minutes, Trevor's arms are full with an electric blanket, heating pad and snacks. I can't help but laugh at him as he gives me a soft smile.

"Couch or bed?"

"Couch," I say as I walk over with him, sitting down before he practically buries me alive.

"Thank you, Trev."

He rolls his eyes like it's a given before grabbing his keys.

"Where are you going? We just got home."

"Let's be real, if not tonight at some point you're going to want movie popcorn. So I'm saving myself the trip for later."

"Isn't that why we have henchmen now? Have them do it."

Trevor laughs and shakes his head.

"We have them to keep you safe. They are in their car outside if you need anything. I'll be back in fifteen."

He comes over to give me a kiss when I make him pause, smiling up at him as I wrap my hand around the back of his neck.

"You're too good to me, you know that, right?"

"Definitely not. You deserve a hell of a lot better than I can give you, but I'm gonna do my best to try to be worthy of you."

Butterflies still manage to race through me, even after the months we've been together, and I can't help but grin as he presses his lips against mine. He gives me a series of short pecks that have me giggling and him winking.

"Be right back."

I wave to him as I grab the remote and flip something onto the TV. I'm only watching the screen for a few minutes when my phone starts ringing. I grab it and pause momentarily when I see who is calling me. I answer it quickly, my pulse skyrocketing as I speak.

"Calista?" I ask.

"Hey sweetie," she says, a watery sound to her voice.

"Where have you been? I haven't heard from you in weeks! What's going on down there."

I hear her let out a staggered breath before a door shuts, and she speaks in a hushed tone.

"We aren't in Santa Fe."

"Okay? Where are you?"

"On the road somewhere outside San Antonio. Shit went down about a month ago. I was laying low, not reaching out much because he almost caught me on the phone with you. I didn't want to risk it but then out of nowhere he flipped a switch. It was like he sobered up enough finally to realize you were gone and went ballistic.

"He killed a prospect, beat me to shit because I told him I didn't know anything and almost killed Hammer. He shot him right in the gut and somehow that big oaf was still able to fireman carry me out of there. We got on our bikes and rode until he couldn't sit up any longer. He had to have surgery, and when we were discharged, we kept driving some more."

"Holy fucking shit. Are you guys okay?"

"We're fine, it's you that I'm worried about. I think he's gonna be coming for you."

"Yeah, I kinda figured when a couple of goons tried to grab me the other day."

"Shit. I should have called sooner. I'm so sorry."

"It's okay. Trevor's house is like a fucking fortress, and he hired two muscle men to watch over me until this shit dies down."

"Who is Trevor?"

I let out a laugh. Holy shit, has my life changed over the last few months.

"Remember that quarterback I told you about?"

"The super douche?"

I can't help but cackle at that.

"That's the one. Well, I sorta love him now."

"Sorta?" she echoes.

I nod even though she can't see me. "And we're dating. Er, I guess that's a little too casual. If he was a biker, I'd already be wearing his cut by now."

"No shit? You settled down with a richy-rich preppy boy?"

Smirking, I look around the house as I shake my head.

"Yeah, I guess I did."

Before she can say more, a piercing sound goes off in the house. I stand up instantly, my stomach instantly turning as I walk to the security room. It has all the camera footage and alarm data for the house inside like something out of an action movie. I look over to the front gate camera when my mouth drops open, and the world around me stills for a moment.

"Oh fuck."

Chapter 42
Trevor

I have to drive with my hand on the bucket as I turn down the road to my house. I love Sage more than anything, but if my leather seats get ruined because of her buttery as sin popcorn, I'm gonna be fucking pissed.

When I pull up to the gate, I roll down the window, ready to enter the code when I freeze.

The fuck?

The gate is already open. I know it shut behind me. It's automatic. Pulling forward, I park beside Alberto's car, throwing the door open before I run over to them.

"Dude, what the fuck? Why the hell is the—"

My words die on my tongue when I look inside the car. Alberto is passed out against the steering wheel, a trickle of blood running down his face while Jake lays in front of the vehicle, gripping his stomach and wincing in pain.

"What happened?" I ask quickly as I rush over to him.

"Four or five guys came out of nowhere," he grits out. "They didn't come through the gate. They were either already here or jumped the fence. They got her," he says as he pulls his hand away from his stomach to reveal a seeping knife wound.

"Got who?" I ask, refusing to believe what I think he just said.

The look on his face though has me running toward the house as fast as I can. The closer I get, the louder I can hear the alarm going off, which means the cops should be here any minute. C'mon, baby. Tell me you're hiding somewhere.

When I get to the front door, I notice it's wide open and the house is fucking trashed. The couch is tipped over, the glass table shattered as well as broken pieces of a vase with a pool of blood beside it. Fear sinks into me like nothing I've ever felt.

"Sage! SAGE! Where are you, baby? It's me! Come on out, baby. They're gone!" I shout wildly, praying to fucking god I hear her sweet voice, but I'm only met with the piercing screech of the alarm.

I dart over to the monitor room, logging in quickly and rewinding it back to when I left. I skim past as I watch Sage take a phone call before the front camera shows several guys jumping the fence before ripping the wiring out of the gate and opening it for a van.

I watch the altercation go down of a guy sneaking up to the driver's side window and bashing Alberto's face against the wheel repeatedly. Jake gets out and draws his gun, but two guys surround him, one knocking his gun out of his hand while the other stabs him and leaves him for dead.

Then they turn simultaneously for the house and dread clenches my chest. I move my attention to the interior cameras, watching as Sage takes off up the stairs just as the front door is opened, four men spreading out in search of her. Fuck. Fuck. Fuck.

She dips into the bedroom, but they've already seen her and seconds later, she's being dragged out, her fingernails literally digging into the floors.

"No, no, no," I mutter as I intently watch the footage, cataloging each of their faces so I'll know exactly who to fucking kill when I find them.

Sage is able to kick free of one of their holds as another comes and kicks her in the side. Her back bends backward before she curls in on herself from the painful blow. Son of a fucking bitch. I can't watch this. Squeezing my eyes shut, I shake my head before forcing myself to open them again. I have to know every single detail possible if I'm going to find her.

When I reopen them, I don't see them on the top-floor camera anymore. I scan over the others to find them in the living room. Sage is bucking against a man who is holding her from behind before she's able to break his grasp on her. She uses her newfound freedom to grab the vase sitting on the table and smashes it against the guy's head, causing blood to pour from his wound and all over the floor.

A little relief fills me knowing that it wasn't her blood in the middle of the hallway. That relief dies though when I watch a larger man grab Sage by the throat and throws her back on top of the glass table. The glass shatters on impact instantly, and she doesn't move once she's on the ground. No matter how hard I try to zoom in, I can't tell if her eyes are open, but when she is lifted up and thrown over a guy's shoulder, there is a small blood pool where her head was that scares the living fuck out of me.

I try to continue tracking them, watching as they carry a limp Sage out the door like they were going for a fucking evening night stroll. They walk past a curled-up Jake and a passed-out Alberto before getting in the van and driving away. I grab the license plate, memorizing it instantly as I grab my jacket and head outside.

When I step through the door, I run right into a police officer who draws his gun.

"Whoa, where are you going?"

"To find the woman you should have put more effort into protecting," I seethe, my anger boiling just near the surface.

"Mr. Michaels, I'm gonna need you to calm down. Let's go sit, and we can go over everything."

"If I go sit down, she could be dead before we are done. Video footage of it all is through the second door on your left," I say as I shoulder check him, rushing out the door and past several other police officers and an ambulance that is just now arriving.

A police officer is helping Alberto come to, and another is pressing something to Jake's wound. I should feel bad that I didn't help them. Taking a minute to help them wouldn't make her any less gone. But for a while now and till the end of time, my sole focus in life will always be Sage, and right now she needs me.

I need to figure out where the fuck they went from here, but I don't know how. I feel out of my depth here, I'm freaking the fuck out, and I know I'm running out of time. She is running out of time. So, I call the one person I'd never expect help from and hope to God he shows me mercy.

"Seb?" I ask.

"What's up?"

I open my mouth to speak before the words really sink in.

"They got her."

The line is dead silent for several seconds before rustling sounds in the background, and I hear the start of an engine.

"I'll be at your place in five."

With that, he hangs up, and I'm left staring at the dark end of my driveway, horrific thoughts flashing in my mind about what Sage must be going through right now. I couldn't have been standing here for longer than three minutes before Sebastian's Suburban pulls in, which is impressive since he is at least a ten to twelve minute drive away.

When he pulls in, it's not just the driver's door that opens. The passenger side and rear doors open as well, revealing Slater and Declan.

"What are you all doing here?"

"We're here to help," Declan says as he pulls out his phone.

"Give me as much info as you can. Did you see them take her?"

I wince as I nod. "On my cameras. I left for ten minutes to get her something, and when I came back, the personal security I hired had been beaten to shit, and she was...gone."

"Did you catch a plate in the video?"

I nod as I repeat it to Declan who begins jotting it down before stepping away. He's dealt with law enforcement a few times when it came to the whole battle over their oldest, and he's also worked with a private investigator for the same case. I don't know what either of those will do right now, but I'm not about to turn away willing help.

I feel a pair of arms wrap around me and look to see Slater squeezing me so hard, I'm not sure if he's trying to hurt me or comfort me. I try to push him away, but he only holds tighter.

"Fall apart, Trev. It's okay to be scared right this second, but when I let go, you're gonna bury it all, and we are gonna go find your girl, okay?"

I squeeze him back, more so because I don't know what to do with this coursing feeling inside of me. It's panic and rage and true gut-wrenching fear all entangled into one. I let out shuddering breaths as I try to regain my composure. Slater's right, me freaking the fuck out isn't going to help find her quicker. We all need to keep our heads on straight.

When I nod, I feel Slater squeeze me one more time before moving away.

"You good?"

I nod for a moment before shaking my head.

"They're armed, obviously. I don't know what I'm gonna do if I even find her. Look at us, we're a bunch of pro football players. We aren't the fucking A-team. We can't roll into a place, guns blazing."

"Mikey and I are packing," Seb says as he lifts up his shirt to reveal a gun tucked into his waistband.

Declan gets off the phone as he nods coming up to us.

"Always."

"What the fuck? Why?" I ask.

Declan gives me a look like I'm ridiculous as he shakes his head.

"You do remember I was born and raised in the south, right?"

"Well fine, what's your excuse," I say to Seb.

"I bought it in case I ever needed to kill you for touching Erica," he says flatly.

I frown at that. "I can't tell if you're being sarcastic or not."

Seb shrugs but doesn't answer. Yeah, I'm not sure he's as level headed as we all assume. I think out of all of us, he should definitely not have a gun.

"Just got off the phone with a friend at the police department. They have the plate, and they are going to track it until they stop."

"So, what until then? We just wait?" I say, equal parts defeated and frustrated.

Declan shrugs but gives me a small nod.

"It's alright. We will wait for Mikey's contact to get back to us, get an address, get the bad guys, and save the girl!" Slater cheers, like this is a fucking game.

"Slater," Seb's irritated voice growls.

"What? I'm the comedic relief of the group. You should know this by now."

I push past him, climbing into the passenger seat while Seb gets in the driver's seat. Slater and Declan get in the back, all of us waiting for Declan's phone to go off.

I try to stay focused, stay positive. If I let my mind go to the dark place of what could be happening right now, I won't make it to her. I have to pull my shit together, for her sake and my own.

I'm coming, baby. I'm coming.

Chapter 43
Sage

The beating of my heart is the first thing I hear, or maybe it's the first thing I feel. It pounds in my head like a hammer over and over again. This is worse than the most lethal hangover I've ever had.

A cool drip constantly hits against my shoulder, causing me to turn my limp neck to the side. Shit, that's blood. That's not good. Flashes of the last things I remember flicker before my eyes. The men storming into the house, me trying to fight back and inadvertently losing.

I look around, fully taking in my surroundings, when I notice that I'm tied to a chair, my hands behind my back and my feet roped together. Could they be any more cliché?

I'm in some old bedroom with all the lights off, I see a twin bed in the corner and a plain wooden side table. Other than that, the room is empty apart from a chair in the corner. The window on the wall tells me it's still nighttime with only a thin stream of moonlight pouring through the window, so at least I haven't been knocked out for too long, assuming it's still Monday.

The door opens, and a tattooed man pokes his head in before whispering behind him into the hallway.

"She's awake."

A rush of fear clenches my stomach, forcing me to hold my breath as the man disappears from the doorway, and a new man appears in his place, shutting the door behind him. It's a familiar man, one who I never thought I'd see again. Or at least, I hoped I never would.

It's funny, being with someone for years who you think you know inside and out, until one day you wake up beside them and have no clue who you're asleep next to, or what they are capable of.

He looks different. It's only been about nine months, but in that time, he looks older, more haggard. He looks every bit the biker Prez that he is, and I spot more than a few new tattoo pieces crawling up his neck apart from the required snake tattoo that is reserved for the column of the neck right over his Adam's apple.

The fear I have for this man isn't for him solely. It's for what he's capable of, for what I feared he would do if he ever found me. I never in my wildest dreams thought that if he did find me and catch me, that he would give me the adoring smile he is right now.

"Hey, firecracker. It's been a while," he says, a soft lilt to his voice as he looks at me like I'm a daydream come true.

I do my best to hide my surprise and confusion. If he wants to be pleasant, I'll play his game until I can figure out how the hell to get out of here.

"Yeah, Alec. How are you?"

"Better now," he says as he takes several steps toward me before reaching out his hand, running his fingers over my face. I wince when he touches my upper cheek, and a thunderous look crosses his face when he inspects the blood on his fingers.

Fuck, when that guy punched me, he must have split me open. Fucker.

"Don't worry, firecracker. I'll kill him before the night is up."

"Didn't you want this, though?" I can't help but ask.

He frowns and shakes his head as he pushes some of my hair out of my face, running his fingers through it like I used to love. Now the motion sends a chill down my spine.

"I never told them to hurt you. I told them to bring you back to me, but not to harm you."

"Yeah, well, the blood dripping down my shoulder doesn't reflect that," I snark.

I can tell he wants to smile at my sass. He always told me it's why he called me a firecracker because I was small and snappy. It was always his favorite.

"I'm so sorry, baby. Do you want to kill him?"

For a moment, I almost think I see the Alec I fell in love with. But the way his eyes spark to life when he says the word kill tells me he's so far gone from that person. I mull over his offer though, if I was going to kill this guy, he'd give me a weapon. A weapon I could use to get out of here.

"Sure. Can you cut me loose?" I ask as I wiggle at my restraints.

He smiles sweetly at me as he shakes his head.

"Not yet. My men told me you were a little violent, and I know you don't cool down that easily. Besides, I haven't forgotten how you left me."

Shit. This is not a good direction.

"Why would you do that, firecracker? We were so happy. We were going to get married, have a baby. Why would you leave?" he asks, his voice becoming more manic with every word.

"I didn't think you missed me. I heard you were fucking Britt after I left. Where is she at?"

That earns me a slap across the face, of course, right across the open cut that has my eyes watering and my teeth sinking into my lip as I bite back my squeal.

"Don't you dare speak to me like that," he says, pointing his finger in my face and truly showcasing how fucking insane he's become.

"She was nothing but a whore to get lost in while I tried to find you. I knew you hated Seattle. I didn't think there was a chance in hell that you'd come back here. But then when I found out your dad had leased a new condo without selling his house, I knew it had to be for you."

I nod more to myself than anything as I confirm what I've honestly suspected from the beginning but didn't want to admit.

"So, you're behind the break-in?"

He shrugs. "It was Pyro's men. He was gracious enough to send a few over while I handled some business in Santa Fe. Gotta say, I'm more than a little surprised that didn't send you running home to me," he says as he runs a hand through his greasy black hair.

I don't speak as he continues, a dangerous glint in his eye as he watches me.

"Then again, I guess you didn't need to when you found a cushy place to stay at the football player's house."

The mention of Trevor on his lips has fear running through me. Of course he already knows everything about Trevor. He knows that we've been together for a while, and he probably already has men after him as we speak. Dear God, I hope he came back to the house and ran like hell. If they find him...I can't even stomach thinking about it.

Alec's fingers dance down my neck before wrapping around it, squeezing tightly enough to show he holds all the power but not so much that I can't breathe.

"That hurt my feelings a lot when I saw the pictures of you two together."

"What pictures?" I ask evenly.

He smiles and shakes his head.

"C'mon, firecracker. You're smarter than that. You think I would have my men take you out of nowhere without assessing my surroundings? I didn't even step foot in Washington until I knew all about Trevor Michaels or Erica Caldwell, Sebastian Caldwell, Slater and Scarlett Santos, and Declan and Vi Daniels. Even the Caldwells' cute twins, Daphne and Rosalie. They seem to have taken a liking to you. I always knew you were going to make a great mother."

I do my best not to let my panic show as I keep my breathing even.

"I get it, Alec. You've been watching me. I'm sorry I left. I was scared. You hurt me," I say, straining to put extra emotion into my sentence.

I have a better chance of appealing to him if I tell him I was scared to be hurt than sick of his psychotic, sociopathic bullshit and him beating the living hell out of me was the last straw. His weakness is me. It always has been. Even after he beat me and came down from his high, he couldn't look at me for days, shame twisting him inside out. I think he truly loves me. I just think this lifestyle combined with the meth has finally gotten to him.

He winces at my words as he brings his forehead to my own, sliding his hand from my throat to the back of my neck to keep me in place.

"I know. I'm so sorry, firecracker. But I won't hurt you again. You're always safe with me. You know that, right?" he practically begs.

God, he's so fucking off his rocker.

"Yeah, baby. I know," I say as I close my eyes like I'm fighting back the tears. "When can we go home? I just want to go home," I say as I nuzzle my head into the crook of his neck.

He latches onto the bait like a fish on a hook. He pulls away, angling my head up slightly before crushing his lips to mine. The foul taste of cheap whiskey, cigarettes, and bad breath invade my mouth, and it takes everything in me not to puke. But I put on a show, act like I've never enjoyed anything more as he pulls away.

"Soon. I just need to tie up some loose ends first."

With that, he walks out the door, shutting it behind him and plunging me back into the darkness of the room. I try to wiggle my hands free, but it's no use. Whoever tied me up did a good fucking job. Too good. Fuck, fuck, fuck.

Trevor obviously made it home by now—he had to have. He will have, no doubt, walked in on what looks more like a warzone than his living room. I tried. I fought with everything I had, and it wasn't enough. Now he has me and a deep vile feeling sinks into my stomach as to what my fate has become, what lies in wait for me.

Chapter 44
Sage

I don't know how much time passes before the door opens up once more, a new face I haven't seen yet stepping inside. He's a younger guy, probably around my age if not a little younger. The prospect patch on his vest clues me in immediately to what his place is here.

"You a prospect for Seattle or Santa Fe?" I ask.

He looks surprised that I'm willingly talking to him before he answers.

"Seattle."

I nod like I'm interested. "What's your name?"

"Chris."

"I'm Sage," I say with a soft bat of my eyelashes that seems to hook him instantly.

His eyes can hardly leave mine as I continue.

"You know you're too cute to be hanging around these guys."

A crooked smile spreads across his face before he ducks his head and rubs the back of his neck nervously. My god, the kid is practically a child. There is no way he'll ever get patched in.

"Yeah?" he asks with that smile as he takes a few steps toward me.

I bite the inside of my lower lip as I let my eyes roam over him in what seems like appraisal.

"Mhmm. Do they take care of you? As well as they can for a prospect?" I ask, arching my back just barely, his eyes snapping to my pushed-out chest as he swallows.

"Sure. Yeah," he says over another swallow as he glances to the open doorway behind him.

I nod before looking down at my feet and back up underneath my eyelashes. "All of your needs?"

The husky lull of my voice seems to be just what he needed to hear as I watch him adjust his stance and tuck his hardening dick to the side. He takes another step toward me, I think subconsciously before he gets a little braver, bracing his hands on either side of my chair as he leans down face to face with me.

"Why, you offering?"

I feign a shy smile before looking up at him, letting my lips hover over his as I speak.

"Definitely. Want to free up my hands so I can put them to better use? I promise you won't be disappointed."

He curses under his breath before looking over his shoulder once more and nodding.

"We gotta be quick," he says, as he reaches behind the chair and grabs the rope.

Excitement runs through me. I can't believe he is actually falling for it. I can practically feel the adrenaline buzzing through my veins as I map out my next move. Once he's undone my hands, I just need to take him down long enough to take off the rope around my feet and get the hell out of here.

When I feel the sharp fraying of the rope freed from my wrists, I let out a steady breath when he grips the back of my head, holding it in place as he begins undoing his pants. Before I can even make my move, though, he's being ripped away from me, his grip on my hair falling instantly as a heaving Alec stands over him. He rains down punch after punch on the kid, and I know this is the only shot I have.

My hands scramble to my feet, desperately untying the knot as fast as possible as the sound of flesh beating flesh echoes through the musty, dark room. I feel my heart thundering so loudly I'm not sure if I'm hearing my heartbeat or Alec's fists.

When the rope falls loosely around my ankles, I could cry in relief as I stand and dart forward. Unfortunately I only make it a few feet before a searing hot pain rips through my skull, yanking me backward before I land on the floor with a loud smack.

Alec's grip tightens, and I feel my scalp burning as he drags me across the room until I'm lying next to the bleeding, unmoving prospect. Fuck. He's dead.

"You fucking WHORE!" Alec roars into my face. "You think you can leave me? You think you can run from me? Not again! You are fucking MINE!"

The steel boot that drives into my stomach takes me by surprise, knocking the wind out of me as he repeats the move again and again before I feel the solid connection of his fist to my cheek. I see stars as he continues again and again, the sound of his consistent hits becoming a dull melody as my vision dulls, and the world around me turns black.

A sharp sting across my face rouses me. I blink hard for several seconds, struggling to open my eyes as a thick liquid cakes my eyelashes.

"Wake up, bitch," Alec's low voice sneers.

I can hardly react as pain radiates from head to toe as Alec moves behind me where I'm apparently sitting in a chair once more. I hear the flick of his blade before it slices through the rope tying my hands together.

"Wake up. We're leaving. Now," he says, freeing my feet next before forcing me to stand.

I do my best to go with him, but I crumble almost instantly. Goddamn it. I think that motherfucker broke my ribs.

"Get up! Hurry, Sage!" Alec practically roars.

"Ribs," I wheeze.

Understanding passes over his face before he rolls his eyes and tosses me over his shoulder like a sack of potatoes. I whimper at the impact it has on my already burning ribs as he smacks my ass.

"Shut the fuck up and keep quiet. They're here."

"Who?" I rasp, my mind foggy and whirling as I try to make sense of his words.

"Your little ball-playing boytoy and his friends. Don't worry, baby. They won't be leaving here alive."

Chapter 45
Trevor

"This is fucking stupid," Declan says again. "The police are on their way. We know where they are, we will follow them if they leave. We can't go in there guns blazing!"

"Why the fuck not?" I snap.

"Well, for starters, we only have two guns?" he fires back. "And I don't know about Seb, but mine is for self-defense only. I don't particularly want to seek out murdering people tonight. Jail doesn't sound like a good time to me."

It took Declan's contact almost three hours to get back to him with an address. Three fucking hours. We were already in the car, and we arrived at this piece of shit shack house in less than fifteen minutes. Apparently it's a safe house for the Snakebacks MC.

I've never felt so out of control than I have in these last three hours. I feel like the whole world is caving in on me and I can't fucking sit and wait any longer. If Declan wants to be a little bitch and wait for the police, he can do that. But it isn't his entire life that was taken and having god knows what done to her in that house.

"Fuck it. Fine. Be a pussy, stay here. I'm going to get my girl," I say as I practically kick the door open before slamming it shut.

I walk around the side of the car to find Sebastian doing the same. I open my mouth to question him when he grips my shoulder.

"I got you."

Seb doesn't say much, even when he didn't hate my guts. He doesn't have to, though, for people to know what he means. I give him a thankful nod as two other car doors open and close. Declan and Slater stand behind me, though the former is still shaking his head like this is a bad idea, before we creep up to the side of the house. There is only a van and two bikes parked out front so there can't be too many guys here. Six at most.

On the front porch, two guys are smoking cigarettes and bullshitting about fuck knows what. Seb and I look at each other before nodding as we climb up the side of the porch. As soon as our feet hit the wood, the two goons' eyes shift to us. I grab the first guy, driving my fist into his jaw as Seb grabs the other in a sleeper hold almost immediately.

The guy tries to fight against Seb, but he has almost a solid foot on him, and in his current position, he's basically incapacitated. Meanwhile, my guy throws a punch that I barely miss before I deliver one to his ribs. He groans out and reaches for what I'm assuming is a gun in the back of his pants when Slater comes out of nowhere, tackling him like a defensive lineman before wrangling him for the gun. Slater takes the gun and pistol whips the guy, effectively knocking him out before standing up.

He smiles at me pridefully as he admires the gun.

"I've always wanted to try that."

We look over to see Sebastian waiting for us, his guy already passed out at his feet. Forgot we had a trailer park scrapper on our side. Declan is standing at the end of the stairs, looking toward the street, no doubt waiting for police that I swear to God are not coming before he nods defeatedly and gestures toward the door.

The guys all hold their guns at the ready, because who the fuck knows what's on the other side of that door. I'm the only one unarmed but that's okay. The amount of fucking fury I have right now is enough to hold my own against anyone who crosses my path.

Seb throws the door open going left, while Slater goes right, and Declan comes up the middle. Three guys are sitting in the living room on the couch watching TV when their eyes swing to us. One of the guys reaches for his gun on the table, but Sebastian is faster. He slaps the gun to the other side of the room before driving his elbow into the guy's temple.

Meanwhile, Slater ends up in a fistfight with the guy in the La-Z-Boy chair as Declan pins the last guy to the ground, driving his meaty fists into him over and over again. Fucking hell. Who knew my friends were such badasses.

Grabbing the gun Sebastian pushed away, I glance at it to make sure the safety is off. I've only shot guns once at a range when I was a teenager, and I'll be honest, I don't know what the fuck I'm doing, but I figure it's better to at least hold it than to walk deeper into the house empty-handed.

I check each room quickly, coming up empty with every one. I'm starting to think she's not here when I see a figure running toward the backyard, a body over their shoulder. My heart seizes in my chest at that.

Sage.

"Hey!" I roar, causing who I assume to be Alec to look over his shoulder at me.

He pulls out a gun from his side and begins shooting aimlessly. Sage's head pops up, eyes full of terror as she screams.

"NO! RUN, TREV! RUN!"

I duck into a side room as I hear Alec fire off six shots before they stop. I'm hoping that means he's out of bullets for now, so I dip back into the hallway to find it empty and the back door open. I tear through the old house, running out into the cool night air to find Sage and Alec fighting.

Sage kicks the side of his knee, causing him to stumble as he goes down. He grabs a fistful of her hair as he does, and they end up in the grass, his hands around her throat.

I run at him at full speed. I may not be a two-hundred-plus-pound linebacker like Declan, but I might as well be with how hard I hit Alec. He falls off Sage as we end up in a tangle. I throw a punch at him that lands then he delivers one right back at me, before he manages his way on top of me.

I feel Sage trying to pull him off me before he swings back and hits her across the face. My vision instantly goes white. Not red. Not black. Blinding fucking white. Swinging my head forward, I headbutt him across the bridge of the nose, causing the thing to crack in a sickening way as I fight like a wild animal, punching, kicking, and hitting him anywhere I can.

"You piece of fucking shit!" I roar as I continue my assault.

Alec, in a daze, shakes it off as he spits a glob of blood into my face and smiles.

"Say good night, pretty boy," before pressing a cool metal barrel against my temple.

I feel panic run through me, not at the fact that there is a gun to my head, that these may be my last moments, but because I don't know what will happen to Sage once he kills me. I won't be able to save her, to protect her. The thought of what would come next for her is far more terrifying than the lights going out for me.

"Good night," Seb's deep vibrato sounds out from above us as he holds the gun to Alec's head.

He freezes just as the sound of sirens ring out in the late-night air.

'Bout fucking time.

In seconds, Slater and Declan along with a couple of police officers are running into the backyard before taking over Sebastian's spot. Alec stares at me in a menacing way that is completely unhinged, but I don't give a fuck about him.

Sage practically jumps on me in the next minute as she runs her fingers over my face and begins patting my body down for injuries.

"You stupid, stupid man. What the hell were you thinking? Who do you think you are, Liam Neeson?"

I let out a laugh that hurts a little as I wrap my arm around her.

"The A-team, babygirl."

"More like the C-team. He was kicking your ass."

Scoffing at that, I shake my head as I look up into those watery purple eyes. Blood is smeared across her face, bruising already blooming across her cheek.

"I'm so sorry I let this happen," I say ashamedly.

"Sorry? You're a rich, pretty boy, NFL player who just busted into a biker gang hideout to save me. You're so fucking dumb, but I love you so much for it."

She presses her lips against mine before laying fully on top of me. I wrap my arms tightly around her, vowing to never let her out of my sight again however unrealistic that may seem. At the very least, I never want to spend a day without her. She so quickly became my whole world, and I know I could never fucking function without her, and I hope to God I never have to.

Her tongue tangles against my own as we deepen the kiss when I hear Slater speak.

"Fuck, think we're gonna get thank you kisses like that when they're done? I think I'll have to call Scarlett to get permission first."

I tear my mouth away from hers, practically growling at him.

"Fuck off!"

Slater and Declan chuckle while Seb just rolls his eyes and shakes his head. Several more police cars show up and even a few paramedics. Slater is sporting the start of a nice black eye, and I have a few marks myself, but out of all of us, Sage looks to be the worst off which fills me with an insurmountable amount of guilt.

They patch her up as best as they can while we gave our statements but told us she needed to go to the hospital for some scans just in case. The cops promise that Alec will be locked up for a long time, but I'm not taking any chances. I'm going to be making some calls and ensuring the best possible prosecutor is on the case, no matter the cost.

When we are all free to go, Sage and I go to get into the ambulance while the guys get into the car, each giving her a tender hug before they leave. Slater and Declan hug me before making their way to the car. Seb pats my shoulder and tries to move past when I stop him.

"Hey."

He turns as I hold out my hand for him. He pauses for a moment, staring at it before he slowly takes it, shaking my hand before I pull him into a hug. He slaps my back as I slap his, and we stay like that for several seconds before he pulls away.

"Thank you, man."

He nods. "I got you, Trev."

That does something to me, heals a once-broken bond, one that I broke. The thing is about breaks, they never grow back the same, but sometimes they grow back stronger.

Seb gets into the car, and they slowly drive away as I get into the ambulance, where Sage is already waiting for me. I come to sit next to her when she reaches out for my hand.

"T-thank you, for coming for me. I didn't want you to. I wanted you to keep yourself safe, but if you hadn't, I—"

"Hey, hey, shhh," I say as I get down on my knees to be beside her. "There isn't a reality where I wouldn't ever come for you. You're mine, Raven, and I'm never letting go."

Chapter 46
Trevor
Epilogue

The roar of a crowd at a Super Bowl is unlike anything you've ever experienced. Some people wait their whole lives to experience one, whether as a fan, a coach, or a player. Others have been blessed to experience multiples, like me. Either blessed or incredibly talented. I think both fit the bill personally.

We miraculously won the NFC championship, by a single fucking point, despite me, Declan, Seb, and Slater all being temporarily suspended for our 'questionable actions' the Monday night before the game. With enough explanation, testimonies from the police, and a phone call from each of our lawyers, the committee allowed us to be reinstated for the Super Bowl.

We are in San Antonio playing and wouldn't you know it? We're playing my old team, the Cobras. I have nothing but respect for all the coaching staff and the players, but it fucking sucks for them because I know how each and every one operates.

The ball is tossed into my hands as I look to my left where Slater is being typical Slater Santos and outrunning every motherfucker on the field, then I look to my right where Sebastian is at least five inches taller than the man covering him. Both are solid options, but we have one minute left in the fourth quarter, and we're all tied up. So, no offense to Slater, I throw it to the person who I know will catch it no matter what. The person who knows where I'm going to throw something before I even do.

The ball lands in Sebastian's outstretched hands perfectly as he turns and runs the remaining fifteen yards to the end zone.

Touchdown.

A feeling basks over me that is so euphoric I can't help but lift my hands to the sky. The stadium goes wild despite the home team losing as the Crusaders fans practically tear the place apart. One voice on the sidelines is louder than the masses, at least to me.

Sage, broken ribs and all is running, well, hobbling, toward me from the sidelines.

When we went to the hospital, they confirmed that she had three broken ribs and some bruising. They did a full work-up of her head, and she came back clean, thankfully. The doctor suggested lots of rest and absolutely no traveling, but have you ever tried to tell her what to do? When I told her she had to stay home and couldn't come to the Super Bowl, you'd think I told her that I was going to massacre all of the puppies in the world.

Alec is in jail along with the goons who kidnapped her. They are all awaiting trial, but the prosecuting lawyer who I may or may not have bribed to take the case says that Alec is facing life, and his men are looking at ten to twenty years at least. I guess Erica and Seb joined in on pressing charges against the men since they technically could have kidnapped Erica. It's a stretch but anything to stick it to these fuckers.

Sage told me it wasn't a good idea for her to press charges because other members could retaliate, but I didn't budge. We need to do everything in our power to ensure he never sees the light of day again, and it starts with her.

Once her dad found out about everything that happened that night, surprising the hell out of all of us, he broke down. He sobbed, begging Sage to forgive him for all the years he had been a shit father. Told her how terrified he was to hear the news and how glad he is that she's okay. I don't think she really knew how to take his shift in attitude.

I can tell she wants a relationship with him but isn't sure where to start. I told her I would support her with whatever that means. I'd kill my contract with the Crusaders if she didn't want to continue to see him. I'd quit the league if she wanted to leave it all behind and start somewhere new, to which she gave me the strangest look as if that wasn't even an option on the table.

We haven't talked much about the future beyond the fact that she doesn't want to work for the Crusaders anymore, that she wants to bake and is thinking of going to school for it. I told her I'd get her into any program she wanted, all she had to do was ask. So, being the brat she is, she picked out a fancy one in Paris that she is starting in two weeks. Good thing the season is over because there is no way in hell I am letting her go to school one town over, let alone an ocean over, at least not alone.

We will come back when she finishes school right before practices start in July. Seb made the public announcement that this is officially his last season, and everyone already knew it was Dec's. Slater and I will finish out our contracts and play it by ear from there.

Scarlett just got her latest scan back, and she is still cancer-free, thank God. They are even talking about surrogacy, and Erica, of all people, volunteered if they were wanting to go that route. Yeah, Erica, the girl who had a pregnancy from hell with the twins, is willing to do it all over again. Scarlett and Slater both cried when she offered, even if Slater said he just has really bad allergies.

Declan and Vi I think are both excited for him to finally retire officially. Their family is only continuing to grow, and if I'm honest, I think they miss Tennessee. They said they'll never get rid of their house up here so they can visit often, but apparently Mama Daniels and Grandma Judy miss all the kids like crazy, and Vi and Declan too, I guess.

Sage is only a few feet away, proudly wearing a number eighty-three jersey as she jumps into my arms, again, strongly against doctor's orders.

"Ow, ow, ow. Fuck," she grumbles.

"Settle down, crazy. Have you forgotten they're broken?" I laugh.

"Sorry, can't help myself. I just saw a really hot quarterback and was wondering if he wanted to go fuck in the tunnel after all this," she says as she gestures all around us.

"Like you have to ask." I smirk.

"Great, I'll go grab Hanson then," she says, pointing toward the new Cobras QB.

A feral growl rips out of me as I pin her tightly against me.

"You're getting your ass spanked raw for that shit."

"Can't wait."

Chapter 47
Trevor
Extended Epilogue

Two Years Later

The season is about to start, and we are having our friends over for dinner before the craziness of the season begins. I have two more seasons until my contract with the Crusaders is up, and I honestly don't know if I'll continue. I love what I do, but during training camp this year my arm started giving me trouble. I've been working with Scarlett, but I've been in the league for over a decade now. No one can say I haven't had a wildly successful career.

I'm not sure Slater will ever want to retire. He will probably need another career-ending injury for that to happen. Despite him still being one of the fastest running backs in the league, it doesn't take away from the dedication he has to his family. Scarlett has been running her own physical therapy practice for about six months now, and they just welcomed baby Jude last May.

Erica was their surrogate, and it ended up turning out amazing for everyone. She had an easy time, hardly any morning sickness or back pain like she had before. The nice thing about it is that Scarlett and Slater were able to be a part of the whole pregnancy. I think Scarlett spent more time at their house than her own, and when Slater wasn't playing ball, he was right there by her side.

Slater and Scarlett are, unsurprisingly, amazing parents, and Jude has quickly become their entire world. As soon as the kid started walking, Slater was trying to show him plays. It ended in lots of falling which had Scarlett scolding him.

Parenthood wasn't always in the cards for them, and I think in some way they had accepted that. But as soon as they held him, it was obvious they were always meant to be parents. He's one lucky kid.

Declan and Vi moved back to Tennessee shortly after our Super Bowl season. They kept their house in Seattle, and they typically spend their summers up here and the rest of the year down there. Their kids are getting so big it's wild. We all joke that Declan must have a breeding kink because they are pregnant with their fourth child, and when the discussion of more kids comes up, neither of them is opposed to it. Crazy bastards.

Vi's floral shop is booming in Tennessee. It's actually doing so well they just opened a second location up here. She's a regular entrepreneur, and Declan is more than happy to spend all of his time either with the kids or helping support his wife's dreams. They are literally the definition of couple goals.

Seb and Erica are really enjoying retirement. They travel a lot as a family to all of Erica's galleries and showings. They are on the move so much they decided to homeschool the girls for a while at least. I don't think I've ever seen a tighter knit family than those four.

After the Super Bowl, Seb took all his girls on a tropical vacation to the Bahamas for almost a month. They said it was the best time, and they even ended up buying a condo out there so they could visit often. Family of globetrotters, I swear.

I figured after Sebastian retired, we'd lose contact, at least a little, but honestly, we are closer than we've been in years. Maybe it's because we finally got all of the shit off our chest, maybe it's the fact that we walked into the literal lion's den together, and he saved my life in the process. Or maybe it's the fact that I'm no longer in love with his reason for existence. Could be any number of things.

Seb, Slater, and I actually get together quite a bit. Whether it is to grab a drink or have a barbecue with the families. I love it. It feels amazing to have my friends back, truly. Guess all it takes is to stop being a narcissistic ass.

Erica and I still talk, and she will never not be one of my closest friends, but we definitely keep a healthier separation between us. The same can't be said for Erica and Sage. They are practically sewn together.

Relief wasn't even close to the right word to explain the feeling we all experienced when we found out that Alec ended up getting nailed with several unsolved murders and was ultimately served a life sentence without parole. Sage cried for a solid hour, mostly happy tears, but I think a little bit of healing ones as well. I just held her through it, and when she looked up at me with red-rimmed eyes and watery cheeks, I knew I would never let anyone or anything put that look on her face again.

I step up behind Sage who is putting the finishing touches on her salmon risotto. Wrapping my arms around her waist, I lean down and press a kiss to her neck. She smiles softly before turning to face me.

"If you think loving up on me is going to allow you a chance at the rolls, you've got another thing coming, Michaels," she says as she moves the basket of her fresh baked rolls away.

"Whatever you say, Mrs. Michaels." I smirk.

"Shhh," she says as she whips around, pressing her finger against my lips as she lowers her voice.

"We haven't even told anyone yet."

"Wasn't that the whole point of this dinner?" I mock whisper back.

She rolls her eyes at me as she continues working. "Yes, hence why you shouldn't ruin it, jackass."

"Love you too, dear." I chuckle before swatting her ass as I move to the dining table where everyone is sitting.

Sage and I were in Vegas a week ago when we decided on a whim to hit up the Little White Wedding Chapel. I proposed to her over a year ago, and though she said yes, she said she wanted a long engagement. I teased that she wanted that in case something better came along, but when the year mark came along and she still didn't even want to talk about a date, I started to wonder if maybe I was right.

We were making our way down the strip when she pointed at a white cocktail dress in a window. We went inside, and when she came out, she did a little spin.

"Yep, I think this is it."

"What? You mean you want it?" I ask as I scroll on my phone.

"Yeah, I think it's about as good a dress as any to do it in."

"Do what?" I say with furrowed brows as I look up at her.

"Get married in," she says flatly like I should be on the same page as her.

My heart thumps in my chest as I quickly stand up from the couch in the shop and make my way toward her. She's smiling at me. Not her typical mischievous smile, but a sweet one. One that melts my heart and fills me up.

"Are you serious?"

She nods. "Tonight."

"Tonight? Like right now?"

She shrugs. "Why not?"

The way I fireman-carried her out of the store, tossing down a few hundred dollars to pay for the dress and didn't stop running until I made it to the Little White Wedding Chapel. It's been so hard to keep it a secret from everyone since we got back, but we decided what better way to tell everyone than at dinner?

She said that she plans on calling her dad tomorrow and telling him. Their relationship isn't the best, but it is getting better. They are slowly building something out of what was essentially nothing. Aberton is less of a dick than usual, at least when he's inside my home, and as long as Sage is happy, I'll deal with the guy.

I haven't spoken to my parents much over the years, honestly. Since I fully removed myself from the business, they haven't made much effort. My mom more so than my dad. That's why an elopement was so perfect for us. It was just me and her. Small, intimate, and completely unconventional.

After the Super Bowl, Sage and I packed up and moved to Paris for the offseason while she took her culinary classes. I didn't think it was possible for her to get any more talented but somehow she did. She took both pastry and regular cooking classes, but her heart came back to the love of baking. When we came back for training camp, she decided that's what she wanted to do.

So, I did what any sensible boyfriend would do, who was completely out of his mind for his woman, and had a couple million in his bank account to burn. I bought her a completely outfitted bakery, built to every request and spec she desired with the request that she make me the first batch of pumpkin cinnamon rolls out of the kitchen, to which she happily agreed.

Despite Sage being an extremely strong and independent woman, she isn't like some of those who would balk at such a lavish gift. She happily accepted it with a giant thank you in the form of an incredible blow job that was well worth the six-figure investment.

"Do you need help, hun?" Vi asks from the table.

"Yeah, like I'm gonna ask the pregnant lady to help," Sage scoffs as she walks over the risotto.

When she sets it on the table, Erica's eyes widen as she leans forward.

"Uh, what the hell is that?" she asks, gesturing to Sage's ring finger.

The three-carat diamond has been there for long enough to where it would be strange not to see it. Of course, eagle-eye Erica would be the one to notice the newly added band.

Sage glances down at her hand before smiling. I can't help but grin as I yank her down into my lap and kiss her cheek.

"Uhm, so we kinda got married." Sage blushes.

"WHAT!" a collective statement shouts from every end of the table.

The kids all cheer in excitement while the adults look at us like we are crazy before they all break out into wide smiles.

"When did this happen?"

"Why didn't you tell me?"

"I need details, like yesterday!"

I look at my new bride, not able to contain my happiness. I never would have imagined I would find happiness like this in my life. Definitely not with someone like Sage either. She's crass, sarcastic, snarky, and a huge pain in the ass, and I wouldn't want it any other way. The only thing we are missing now is a couple of babies, though I haven't quite talked Sage into it just yet. I'll give her another year or so to get on the bandwagon.

Maybe.

Glancing around the table, so full of love and laughter, it's funny to me how we all came to be here right at this moment. We've all gone through hell, in our own ways, on our own journeys, and we've all seemingly made it out the other side. Life is so unpredictable, but I think that the best parts of life are lived in those unpredictable moments. They're lived in laundry rooms, small diners, simple family homes in a tight-knit neighborhood or even a packed nightclub. Some of the most important moments are the ones we never see coming.

If there is anything I've learned so far in my life, though, it's that nothing is permanent. Things break. Whether it's Loyalties, Walls, Hearts or Rules. It's all about having the right person by your side to help put the pieces back together.

Chapter 48
Thank you

And there we have it. The Alphaletes Series is completed. It's a bittersweet feeling to say goodbye to these characters. They have been with me through so much. I have cried over these characters, bled over them, and grew with them. I wasn't always certain Trevor was going to get his own story, but now that he has, it feels like the perfect ending to these characters, to this series.

If you haven't gotten a chance to read about the other characters in the series, check them out below! Below is also listed my standalones.

The Alphaletes Series –

The Loyalties We Break – Ex-boyfriend's best friend sports romance. (Seb & Erica)

The Walls We Break – Single mom sports romance. (Declan & Vi)

The Hearts We Break – Friends to lovers sports romance. (Slater & Scar)

Stand Alones –

Gratify – Forbidden age gap romance

Jagged Harts – Enemies to lovers MMA romance.

Reviews mean everything to indie authors, so if you could take a moment to leave a review, I would be so thankful!

Review on Amazon

Review on Goodreads

Make sure you are subscribed to my newsletter and following me on socials to stay up to date on any upcoming releases, special announcements, and give-aways!

Instagram

TikTok

Facebook
Facebook Reader Group
Newsletter

Chapter 49
Acknowledgments

To my Alpha, Courtney, to put it simply, I adore you. The amount of extensive voice messages you receive from me in the time I draw an outline of a book to finishing one is honestly insane. Thank you for being there for me inside and outside of the writing process. I'm so blessed to call you one of my closest friends and your feedback and support is completely invaluable. Love you forever and ever.

To my Betas, Kenzie, Elena, Sara, and Lynds, thank you all so much. From your incredible insight, your overdramatic but extremely entertaining voice messages (*cough* Elena), and your special eyes catching the little things my tired author brain missed, I'm so grateful to have had you all a part of my team! I appreciate each of you and am so thankful for you taking the time to help mold Trevor and Sage.

To Skarlet, of course you need a special shout out, you're this series' godmother after all. You have been with me literally from the bottom of the barrel. And it was bad at times, remember that horrible ending I originally had for Loyalties or the third-act breakup I had planned for Hearts. I think there are thousands of readers out there who would be indebted to you if they knew the atrocities you convinced me to abolish. More than any of that, thank you for all of your love, support, insight, and vision. I truly believe I would not be standing in the place I am today if it wasn't for meeting you, and I'm so freaking blessed to have you in my life.

To my wonderful editor, Ellie, I'm so thankful I met you! To have you as an editor is an honor but having you as a friend is so much better. Thank you for all you do. I appreciate you more than you know!

To my Street Team and ARC Team, since most of you overlap, I might as well get on my knees all at once for you all. YOU guys are so incredible. The amount of support you all bring to me, whether it's the announcement of a new book, a playlist or release day, you all come in droves, and I couldn't be more grateful! Authors truly aren't anything without having good people to back them, and I'm going to arrogantly boast that I've found some of the best people out there. Thank you all for being by my side whether this was your first book or ninth with me, thank you so much. I love you all infinitely.

To my readers, I adore every single one of you. Thank you for reading my books, for leaving a review, and for supporting me in the best way possible. I may be a new to you author, and if so, thank you for taking a chance on the perpetually sarcastic (but biasedly super funny) indie author. To those of you who have already binged my backlist, and this is your latest read of my books, I could never thank you enough for your support. Every page read, every book picked up is quite literally changing my life, and I hope, at moments, it changes yours too.

All of my love!